Francis Bacon, Edwin Abott

Essays. With introd.,

Notes, and index by Edwin A. Abbott - Vol. 1

Francis Bacon, Edwin Abott
Essays. With introd.,
Notes, and index by Edwin A. Abbott - Vol. 1

ISBN/EAN: 9783337809539

Printed in Europe, USA, Canada, Australia, Japan

Cover: Foto ©ninafisch / pixelio.de

More available books at **www.hansebooks.com**

BACON'S ESSAYS

WITH

INTRODUCTION, NOTES, AND INDEX

BY

EDWIN A. ABBOTT, D.D.

HEAD MASTER OF THE CITY OF LONDON SCHOOL

IN TWO VOLUMES

VOL. I.

FOURTH EDITION

LONDON
LONGMANS, GREEN, AND CO.
1881

All rights reserved

PREFACE.

THE object of the present edition of Bacon's Essays is to illustrate them as far as possible, not merely by disconnected notes, but by a continuous Introduction, bringing to bear upon the Essays such knowledge of Bacon's thoughts, as can be derived from his life and works. The basis of this Introduction is, of course, the edition of Bacon's Works issued by Mr. Ellis and Mr. Spedding; and the 'Letters and Life' recently completed by Mr. Spedding. Allusions and textual difficulties are explained by notes; but the writer's experience, while reading the Essays with a class of advanced pupils, led him to the conviction that, for the proper understanding of the Essays, more is wanted than mere annotation, however accurate and judicious. Bacon's Essays can hardly be understood without reference to Bacon's life.

The text adopted is generally that of the accurate and scholar-like edition of Mr. Aldis Wright; but I have ventured to depart from his example in the matter of spelling and punctuation. As regards spelling, the principle adopted in the following pages is this : whatever quotations or extracts are made for critical or antiquarian purposes are printed with the old spelling, but the Essays themselves are placed on the same footing as the Bible and Shakespeare; and, as being not for an age but for all ages, they are spelt with the spelling of this age. Still less scruple has been felt in departing from the old punctuation; it has no right to be considered Bacon's; it often makes absolute nonsense of a passage; it sometimes produces ambiguities that may well cause perplexity even to intelligent readers; and its retention can only be valuable to archæologists as showing how little importance should be attached to the commas and colons scattered at random through their pages by the Elizabethan compositors.

By way of illustrating Bacon's style and method, the ten Essays of 1597 are printed (and, in accordance with the principle stated above, in their original spelling) below the corresponding Essays of A.D. 1625. The comparison of these may furnish a useful exercise in composition; but it has not been thought necessary to add in full the edition of A.D. 1612, some account of which will, however, be found in the Notes, and in the Appendix in the second volume.

It is hoped that this edition may be of some use in the highest classes of schools; but the object has been, not the compilation of a book adapted for the use of persons desiring to pass examinations, but of

Preface

a work that may enable readers of all ages and classes to read Bacon's Essays easily and intelligently.

I am indebted to Dr. Kuno Fischer's 'Francis of Verulam' for some valuable hints, which will be found acknowledged severally where they occur. Of Mr. Spedding's work I have made so much use that the words 'debt' and 'obligation' cannot sufficiently express what I owe to it. Though (as I regret to learn from Mr. Spedding, who most kindly and laboriously criticised my proofs) my interpretation of Bacon's character differs widely from his, yet it is founded almost entirely upon the evidence that he has himself collected. I have endeavoured to throw a little additional light on Bacon through Machiavelli.

In the notes, I have gained much from Mr. Aldis Wright's edition, and especially from his references. I regret that I did not see Mr. Gardiner's *History of England from the Accession of James I.*, &c., in time to do more than add a few foot-notes from it. I find myself in complete accord with almost every word referring to Bacon in those valuable volumes.

In the Second Edition some misprints have been corrected, and an alteration of some importance has been made in the last sentence of the Introduction.

CONTENTS

OF

THE FIRST VOLUME.

	PAGE
PREFACE	iii
PRINCIPAL EVENTS IN BACON'S LIFE AND TIMES	ix

INTRODUCTION—

CHAP.
I. WHAT BACON WAS HIMSELF	xvii
II. BACON AS A PHILOSOPHER	lxv
III. BACON AS A THEOLOGIAN AND ECCLESIASTICAL POLITICIAN	xcviii
IV. BACON AS A POLITICIAN	cxvi
V. BACON AS A MORALIST	cxxxiv

DEDICATION OF THE ESSAYS	clxi
TABLE OF CONTENTS	clxiii
ESSAYS	1–112

PRINCIPAL EVENTS IN BACON'S LIFE, AND TIMES.

A.D.

Born (youngest of eight children, six of whom were by a former marriage). Son of Sir Nicholas Bacon, Jan. 22	1560–1*
The Council of Trent breaks up.	1563
Revolt of the Netherlands; Execution of Counts Egmont and Horn.	1566–7
Elizabeth is excommunicated	1570
The Turks are defeated off Lepanto	1571
Massacre of St. Bartholomew	1572
Bacon goes to Trinity College, Cambridge	1573
Union of Utrecht between the seven northern provinces of the Netherlands	1575
He is admitted 'de societate magistrorum' at Gray's Inn	1576
In France with Sir Amias Paulet.	1576–8
His father dies, and he returns to England	1579
Admitted 'Utter Barrister'	1582
Conspiracies against Elizabeth; The Parliament sanctions the Voluntary Association formed in defence of the Queen; Severe laws passed against Priests and Jesuits	1583–4
Represents Melcombe Regis in the House of Commons.	1584
William of Orange assassinated	1584
Writes *Letter of Advice to Queen Elizabeth*†	1584
About this time was written the *Greatest Birth of Time*‡	1585
Becomes a Bencher of Gray's Inn.	1586
Execution of Mary Stuart	1587
Destruction of the Spanish Armada	1588
Assassination of the Duke of Guise	1588

* This is *our* 1561. But in Bacon's time the 'civil' year began with March 25, the 'historical' year with January 1. The dates that follow will be given according to the *modern* reckoning.

† Mr. Spedding inclines to think this letter was written by Bacon.

‡ Writing in 1625, Bacon says: 'It being now forty years, as I remember, since I composed a juvenile work on this subject, which, with great confidence and a magnificent title, I named "The Greatest Birth of Time."'—Life, Vol. vii. p. 533.

	A.D.
Asks the Earl of Leicester to further a suit urged in his behalf by Essex*; death of Leicester	1588
Assassination of Henry III. by Friar Clement	1589
Advertisement touching the Controversies of the Church of England	1589
Elizabeth adopts as her favourite the Earl of Essex	1589
The clerkship of the Council in the Star Chamber is granted to Bacon in reversion	1589
A Conference of Pleasure containing '*the Praise of Fortitude*,' '*the Praise of Love*,' '*the Praise of Knowledge*,' '*the Praise of the Queen*.'	1593
Certain Observations made upon a Libel† published this present year	1593
Some Members of Parliament are imprisoned for presenting a Petition touching the succession	1593
Bacon opposes the Government in a speech on a motion for a grant of three subsidies payable in four years‡: he is consequently forbidden to come into the Queen's presence	1593
A true Report of the detestable treason intended by Dr. Roderigo Lopez, a physician attending upon the person of the Queen's Majesty	1594
Sues unsuccessfully for the place of Attorney and then for that of Solicitor-General	1593-5
Gesta Grayorum, a Device represented at Gray's Inn	1594
Rebellion of Tyrone; End of Religious Wars in France	1595
Essex makes a present of an estate to Bacon to console him for his disappointment; Bacon's *Device*, written for Essex	1595
Alliance between Elizabeth and Henry IV.	1596
Essays (first edition) with *Colours of Good and Evil* and *Meditationes Sacræ*	1597

* Mr. Spedding informs me that this letter, which fixes the acquaintance of Bacon with Essex a little earlier than was supposed, was mentioned to him by Mr. Bruce, after the publication of his earlier volumes.

† The 'Libel' is described by Mr. Spedding as 'a laboured invective against the government, charging upon the Queen and her advisers all the evils of England and all the disturbances of Christendom.'

‡ 'The gentlemen,' he says in his speech, 'must sell their plate, and the farmers their brass pots, ere this will be paid.'

	A.D.
Speaks in Parliament against Enclosures	1597
Quarrel between Essex and the Queen	1598
Edict of Nantes	1598
Death of Lord Burghley	1598
Victory of Tyrone in Ireland	1599
Essex goes over to Ireland	1599
Essex suddenly makes truce with Tyrone, and returns, against orders, to England	1599
Essex placed under restraint, and not restored to favour, though set at liberty	1600
Outbreak of Essex: his arraignment (in which Bacon takes part) and execution	1601
Speaks against Repeal of 'Statute of Tillage'	1601
A declaration of the Practices and Treasons attempted and committed by Robert, late Earl of Essex, and his Complices	1601
Death of Bacon's brother Anthony	1601
Bacon mortgages Twickenham Park	1601
Death of Elizabeth	1603
Accession of James I.	1603
Bacon seeks to get himself recommended to the King's favour	1603
About this time comes *Valerius Terminus*, written before the *Advancement of Learning*	1603
The First book of the *Advancement of Learning* probably written during this year	1603
Bacon is knighted	1603
A brief discourse touching the happy Union of the Kingdoms of England and Scotland	1603
He desires '*to meddle as little as he can in the King's causes,*' and to '*put his ambition wholly upon his pen.*' He is engaged on a work concerning the '*Invention of Sciences,*' which he has digested in two parts, one being entitled *Interpretatio Naturæ*. At this time he probably writes the *De Interpretatione Naturæ Proœmium*	1603
Certain considerations touching the better pacification and edification of the Church of England	1603
Conference at Hampton Court; Translation of the Bible into the Authorised Version; Proclamation of the Act of Uniformity	1604

	A.D.
Sir Francis Bacon his Apology in certain imputations concerning the late Earl of Essex, first printed copy is dated	1604
Bacon repeatedly chosen to be spokesman for Committees of the House of Commons in Conference with the Lords	1604
Draft by Bacon of *An Act for the better grounding of a further Union to ensue between the Kingdoms of England and Scotland*	1604
Appointed an 'ordinary member of the Learned Counsel'	1604
Certain Articles or considerations touching the Union of the Kingdoms of England and Scotland	1604
Draft of *a Proclamation touching his Majesty's Stile. Prepared, not used*	1604
The most humble Certificate or Return of the Commissioners of England and Scotland, authorised to treat of an union for the weal of both realms. 2 Jac. 1. Prepared but altered	1604
Publication of the *Advancement of Learning*	1605
The Gunpowder Plot	1605
Marriage of Bacon to Alice Barnham	1606
Bacon requests Dr. Playfair to translate the *Advancement of Learning* into Latin	1606
Bacon made Solicitor-General	1607
Colonisation of Virginia	1607
Bacon shows Sir Thomas Bodley the *Cogitata et Visa de Interpretatione Naturæ*	1607
Conversion of Toby Matthew (one of Bacon's most intimate friends) to the Romish Church	1608
Matthew imprisoned and banished; writes *In felicem memoriam Elizabethæ; Calor et Frigus; Historia Soni et Auditus*	1608
Begins *Of the true Greatness of the kingdom of Britain;* The Clerkship of the Star-Chamber falls in	1608
Certain considerations touching the Plantation in Ireland presented to his Majesty	1609
Bacon sends to Toby Matthew a part of *Instauratio Magna* (the part is supposed to be the *Redargutio Philosophiarum*)	1609
Bacon sends to Bishop Andrewes a copy of *Cogitata et Visa*, with the last additions and amendments	1609

Events in Bacon's Life

	A.D.
He also sends to Toby Matthew his *De Sapientia Veterum*	1609
Twelve years' truce between Spain and Holland	1609
Bacon is chosen by the Commons as their spokesman for presenting a Petition of Grievances	1609
Sends to Toby Matthew a MS. supposed to be the *Redargutio Philosophiarum*	1609
Assassination of Henry IV. by Ravaillac	1610
Newfoundland is colonised	1610
The thermometer invented	1610
Death of Bacon's mother	1610
Writes a fragment entitled *The Beginning of the History of Great Britain*	1610
Disputes between King and Parliament	1610
Publication of the Authorised Version of the Bible	1611
Death of Salisbury (Cecil)	1612
The first English settlement in India is founded at Surat	1612
Death of the Prince of Wales	1612
Second Edition of the *Essays*	1612
Writes *Descriptio Globi Intellectualis* and *Thema Cœli*	1612
Bacon made Attorney-General	1613
The Princess Elizabeth marries the Elector Palatine	1613
Michael III. founds the dynasty of the Romanoffs in Russia	1613
Bacon returned for Cambridge University	1614
Napier invents Logarithms	1614
Prosecution and examination (with torture) of Peacham	1614
The 'Addled Parliament' meets April 5, and is dissolved June 7	1614
Prosecution of Oliver St. John for a seditious libel concerning the Benevolence	1615
The last Assembly of the States-General in France	1615
Discovery of the murder of Sir Thomas Overbury	1615
Commencement of Bacon's acquaintance with George Villiers	1615
Bacon appointed Privy Councillor	1616
Coke suspended from his office of Chief Justice of King's Bench	1616
A letter of advice written by Sir Francis Bacon to the Duke of Buckingham when he became favourite to King James	1616

Events in Bacon's Life

	A.D.
Bacon made Lord Keeper	1617
Episcopacy introduced into Scotland	1617
Buckingham alienated by Bacon's opposition to the marriage of Buckingham's brother with Coke's daughter	1617
Buckingham made a Marquis	1618
Bacon Lord Chancellor	1618
Commencement of the Thirty Years' War	1618
Bacon created Baron Verulam of Verulam	1618
Execution of Ralegh	1618
Official declaration concerning Sir W. Ralegh, which is supposed to have been, in part, composed by Bacon	1618
Bacon's 'great sickness'	1619
The Bohemians offer the crown to the Elector Palatine	1619
Arminius is condemned by the Synod of Dort	1619
Preparations in Germany to attack the Palatinate	1620
Volunteers levied by Frederick's agents in England	1620
Movement of the Spanish forces against the Palatinate	1620
The King resolves to defend it and to call a Parliament	1620
Publication of the *Novum Organum* and the *Parasceue*. To the *Novum Organum* he prefixed a *Proœmium* beginning with the words *Franciscus de Verulamio sic cogitavit*; a dedication to King James; a general Preface; and an account (entitled *Distributio Operis*) of the parts of which the *Instauratio* was to consist. Of these the *Novum Organum* is the second; the *De Augmentis*, which was not then published, occupying the place of the first	1620
Bacon created Viscount St. Alban	1620
Bacon charged by a disappointed suitor with taking money for the dispatch of his suit	1620
The charge investigated	1620
Bacon's illness	1620
Makes his will	1620
The confession and humble submission of me the Lord Chancellor	1621
Bacon is imprisoned in the Tower, but almost immediately released	1621
Retires to Gorhambury	1621
Begins his *History of Henry VII.*	1621

	A.D.
Alienates Buckingham by his refusal to sell York House	1621
His pardon is stayed at the seal	1621
Consents to part with York House to Cranfield, a creature of Buckingham's, and thereupon obtains Buckingham's help in his suit for leave to come within the verge	1621
The Commons make a Protestation of their Rights, the entry of which is torn from their Journal by the King	1621
Publishes *Henry VII.*; speaks of the *De Augmentis* as a work in the hands of the translators, likely to be published by the end of the summer; writes *Historia Naturalis*, &c., containing *Historia Ventorum*, with titles of five similar *Histories*, proposed to be published month by month; writes the *Advertisement touching a Holy War*	1622
Parliament is dissolved	1622
Writes *Historia Vitæ et Mortis;* sues in vain for the Provostship of Eton; publishes the *De Augmentis;* writes a few lines of the *History of Henry VIII.*	1623
Prince Charles visits Spain to negotiate a marriage with the Infanta	1623
War is proclaimed against Spain and Austria	1624
The *New Atlantis* is supposed to have been written about this time; The *Apophthegms*	1624
Extinction of hopes of being enabled *to live out of want;* his anxiety now is to *die out of ignominy*	1624–6
Third edition of the *Essays*	1625
Dies, April 9	1626

The following is a description given by Bacon himself, in the year 1625, of his intentions with regard to his writings:—

Most reverend Father Fulgentio,

..... I wish to make known to your Reverence my intentions with regard to the writings which I meditate and have in hand; not hoping to perfect them, but desiring to try; and because I work for posterity; these things requiring ages for their accomplishment. I have thought it best, then, to have all of them translated into Latin and divided into volumes. The first volume consists of the books

concerning the 'Advancement of Learning'; and this, as you know, is already finished and published, and includes the Partitions of the Sciences; which is the first part of my Instauration. The Novum Organum should have followed; but I interposed my moral and political writings, as being nearer ready. These are: first, the History of the reign of Henry the Seventh, king of England, after which will follow the little book which in your language you have called Saggi Morali. But I give it a weightier name, entitling it Faithful Discourses, or the Inwards of Things. But these discourses will be both increased in number and much enlarged in the treatment. The same volume will contain also my little book on the Wisdom of the Ancients. And this volume is (as I said) interposed, not being a part of the Instauration. After this will follow the Novum Organum, to which there is still a second part to be added: but I have already compassed and planned it out in my mind. And in this manner the Second Part of the Instauration will be completed. As for the Third Part, namely, the Natural History, that is plainly a work for a king or a Pope, or some college or order; and it cannot be done as it should be by a private man's industry. And those portions which I have published, concerning Winds and concerning Life and Death, are not history pure, because of the axioms and greater observations that are interposed: but they are a kind of writing mixed of natural history, and a rude and imperfect form of that intellectual machinery which properly belongs to the Fourth Part of the Instauration. Next therefore will come the Fourth Part itself; wherein will be shewn many examples of the Machine, more exact and more applied to the rules of Induction. In the Fifth Place will follow the book which I have entitled the 'Precursors of the Second Philosophy,' which will contain my discoveries concerning new axioms, suggested by the experiments themselves, that they may be raised as it were and set up, like fallen pillars: and this I have set down as the Fifth Part of my Instauration. Last comes the Second Philosophy itself, the Sixth Part of the Instauration, of which I have given up all hope; but it may be that the ages and Posterity will make it flourish. Nevertheless in the Precursors—I speak only of those which almost touch on the Universalities of Nature—no slight foundations will be laid for the Second Philosophy. *

* Life, Vol. vii. pp. 531–2.

INTRODUCTION.

CHAPTER I.

WHAT BACON WAS HIMSELF.

'I NEVER LOOK,' says Montaigne, ' upon an author be they such as write of virtue and of actions, but I curiously endeavour to find out what he was himself.'[1] This hint, useful for the students of any book, is especially useful for those that want to understand Bacon's Essays, for they spring directly out of Bacon's life. They are not the results of his reading, nor the dreams or theories of his philosophy; they are the brief jottings of his experience of men and things. On this ground he tells the Prince he can commend them: he has endeavoured to make them, *not vulgar, but of a nature whereof a man shall find much in experience, little in books, so as they are neither repetitions nor fancies.* Moreover, the experience of the author's old age, as well as that of his youth, finds condensed expression in the little volume of the Essays: for, besides the fact that they embody the *Antitheta*, which he is known to have collected during his youth or early manhood, the first edition was published when he was thirty-six, the second when he was fifty-two, the third when he was sixty-four, so that the different editions cover the whole period of his active life. Nor again need we suspect that in the Essays we have, not

[1] Florio's Montaigne, p. 411.

the true Bacon, but an artificial essayist, wishing to found a literary reputation, or a reputation for morality or statesmanship. Such a suspicion might attach to some of his more formal compositions; but it is out of place here, and it is disproved by internal evidence. For the Essays are strewn thick with Bacon's *household words*, with maxims, arguments and illustrations, to be found elsewhere in letters to friends, in charges to judges, in parliamentary or legal speeches, in diaries and the like, as well as in his formal philosophic works. Sometimes, though rarely, we find here a notion in its germ developed and matured in Bacon's later works; more often these terse pages give us a condensation of some old familiar, oft-repeated thought, abridged here almost to the excess of obscurity, because the writer has repeated it so often that he thinks we must be, by this time, in his confidence, able to catch his meaning from a bare hint. But whether pruned or germinating, the thoughts are the thoughts of Bacon; hints of his life's experience, *certain brief notes* of it, *set down rather significantly than curiously*—that is, thinking of meaning more than of style. Of no other of Bacon's works can it be said so truly that what he was, they are. Bacon's habit of thinking with a pen in his hand has been kind to us: for it has photographed his portrait for us. Perhaps no man ever made such a confidant of paper as he did. He might have said with Montaigne, 'I speak unto paper as to the first man I meet.' Not that he ever rambles or chats colloquially or egotistically on paper as Montaigne does: the difference between the two is very striking. Montaigne lets us into all his foibles: Bacon either describes his character as that of a Prophet of Science, or suppresses the description on second thoughts with a—*de nobis ipsis silemus*. 'My thoughts,' says the genial rambler, 'slip from me with as little care as they are of small worth': but the philosopher has no thoughts 'of small worth': *With me it is thus, and, I think, with all men in my case; if I bind myself to an argument, it loadeth my mind, but if I rid myself of the present cogitation, it is rather a recreation.* Some counsellor he must have to whom he may disburden his thoughts. He often speaks, and with something like pathos, of the value of a friend in helping one to clear one's thoughts, and of his own friendless and solitary condition in his arduous search after truth. *A man were better relate himself to a statua than to let his thoughts pass in smother*, and Bacon's *statua* was pen and paper. Perhaps some dim sense of his own principal deficiency was one reason why Bacon so systematically *related himself* to paper. *Writing*, he said, *maketh an exact man;* and exactness, as he knew, was not a strong point with him. He was singularly inexact, and by nature indifferent to details; and however strenuously he may have laboured to remedy this defect, yet a defect it always remained, seriously influencing his philosophic investigations, his statesmanship, and his morals. 'De minimis non curat lex,' said King James good-humouredly of his great Chancellor; and the Chancellor good-humouredly admits the justice of the charge. He was by nature indifferent to small things; but he strove to remove this inexactness, and one of his remedies was the abundant use of writing. Writing seemed to Bacon profitable for all things. *No course of invention*, he said, *can be satisfactory unless it be carried on in writing.*[1] But it was not for great inventions merely: for every kind of work, philosophic, political, private, be it an onslaught on the ancient philosophy, or a speech in parliament, or a council meeting, or an interview with some great lord or lady, Bacon in each case begins by relating himself to paper. Even if his object was no

[1] *Novum Organum*, Aphorism CI.

more than to win credit at the expense of some legal rival by being more *round* or *resolute*, or to exchange his shy and nervous manner for a more confident carriage— for each and all of these things Bacon did not think it amiss to take counsel with paper.[1]

Hence it comes to pass that, though throughout the whole of the Essays one can scarcely find a word about the writer, yet they really make up a kind of autobiography. The very names, and perhaps the order of the Essays, in the earlier and later editions, tell the story of youth passing into age, and the student making way for the statesman. In the edition of 1597 the student is predominant. *Studies* lead the way, and the few essays that follow in that short edition turn almost all upon the subjects that would interest an ordinary student or gentleman leading a private life—*Discourse, Followers, Suitors, Expence, Health, Honour.* The only two that have any savour of the politician, *Faction* and *Negociating,* come last in order, and they are short and incomplete. Passing to the edition of 1612, we find the first place occupied by *Religion;* but it is religion treated from the statesman's point of view, as the most interesting subject in the politics of the day. But in 1625 the old man, drawing near his grave while the work of his life is yet unaccomplished, is driven back on that which he had made the object of the fresh ambitions of his hopeful youth. *Death* comes near the beginning, but not first: the first place is given to *Truth.* And so the final edition of the Essays of the author of the *Instauratio Magna* will

---

[1] See p. xlix., also *Life,* Vol. vii. p. 197, 'Everybody prepares himself for great occasions. Bacon seems to have thought it no loss of time to prepare for small ones too.' See also Mr. Spedding's note on the *Temporis Partus Masculus* as an 'experiment' in 'a spirit of contemptuous invective,' *Works,* Vol. iii. p. 525; 'To assist his memory and perhaps also to excite his thoughts, he was in the habit of jotting down in common-place books such reflexions and suggestions as occurred to him on the sudden.'

begin for all posterity with the indignant protest against the indolence of mankind, who question Nature in jest, and will not believe that the Truth—Nature's answer—is attainable, if they will but wait to be taught. *What is Truth? said jesting Pilate, and would not stay for an answer.*

Thus, then, the Essays contain an abridgment of Bacon's life, the essence of his manners, his morals, and his politics, tinged throughout with his philosophy: and, in order thoroughly to understand the Essays, we must endeavour to understand their author as a philosopher, a politician, and a moralist, or—to return to Montaigne, with whom we set out—' we must curiously endeavour to find out what he was himself.'

Multum incola: my soul hath long dwelt with those that are enemies unto peace—this is the text that Bacon himself has given us as the key-note of his life.[1] No other words are so often on his lips as these. He is a pilgrim in an unfriendly land, a stranger to his work; his occupations are alien to his nature. He was intended to be a Prophet of Science, mouthpiece of the discoveries of Time, and fate has diverted him to the petty details of a lawyer's, or a courtier's, or a statesman's life. Whether engaged in writing the histories of monarchs, or preparing *devices* for the royal pleasure, in legal practice, in parliamentary business, in drawing up royal proclamations, in giving judgments from the bench, in discussing the highest matters of national policy, or defending the pettiest rights of the royal prerogative, it is always the same; Bacon is still *multum incola*, not at home in his work, a Prophet who has missed his vocation. *I think no man may more truly say with the Psalmist, Multum incola fuit anima mea, than myself: for I do confess, since I was of any understanding, my mind hath been in*

---

[1] Bacon never uses these words in their full force. He means that he dwells amid *alien* occupations.

effect absent from that I have done.[1] The history of Bacon's life is a record of the temptations by which he was allured from philosophy, of struggles, penitences, relapses, and final failure.

We cannot definitely say how soon Bacon conceived the idea of his philosophic mission. However much he may have been endowed—as his biographer Rawley tells us he was—even in 'his first and childish years with pregnancy and towardness of wit,' yet it would be absurd to suppose that, when he went up to Trinity College, Cambridge, a boy between twelve and thirteen years of age, 'at the ordinary years of ripeness for the University, or something earlier'—he had the *Instauratio Magna* already in his mind. Yet, we are informed that while still a resident at the University, he had already conceived a dislike for the philosophy of the schools. Aristotle's philosophy was then, as always, his aversion, not merely for its barren logic and puerile induction, but also as embodying the evil Spirit of Authority, barring the way to improvement and thus retarding science. Already the young student had noted the 'unfruitfulness of a philosophy only strong for disputations and contentions, but barren of the production of works for the benefit of the life of man.'[2] Such is the testimony of his biographer, speaking of what had been 'imparted from his lordship'; and we have Bacon's own confession that the ardour and constancy of his mind in his pursuit of truth had been protracted over a long time, *it being now forty years* (he is writing thus in his sixty-fifth year) *since I composed a juvenile work on this subject, which, with great confidence and a magnificent title, I named the Greatest Birth of Time.*[3]

Between his fortieth and fiftieth year, looking back

---

[1] *Life*, Vol. iii. p. 253.   *Works*, Vol. i. p. 4.
[2] *Life*, Vol. vii. p. 533.

upon and justifying his past life, he speaks as one who had from the first recognised that he was *born to be useful to mankind and specially moulded by nature for the contemplation of the truth.* He justifies his divergence into law and politics on the ground that his country had claimed such a sacrifice at his hands. But *he found no work so meritorious as the discovery and development of the arts and inventions that tend to civilize the life of man. I found in myself*—he thus continues—*a mind at once versatile enough for that most important object the recognition of similarities, and at the same time steady and concentrated enough for the observation of subtle shades of difference. I possessed an earnestness of research, a power of suspending judgment with patience, of meditating with pleasure, of asserting with caution, of correcting false impressions with readiness, and of arranging my thoughts with careful pains: I had no passion for novelty, no fond admiration for antiquity; imposture in every shape I utterly hated. And, thus endowed, I considered myself as it were a relation and kinsman of truth.*[1]

There was no exaggeration in this self-painted portrait. One at least of the qualities here enumerated he possessed even to excess, that most dangerous faculty of *recognising similarities.* It is curiously characteristic of Bacon that he lays more stress upon *that most important object the recognition of similarities,* than upon the *observation of subtle shades of difference.* Yet the latter is pre-eminently the philosopher's faculty, while the former is the poet's. But Bacon was a poet, the poet of Science. His eye, like the poet's—

in a fine frenzy rolling,
Doth glance from heaven to earth, from earth to heaven

---

[1] *Works,* Vol. iii. p. 519. He also speaks of himself (1592) as willing 'to serve Her Majesty,' but 'not as a man born under Sol, that loveth honour: nor under Jupiter, that loveth business (*for the contemplative planet carrieth me away wholly*).' *Life,* Vol. i. p. 108. See also pp. liii, lxiii.

—catching at similarities and analogies invisible to uninspired eyes, giving them names and shapes, investing them with substantial reality, and mapping out the whole realm of knowledge in ordered beauty. Well have Bacon's analogies been described as 'attractive points of view affording a rich and fertile prospect'[1] over the Promised Land of Science. But though they are natural to Bacon, they are not natural to his philosophy: they are examples to show that 'the mind of Bacon extended beyond his method.'[2] He himself says of them that *they sometimes lead us as if by the hand to sublime and noble axioms:* but they also led him into error. They afford rich and fertile prospects; but the richness and fertility are often a mere mirage.

Put aside this dangerous excess of the poetic faculty, and we must recognise in Bacon many faculties fitting him for his scientific mission. Above all he had—whenever the unity and harmony of things, or the honour of Science was not called in question—that cool, dispassionate, impartial way of looking at things which a man of science should have. He knew the necessity of obeying Nature if he would command her: and he had a supple and compliant nature[3] convenient for obeying. He was aware of the scientific danger of ignoring inconvenient facts and constructing convenient facts: and he had something of the scientific simplicity, taking things as they are and not as he would have liked them to be. Above all he had a sanguine confidence, not so much in his own powers as in the divine order of the Universe, and in the adaptation of the human mind to the special purpose of finding what that order is.

Believing himself therefore to be born *to be useful to mankind*, the young philosopher looks round the world

[1] Dr. Fischer's *Francis of Verulam*, p. 133.
[2] Ib., p. 139.   [3] Ib.

to see what special work he is to do. He finds that the dominating influences around him appear to be the inventions of men. Gunpowder, printing, the compass, had shaped the destinies of mankind : *no empire, sect or star, seems to have exercised greater power or influence upon human affairs than these mechanical inventions.* But most of these and other great inventions have been discovered in a manner most discreditable to mankind. They have stumbled upon them, as by accident; sometimes even beasts—deservedly worshipped as gods by the ancient Egyptians—have led the way to them, surpassing with their brute instincts the reasoning faculties of men. This was not meant to be. *God hath set the world in the mind of men,* that men may find it out. All knowledge is divine; but to enter the Kingdom of Knowledge we must become as little children, and learn to read with a simple eye the world, the Second Scripture of God. All the world being made according to Law, all true knowledge consists of knowing the Laws and Causes of things. But if we know the Causes, we shall be able to cause. As by mastering the alphabet we can make words, so by mastering the first principles or causes of things, we shall be able to construct. Hence, all knowledge should result in invention.

'Thoughts without good acts are poor things.'

The contemplative life of the Greek philosophers is a despicable affair, *and good thoughts, though God accept them, yet towards men are little better than good dreams, except they be put in act; and that cannot be without power and place, as the vantage and commanding ground. Merit and good works is the end of man's motion, and conscience of the same is the accomplishment of man's rest.*[1]

[1] *Essay* xi. ll. 35-40.

Power and place were necessary then to Bacon, or at least to him seemed necessary. Let us remember this, throughout his life. The path of his philosophy, he tells us, was of such a kind that no man could pass over it alone. It was to be a social work, employing hosts of workers in different ways, observers, experimenters, supervisors, and the like. The accumulation of the facts that were to form his Natural History was a stupendous work, *fit for a King or a Pope*. No recluse, how self-denying and industrious soever, pore though he might upon the musty books of old philosophy, could ever charm out the secret of Nature. Merlin has exactly described for us that kind of student which Bacon could never be, if he meant to be faithful to his own Induction,—'the hairless man'

> Who lived alone in a great wild on grass,
> Read but one book, and ever reading grew
> So grated down and filed away with thought,
> So lean, his eyes were monstrous; while the skin
> Clung but to crate and basket, ribs and spine.
> And, since he kept his mind on one sole aim,
> Nor ever touch'd fierce wine, nor tasted flesh,
> Nor owned a sensual wish, to him the wall
> That sunders ghosts, and shadow-casting men,
> Became a crystal, and he saw them through it,
> And heard their voices talk behind the wall,
> And learnt their elemental secrets, powers
> And forces.

The part Bacon had to play and set himself to play was harder: he had to be in the world but not of the world, to *keep his mind on one sole aim*, and yet to take up other by-aims and by-works as tending to the one aim on which his mind was fixed. Instead of 'living alone in a great wild,' proclaiming in the wilderness the news of the Kingdom of Man over Nature, he had to bring himself to wear 'soft clothing' and enter 'kings' houses' as a sleek courtier, because the new knowledge was to be thought *put in act; and that cannot be without power and place as the vantage and commanding ground.*

Circumstances combined with the suggestions of his philosophy to divert Bacon from a contemplative to a public life. The death of Sir Nicholas Bacon occurring before he had been able to make any provision for Francis, the younger son of a second marriage, threw the youth at the age of eighteen on his own resources. Returning from France, where he had been placed by his father with Sir Amias Paulet, the Queen's Ambassador, he found himself obliged, sorely against his will, to devote himself to the law for the purpose of earning his living. Had he been able to secure a competency he would gladly have devoted himself to philosophic study: and he applies to Lord Burghley with this view in his twentieth year. But it is not till his twenty-ninth year that his applications are in any way successful, and even then their only result is the reversion of an office, valuable, it is true, but it did not fall in for twenty years. Meantime he had been admitted as a barrister, and in his twenty-fourth year had been elected Member of Parliament.

In his thirtieth year, still unrewarded by place of any kind, he made the acquaintance of Essex. *I held at that time my Lord to be the fittest instrument to do good to the State, and therefore I applied myself to him in a manner which I think rarely happeneth among men:*[1] such is the account given by Bacon fourteen years afterwards of the commencement of their friendship. It is no doubt true, but probably not the whole truth. The *State*, high as it stood in Bacon's mind, was subordinate to Science. We shall find him afterwards in his diary noting down

---

[1] *Life*, Vol. i. p. 106. This deliberate and cold-blooded friendship seems inconsistent with expressions of affection such as 'my affection to your Lordship hath made mine own contentment inseparable from your satisfaction.' *Life*, Vol. i. p. 235. But there is no reason to doubt that Bacon really *liked* Essex, though he hardly *loved* him.

the names of lords and bishops, and other eminent men, who are to be *drawn in* for the purposes of Science. Rich people, sickly people, medical men, scientific men, all who can by wit or money help the good cause, are to be made friends of, or, as he expresses it, *drawn in*. Add *Science* to *State* above, and we have the full account of the origin of Bacon's friendship for Essex. The young nobleman appeared to him more likely to forward high plans of science and of policy than the cautious, jealous Cecils, *in whose time able men were suppressed of purpose*. Essex, by advancing his client Bacon, would advance alike the State and Science : it was as the ministers or tools of Science that Bacon regarded his friends. Not that Bacon had no affection for Essex ; but it was affection of a subdued kind, kept well under control, and duly subordinated to the interests of the Kingdom of Man. Bacon could not easily love friends or hate enemies though he himself was loved by many of his inferiors with the true love of friendship. But his scientific passionless disposition, taking men as they are and not as they ought to be, was fatal to true love ; and his scientific compliance with circumstances was no less fatal to constancy. The *precept of Bias* commends itself to his scientific mind, always provided that it be *not construed to any purposes of perfidy : Love as if you were sometime to hate, and hate as if you were sometime to love*. Bacon could not help liking Essex : indeed, he liked almost everybody with whom he was brought into close intercourse ; he liked James, he liked Villiers, but he loved and could love no one.

Meantime, Bacon was running into debt. Partly for himself, and partly for his brother Anthony, just returning from a long course of foreign travels, he had been obliged to borrow. Anthony's knowledge of foreign politics and foreign connections enabled him to procure for the

Queen secret information of importance, duly valued by Elizabeth. But to procure this information money was going out, and meantime money was not coming in. *Voluntary undoing may be as well for a man's country as for the Kingdom of Heaven:* so runs the Essay on Expence; and both Bacon and his brother exemplified this *voluntary undoing.* More than once he was threatened with arrest for debt; and all this while place and office were still withheld. The Queen, he says, condescended to call him *her watch-candle: and yet she suffered him to waste.*

At this crisis Bacon lost the favour of the Queen, and with it all hope of office, by an independent speech in the House of Commons. Even in the days when he was, as he describes himself, a *peremptory Royalist,* under King James, his mind always recoiled against the haggling and chaffering by which the courtiers thought it necessary to secure subsidies: and it is possible that on the present occasion Bacon sincerely believed that the influence of the crown was in danger of being weakened by an undue insistance on an unpopular and excessive imposition. At all events, he protested in no measured terms against it. The protest was unsuccessful, and the subsidy appears to have been raised without difficulty; but the Queen was seriously displeased, and banished Bacon from her presence. It is worthy of note that, among the many expressions of regret at the royal displeasure, there is no record of any apology tendered by Bacon for his speech: but all that he could do to obtain access to the royal ear he did assiduously. He was strenuously backed by his friend Essex, who for two or three years urged Bacon's claims for the place of Attorney, and then for that of Solicitor-General, in both cases unsuccessfully. To console his disappointment Essex presented Bacon with an estate, which he afterwards *sold for* 1,800*l. and thought* *was more worth*. But to the end of the Queen's life office was withheld. He was restored to the royal favour, but still *suffered to waste*.

It was now ten years since Bacon had composed *the juvenile work which with great confidence and a magnificent title* he had named *the Greatest Birth of Time:* and he was still as far off as ever from obtaining that place and power which he thought he needed to convert his thoughts into acts. Conscious of high powers, political as well as philosophical, he chafed under the deliberate suppression to which he was subjected by his kinsmen. As Machiavelli piteously petitioned to become the servant of the Prince by whom his country had been deprived of her liberties and he himself had been tortured, so Bacon asked nothing better than to be employed by the Queen who had neglected and rebuked him : and in both these two great men it was not avarice or the lust of power that dictated the request. It was the sense of high faculties rusting unused, and a restless desire to do something, even though they could not do what they wished—the intolerable disgust at seeing mediocrity preferred to genius :

> And right perfection wrongfully disgraced,
> And strength by limping sway disabled ;
> And art made tongue-tied by authority,
> And folly doctor-like controlling skill,
> Aud simple truth miscalled simplicity,
> And captive good attending captain ill.

In the sanguine confidence of youth, Bacon had dreamed that knowledge was power, not only in the immaterial world, but also in the world of men. But now at last, weary of the *exquisite disgrace* of continual suing and continual rejection, and sick of *asserviling himself to every man's charity*, the Apostle of the New Logic and herald of the Kingdom of Man began to learn, after years of degradation, that it is one matter to be *perfect in things*, and quite another to be perfect in the *drifts of men*. He begins to see that, if he is to succeed in the world, he must do as the world does. It is not enough to know what is best, it is necessary to be able to persuade others that it is best. Hence the *knowledge of the art of advancement in life* must include careful observance of the humours and weaknesses of the great. *Clear and round dealing* is undoubtedly the honour of human nature: but when human bodies are diseased, physic must not be despised; and when society is diseased, the physic of society is falsehood. There are different degrees of falsehood; there is reserve, there is dissimulation, there is simulation: the latter is not to be used except there be no remedy, but it is not always to be rejected. Thus is Bacon gradually breaking himself to obey the rules of the *Architect of Fortune*, not for his own sake—so he would have said—but for the sake of his mistress Science.

Yet his nobler nature rebels against the hard apprenticeship to which he is training himself. Among the other literary trifles with which he endeavoured to solace the anxieties of this unhappy period of his life, we have a Device prepared by him for his friend Essex, and exhibited to Elizabeth in 1595 A.D.; and in this there is introduced the character of a *hollow statesman* who, instead of serving the true Queen Gloriana, devotes himself to the false Queen Philautia or Selfishness. With bitter irony the writer lays down fit precepts for the conduct of such an impostor: *Let him not trouble himself too laboriously to sound into any matter deeply, or to execute anything exactly; but let him make himself cunning rather in the humours and drifts of persons, than in the nature of business and affairs. Of that it sufficeth him to know only so much as may make him able to make use of other men's wits and to make again a smooth and pleasing report. And ever rather let him take the side which is likeliest to be followed, than that which is soundest and best, that everything may seem to be carried by his direction.*[1] This was an apt description of the hand-to-mouth policy too common among the Queen's ministers, which Bacon contrasts with true foresighted policy, and stigmatizes by the name of *fiddling:* but whoever may have been alluded to by the words, the irony of fate has made them recoil with special force upon the writer. They predict with startling exactness the policy to which Bacon was hereafter to degrade himself, making himself cunning in the humours and drifts of a pedant king and a fickle favourite.

. It was hard for Bacon to learn the seven rules of the *Architect of Fortune:* he was not meant by nature for flattery and the tricks of courtiers. He had deliberately made up his mind that a philosopher ought to study *Advancement in Life*, and that pragmatical men should be taught that the philosopher was not always like the lark soaring heavenwards without object, but could sometimes imitate the hawk and strike down upon an earthly prey; and for this purpose he had drawn up appropriate precepts. But he did not find it easy to stoop to them. When he stoops he has to prepare himself for his degradation with art and deliberation, often on paper. His health and physical constitution were against him here. He was not only an invalid from his youth, but also by nature shy, retiring, and nervous. He includes himself among the class of *persons that are of nature bashful, as myself is, who are often mistaken for proud.* He gasped and *spoke with panting* in public, as nervous men are apt to do. His mother holds up his student meditative way of living as a warning to Anthony, showing him what to avoid. *I verily think your brother's weak stomach*

[1] *Life*, Vol. i. p. 382.

to digest hath been much caused and confirmed by untimely going to bed, and then musing nescio quid *when he should sleep, and then in consequent by late rising and long lying in bed, whereby his men are made slothful and himself continueth sickly.* One of his brother's friends is so deeply offended at his reserve as to complain of it to Anthony. We shall soon find him recognising this defect in his note-book and preparing himself (on paper) to grapple with it; but years afterwards, when he rides to court as Lord Chancellor, with three hundred gallants attending him, he writes that *this matter of pomp, which is heaven to some men, is hell to me, or purgatory at least.* His manner of life and meditative habits seriously interfere with the arrangement of his household, but he cannot shake them off. In vain his precise strict mother lectures him on his unthrifty ways, and declares that she will contribute nothing to his support so long as he persists in keeping his dissolute servants preying upon him. To the end of his life, with all his parade of account-books and note-books, his servants remained uncontrolled and his household laxly supervised. *De minimis non curat lex:* such petty details were beneath the attention of one who was *born for the service of mankind.*

To the obstacles of a retiring and nervous nature, sensitive and unconventional, was added that greatest of all obstacles, at least in the way of *Advancement in Life*—ill-health. His diary is full of recipes for medicines and notes of their effect: and his mother's letters often refer to his weakness and sensitiveness: 'I am sorry,' she writes to Anthony, 'your brother with inward secret grief hindereth his health; everybody saith he looketh thin and pale.' As the newly-appointed Chancellor, he is pronounced by public opinion to have 'so tender a constitution of body and mind that he will hardly be able to undergo the burden of so much business as his place requires.'[1] Nothing but his perpetual hopefulness and the sense of a noble purpose, and the excitement of aspiring action, could have enabled Bacon to protract for more than sixty years 'that long disease, his life.' His mother's intuition guided her rightly when she attributed his bad health to 'inward grief': and Bacon himself gives us the secret of his ailments, as well as an insight into his character, in the following curious passage written a few years later, and extracted from his diary: *I have found now twice, upon amendment of my fortune, disposition to melancholy and distaste, specially the same happening against the long vacation, when company failed and business both. For upon my solicitor's place I grew indisposed and inclined to superstition. Now, upon Mill's place,*[2] *I find a relapse unto my old symptoms, as I was wont to have it many years ago.* Prosperity, without something to hope and strive for, did not suit Bacon: nor did he need or enjoy rest. He throve on work, as long as he could work in hope. When indeed the fatal blow fell on him, and he who was born for the service of mankind had been convicted of corruption, then the fear that he expresses *lest continual attendance and business, together with these cares, and want of time to do my weak body right this spring by diet and physic, will cast me down*, was fully realised, and health and hope gave way together.

Besides these disadvantages, Bacon was weighted in the practice of the Arts of Advancement by what we may call the magnificence of his character. Supple and cool and compliant though he was, he was altogether too vast and grand for a successful and easy flatterer. His philosophy and his policy were all on a scale too magnificent

---

[1] *Life*, Vol. vi. p. 200.
[2] The Clerkship of the Star Chamber, of which Bacon had held the reversion since 1589. He received it in 1609. Its value is reckoned by him at 2000*l.* a year

for the court of James I. His Novum Organum was
described by the king as being 'like the peace of God
which passeth all understanding'; as for his high dreams
of a warlike Western Monarchy uniting all the Protestant
powers, they must have seemed intolerable to the monarch
who detested the sight of a drawn sword. Even his
language was likely to be displeasing in its exuberant
vigour: on one occasion, at least, we are told that Bacon,
while attempting to explain the desires of the House of
Commons, was interrupted by the king because he spoke
in a style more extravagant than His Majesty delighted to
hear, and Sir Henry Neville was requested to take his
place. If Bacon was, as indeed he tells us he was,
multum incola, a stranger amid his work, he must have
been most of all a stranger amid the alien servility imposed upon him by the court of James I.

Yet in spite of all these obstacles, ill-health, natural
aversion to petty things, and a retiring disposition, Bacon
deliberately sat down to build his fortunes upon the approved precepts of art, and, as we shall see, succeeded.
He was resolved to gain advancement, because advancement was necessary—so he persuaded himself—to secure
scientific success: and in the true practical spirit he
despises those who desire an object and will not work for
it: *it is the solecism of power to think to command the end
and yet not to endure the mean.*[1] Writing between his
fortieth and fiftieth year, at a time when he had resolved
to give up politics and to devote himself to philosophy,
he thus justifies his temporary desertion of the latter. He
acknowledges that he was born for the Truth, *but*, he adds,
*being imbued with politics by birth and breeding, finding
myself moreover shaken at times in my opinions*[2] *as young*

[1] *Essay* xix. l. 56.
[2] *Works*, Vol. iii. p. 519. He does not say whether the 'opinions'
refer to philosophy or not: but the context implies that they do. If so, this
would be an additional excuse of no little weight.

men are apt to be, conceiving myself to be indebted to my country in a debt special and peculiar and not extending to other relations, and lastly, hoping that, if I could obtain some honourable place in the State, I might accomplish my objects with greater helps to back my own ability and industry, I not only studied law and policy, but also endeavoured, with all due modesty and by such methods as were consistent with my honour, to commend myself to my influential friends. This is the way then in which we must be prepared to find Bacon regarding his *influential friends*, even such benefactors as Essex: they are to him not much more than stepping-stones to knowledge.

Commonplace people will never believe that Bacon sought power for the sake of Science : naturally, because they care greatly for power and little for Science. Nor will they readily understand the confidence with which Bacon anticipated scientific success. It seems at first sight to be mere self-conceit. But no correct notion can be formed of Bacon's character till this suspicion of self-conceit is scattered to the winds and his love of Science is, if not sympathized with, at least understood.

First then for self-conceit. If the question is asked what was the ground of Bacon's unflagging scientific confidence, it would be quite a mistake to reply 'A sense of his own powers.' True, he knew his own powers, but he did not trust to them : there never was a Prophet who trusted less to himself. Even in his youthful effervescence, when he began to write his *Greatest Offspring of Time*, he always bore in mind what that title indicates. It was great, yes *Greatest*, but still the Child of *Time*. Speaking of his own discoveries, he says, *certainly they are new, quite new, totally new in their very kind, and yet they are copied from a very ancient model, even the world itself, and the nature of things, and of the mind. And, to say truth, I am wont for my part to regard this* work as a *Child of Time rather than as a Child of Wit*.[1] The New Logic is expressly declared to be of a nature to level all understandings. And besides, the very grandeur and novelty of his discoveries, so far from stimulating, are antidotes against conceit. A Prophet does not speak or think about himself; and Bacon is the Prophet of the New Logic.

What therefore gave Bacon his great confidence, untired by forty-five years of philosophic work, was not his sense of his own powers, but his insight into the unity of nature. The sense of the simplicity of the universal order had so taken hold of him that it inspired him with such certainty as might be felt by one who had seen and touched the very springs of the machinery of Creation. We have seen above what importance he attached to his possession of a mind *versatile enough for the recognition of the similitudes of things*. This versatile mind, blending itself compliantly with the phenomena of earth and heaven, giving to its owner a *Filum Labyrinthi*, a clue to thread the mazes of Nature, and enabling him to trace unity and similitude where others could see nothing but dissimilitude and confusion—this is the secret at once of Bacon's scientific successes and moral failures, and it is an essential part of his nature, peeping out of his versatile style, his versatile handwriting, and many other trifling traits in his character. For example, it is the sense of likeness, the *recognition of similitudes*, that is the source of wit and playing upon words: and that Bacon was given to this kind of word-playing, although he disliked it and suppressed it on paper, is clear from the suggestive exception made by his eulogist Ben Jonson, when speaking of his eloquence: 'his language (where he could spare or pass by a jest) was nobly censorious.' Again, it is the *recognition of similitudes* that originates

---

[1] *Works*, Vol. iii. p. 519.

the rich exuberance of metaphor, and the picturesque names with which Bacon maps out the Provinces of Science before subduing them. Even in music (and perhaps in colour) the same power of *recognition of similitudes* appears in his dislike of complications and love of simple effects. *In music,* he says, *I ever loved easy airs that go full, all the parts together, and not these strange points of accord or discord.* As it was with Bacon in music, so was it in his views of nature: he loved easy airs that go full, all the parts together, not the accords and discords that make up the Universal Harmony. In many cases this faculty guided him right, as when it taught him that the *rainbow is made in the sky out of a dripping-cloud; it is also made here below with a jet of water. Still, therefore, it is nature which governs everything;*[1] or when he protests against the doctrine that the heat of the sun and fire differ in kind, as being the useless fruit of *that philosophy which is now in vogue, the purpose of which is to persuade men that nothing difficult, nothing by which nature may be commanded and subdued, can be expected from art or human labour—which things tend wholly to the unfair circumscription of human power, and to a deliberate and factitious despair.*[2] But in other cases this faculty led him wrong, inducing him to expect to arrive too easily at the underlying causes of phenomena, and, in this expectation, to ignore slight differences and points of detail apparently unimportant, but really essential to the formation of a just conclusion. It is the singular predominance of this faculty in Bacon that justifies the saying[3] that his character is a prominent instance of the rule that 'the will produces the understanding.' In despite of all his aphorisms, Bacon's philosophy sprang from

[1] *Works,* Vol. iv. p. 294. [2] Ib. p. 87.
[3] Fischer's *Francis of Verulam,* p. 29.

his will, and from the same source came perhaps his imperfect morality. He saw unity in the Universe, the *Great Common World*, as he was fond of calling it, because he willed to see it; and there he was often right: he saw unity and consistency in his own tortuous morality, in *his own Little World*, because he willed to see it; and there he was often wrong. Few men were so self-deceived as he was, or did such bad deeds as he did without being hypocrites. But this dangerous power of seeing what he willed to see was the secret source of that confidence which enabled him amid the pressure of debt, and the cares of place-hunting, and the anxieties of fruitless expectations, and the distractions of legal practice and parliamentary business, and, in later years, amid the duties of office and the necessities of flattery, to maintain, still unimpaired, his zeal for philosophic Truth.

Of this he never despairs. A stranger in all other occupations, he is always longing to return to his true home, philosophy, to *all knowledge which he has taken as his province*. Grant him but life and leisure, and he is certain of success. It is the hope of his life, and he offers up earnest prayers to God for it. But, when he prays, it is not so much that he may succeed, as that success may not make him vain, presumptuous, and faithless: that, not failure, is the danger. His fear is not for science but for religion; not that he may fail of gaining scientific light, but that scientific light may blind the mind to celestial mysteries. Nothing can be more sublimely confident, and yet free from all suspicion of self-conceit, than his prayer *that men confine the sense within the limits of duty in respect of things divine: for the sense is like the sun, which reveals the face of earth, but seals and shuts up the face of heaven.*

In the next place, as to Bacon's love of Science, we

shall best express it by saying that he was enamoured of it. This is the only subject on which his passionless nature can express itself passionately. Science is his substitute for love, for friendship, we may almost say for religion itself. Indeed, it is Science that makes him in any sense a religious man. Non-religious in conduct, he rises nearest to the language of prophetic ecstacy when he speaks of his great Mission to reunite in wedlock the Universe and the Mind of Man. He believes in a God, it is true; he would *rather believe all the fables in the Legend and the Talmud than that this universal frame is without a Mind.* But this belief in the existence of a Mind of the Universe does not materially affect his advice upon conduct or matters of morals. So far as it influences him at all, his belief in a God influences him rather scientifically than morally, strengthening his sanguine trust that all nature is based, by one divine Mind, upon one divinely simple order, which it is the highest privilege of man to discover and proclaim. That God is in any sense a Person, that is to say, a Being capable of loving and of being loved, or that He is a Father conforming His human children more and more nearly, century by century, to the divine image—this, the Christian theory—seems to form no perceptible part of Bacon's moral system. What he needs, and feels sure of, is the existence, not of a Person, but of a Mind. Even in the Essay where he condemns Atheism as destroying *magnanimity and the raising of human nature*, it is obvious that he attaches no special importance to the Christian faith. Some god, or *Melior Natura*, is useful as a point to draw towards itself the aspirations of humanity; without it, the pyramid is incomplete; there is a sense of something missing and unfinished. But any *Melior Natura* will answer the purpose: and, as his example of its utility, he chooses the magnanimity derived from their religion by the ancient Romans. Whatever passages may be quoted to the contrary from the formal philosophical works, it is an undoubted fact that in the Essays—a far more trustworthy guide to Bacon's real thoughts on such a subject—the Christian religion is seldom recognised as a powerful influence on conduct, except in the perverted form of Superstition.

We are dealing at present with what Bacon was in himself, not with what he taught as a theologian, or as a moralist; but it is important, even for the appreciation of his conduct, to note how his views of human nature were affected by his too sharp distinction between theology and philosophy. He will not, like Plato, *intermingle his philosophy with theology*,[1] and therefore he accepts human nature and life as they are, without taking account of tendencies, aspirations, and impossible ideals. Hence his hopelessness in morals as compared with his hopefulness in science: hence his preference of youth as being, morally at all events, superior to old age; hence his deficiency in the Christian Enthusiasm of Humanity, so that his nearest approximation to it is a pity for the miseries of mankind; hence his want of the virtue of resentment, that righteous recoil from injustice and oppression; hence his general distrust of human nature, and his low standard of conduct for himself and others. *If any man should do wrong merely out of ill nature, why yet it is but like the thorn or briar which prick and scratch because they can do no other;* hence his coldness in friendship; hence his tolerance of falsehood, not as being pleasant, but as being necessary, like physic for a frame diseased.

If philosophy was Bacon's religion, it was also his love, his first love and his last. Human love finds small space in his writings. He had no children to teach him

[1] *Works*, Vol. iii. p. 293.

a father's love. As for marriage, at the ripe age of forty-six he married, as he tells Cecil, an alderman's daughter, a handsome maiden whom he had found to his liking, with whom, his biographer adds, he received a sufficiently ample and liberal portion in marriage. In a codicil to his will he revoked, *for just and grave causes,* the bequests made to his wife in the former part of the will; and shortly after his death she married her gentleman usher. Whatever may have been the relations between them, thus much is certain, that of the love between husband and wife Bacon has no more to say than that *nuptial love maketh mankind:* the love that *perfecteth mankind* is the love of friends. Of friendship he has more to say, and it cannot be denied that among his inferiors (who were not *influential persons*, and therefore could not be regarded as stepping-stones to scientific objects) he made many friends, whom he attached to himself indissolubly by his genial, placid, bright, and unvarying goodness. Yet even in the Essay on Friendship, it is characteristic that he entirely discredits the ancient ideal of friendship as the bond between two differing equals: *there is little friendship in the world, and least of all between equals, which was wont to be magnified. That that is, is between superior and inferior, whose fortunes may comprehend the one the other.* His notion of friendship therefore appears to be little more than kindness answered by gratitude: and even this has to be tempered by the *ancient precept of Bias,* warning men not to be friends as though they could be friends for ever.

Of the other natural outlets for human energy we find little mention in Bacon's works. Of war he speaks with spirit, but as a statesman, not as a warrior. There is nothing of the ring of the trumpet in the persistence with which he recommends external conflict as the natural exercise for the energies of a healthy nation. As for hunting, or other field sports, omit an allusion or two to the game of bowls, and there is scarcely a trace in the Essays that Bacon cared for them. He seems to have no liking or care for birds or beasts, wild or tame. The torture of a long-billed fowl by a *waggish*[1] Christian, who called down on himself the resentment of the Turks by his cruelty, inspires him with no deeper feeling than amusement; and, though he objects to experimenting upon men, he has not a word to say, nor dreams that a word can be said, against the vivisection of animals for scientific purposes. Such petty matters dwelt not in the Philosopher's thoughts. What are they to him compared with the one great object of life? Amusements, interests, occupations, friendship, wife, children, religion, he finds them all in the pursuit of Truth, and the furtherance of the Kingdom of Man.

To a man of this nature, versatile, supple, passionless except where science is concerned, born for the service of all men collectively, and thinking himself justified in using each man individually as a tool and instrument for so high an object, what must have been the feelings suggested by the increasing restlessness and final outbreak of a patron such as Essex? Even before any serious symptoms of such a grave calamity had appeared, Bacon seems to have felt uneasy about the future. He tells his benefactor significantly that he regards himself *as a common (not popular but common)*, and *as much as is lawful to be enclosed of a common so much your Lordship shall be sure to have*. He had long warned his too blunt and impulsive patron against his neglect of the Queen's humours. He had entreated him to study Her Majesty's nature more closely and to flatter her, or, as he expresses it, *to do Her Majesty right*, not in a dry and formal manner,

[1] *Essay* xiii. l. 20. See note there.

but *oratione fida*, with face as well as words.[1] He had instructed him how to imitate Leicester in taking up plans never seriously intended to be carried into effect, but proposed for the mere purpose of appearing to yield to the Queen by dropping them at her desire. Among other arts of a politician, he had written a letter to himself in the name of Essex for the express purpose of showing it to the Queen, so as to conciliate her to her fallen favourite; nay, to make the forgery more complete, he had added a postscript (as from Essex) requesting Bacon to burn the letter. All this and more Bacon had done: the three degrees of falsehood—reserve, dissimulation, and simulation—all had been tried; none of the precepts of the Architect of Fortune had been forgotten; but all had failed. This being the case, what was to be done? Was he to allow his opening career to be shut for ever by a false and foolish sentiment? Surely not; the interests of Science forbade, and the *precept of Bias* condemned it. He had no sympathy with the plot of Essex; on the contrary, his sympathies were with England against all who would divide or weaken England, and with the Queen as representing the unity of England. But if he could no longer defend his former benefactor, might he not at least have avoided prosecuting him? Even if urged to such a task, might he not have excused himself on grounds intelligible to all? Yes, he might have done this; and most commonplace people, obeying commonplace instincts, would have done this, and would have avoided Bacon's fatal error. But the Prophet of Science, not being a commonplace person, acted very differently. Looking at the matter in the dry light of reason, he saw no cause why he should not take such part in the pro-

---

[1] *When at any time your Lordship upon occasion happen in speeches to do her Majesty right (for there is no such matter as flattery amongst you all), I fear, &c. Life,* i. p. 42.

secution as might naturally devolve upon him. To avoid such a duty might engender suspicion ; to court it could do his former friend no harm, and might advance his own fortunes. He therefore wrote, volunteering his services in the prosecution ; he performed the petty part entrusted to him with a vigour approaching acrimony, and as the Queen *took delight in his pen*, he afterwards drew up a narrative detailing the ruin of his unhappy friend, entitled *A Declaration of the Practices and Treasons attempted and committed by Robert, late Earl of Essex.* Defence or justification of such conduct can never be satisfactory. But at least it is well to recognise that we are dealing with an extraordinary man, who did not bind himself by ordinary rules. Bacon's desertion of Essex was not the result of a sudden or unusual impulse : it was the natural result of some of those qualities that contributed to his scientific greatness. It was a sin, but not a sin of weakness, or pusillanimity, or inconsistency : it was of a piece with his whole nature, not to be justified, nor excused, nor extenuated, but to be stored up by posterity as an eternal admonition how easy it is for a gigantic soul, conscious of gigantic purposes, to make shipwreck upon indifference to details, and how morally dangerous it is to be so imbued and penetrated with the notion that one is born for the service of mankind as to be rendered absolutely blind to all the claims of commonplace morality, and to the vulgar ties that connect individuals.

A reactionary feeling seems to have seized Bacon soon after the death of Essex. He gained no promotion by his desertion of his friend, so that he had in no way furthered Science by it; moreover, he had created an unfavourable impression which, injuring him, might so far injure the cause of Science. We have no proof that he even felt a touch of remorse for his conduct to his benefactor; but circumstances seem to show that he felt uneasy under the construction put upon his actions. Possibly the death of his brother Anthony at this time —and Anthony was an avowed and faithful friend to Essex—may have increased this feeling of uneasiness. At all events we find him resolving, about two years after the death of Essex, to have done with politics and to devote himself wholly to philosophy. He gives several reasons for this resolution,[1] and the first is, that *his zeal had been set down as ambition.* But his great reason is philosophy. *I found my zeal set down as ambition, my life past the prime, my weak health chiding me for delay, and my conscience warning me that I was in no way doing my duty in omitting such services as I could myself unaided perform for men, while I was applying myself to tasks that depended upon the will of others: and therefore I at once tore myself away from all those thoughts, and in accordance with my former resolution I devoted my whole energies to this work*—i.e. the Art of Interpreting Nature. Writing thus in 1603, he also tells Cecil that he and politics have shaken hands. *I desire to meddle as little as I can in the King's causes, His Majesty now abounding in counsel, and to follow my private thrift and practice. For as for any ambition, I do assure your Honour mine is quenched. My ambition now I shall only put upon my pen, whereby I shall be able to maintain memory and merit of the times succeeding.*

It was in this year that the *Advancement of Learning* was probably written; and the *Apology in certain imputations concerning the late Earl of Essex* (of which the first printed copy is dated the following year, 1604) may have been at the same time receiving his attention. Probably therefore Bacon, immersed in his favourite literary work, was sincere in his disavowals of all poli-

[1] *Works,* Vol. iii. p. 519.

tical ambition. But even at this time, only three or four months before thus renouncing politics, he does not think it amiss to practise some of the precepts of the *Architect of Fortune.* Among the courses enjoined by that art is *morigeration,* or *applying oneself* to one's superiors. Bacon justified morigeration on principle. *To apply oneself to others is good:* but he adds an important qualification, *so it be with demonstration that a man doth it upon regard, and not upon facility.* Yet in practice Bacon disregards this qualification, and carries his flattery to an unscientific excess of which a master of the art would have been ashamed. When the Queen died, and new favourites were expected to come into power, it was perhaps natural that he should wish to strengthen his connection with Cecil, and to conciliate a few Scotchmen of influence. But was it like a scientific Architect of Fortune to exaggerate his liking for Cecil—between whom and himself there was probably a physical antipathy[1]— so far as to write to Cecil's secretary, *Let him know that he is the personage in this State which I love most; and this, as you may easily judge, proceedeth not out of any straits of my occasions, as might be thought in times past, but merely out of the largeness and fulness of my affections?*[2] And again, in writing to the Earl of Northumberland, who was at first expected to have great influence with the new King, there is something quite naïve in the simplicity with which Bacon suddenly discovers that *there hath been covered in my mind, a long time, a seed of affection and zeal towards your Lordship.*[3] In such *morigeration*

---

[1] *Life,* Vol. iv. p. 52. Yet (Ib. p. 12) he can say to Cecil: *I do esteem whatsoever I have or may have in the world as trash, in comparison of having the honour and happiness to be a near and well-accepted kinsman to so rare and worthy a counsellor, governor, and patriot. For having been a studious, if not curious observer, as well of antiquities of virtue as of late pieces, I forbear to say to your Lordship what I find and conceive.*

[2] Ib. Vol. iii. p. 57.   [3] Ib. Vol. iii. p. 58..

as this, there is little demonstration that it is *done upon regard.* It is refreshing to find Bacon, in spite of all his study, such a child in the art of flattery; but these and other letters seem to indicate that, although he had resolved to give up politics for philosophy, yet he wished so far to keep his footing in the political world as to make his retirement not irrevocable.

Accordingly, he is soon called back to politics. The very year after his *ambition was quenched,* he was appointed an ordinary member of the King's Counsel, and is found drawing up an *Act for the better grounding of a further union to ensue between the Kingdoms of England and Scotland;* and three years afterwards he is made Solicitor-General. Thus in 1607 we find him drawn once more away from Philosophy. And now in the following year, at the beginning of a vacation, Bacon sits down in his practical scientific way to review his prospects. After his fashion he *relates himself to* a note-book, and the note-book has been preserved. During four consecutive days in July, 1608, he jots down entries as they occur to him, about money matters, health, politics, moral maxims, tricks of rhetoric, forms of compliment, great men to be conciliated, philosophy, farming, building, and what not, all unarranged. It is not too much to say that no account of Bacon, however brief and incomplete, can afford to pass over this Diary; for, if we bear in mind steadily, throughout the perusal of it, Bacon's peculiar nature and his entire concentration on science, we shall gain more knowledge of him from these few pages than from any other of his works. The following is a summary of the entries.

Beginning with a determination to *make a stock of 2,000l. always in readiness for bargains and occasions,* he proceeds to touch next on the means of obtaining access to the King, and the names of the Scotchmen who

What Bacon was himself

can help him here; he makes notes of the notions and likings of the King and of Salisbury; he reminds himself *to have ever in readiness matter to minister talk with every of the great counsellors respective, both to induce familiarity, and for countenance in public place;* also, *to win credit comparate to the Attorney in being more short, round, and resolute. (All this is nothing except) (there is more);*[1] and again, a few lines lower down, *to have in mind and use the Attorney's weakness.* It must be remembered that Bacon wishes to succeed the Attorney, and then this will explain the following notes of the Attorney's weak points, to be used as occasion should arise—*The coldest examiner, weak in Gunter's cause, weak with the Judges, Arbe* (Arabella) *cause, too full of cases and distinctions, nibbling solemnly, he distinguisheth but apprehends not.* Salisbury's friendship seemed most important to him at this time, and accordingly he makes a note: *to insinuate myself to become privy to my Lord of Salisbury's estate,* and again, *to correspond with Salisbury in a habit of natural but noways perilous boldness,* so as to get rid of the obstruction; or, to quote Bacon's words, *to free the stands* in his cousin's suspicious nature. Soon afterwards follows a detailed account of the effect of certain medicines upon his constitution, and then—*to think of matters against next Parliament for satisfaction of King and people in my particular* (*and*) *otherwise with respect to policy e gemino*—i.e., the double policy of replenishing the exchequer and also of contenting the people. Then follow some notes about letting lands and houses, and building. Then he reminds himself to send message of compliments to my Lady Dorset the widow, and jots down a *form* appropriate to the occasion: *Death comes to young men, and old men go to death, that*

---

[1] The bracketed words are, I suppose, the phrases in which Bacon intended to correct the Attorney's inadequacies.

is all the difference. Then follow more *forms*, then another note about his health, then legal notes, then the titles of his different literary works, and plans for the arrangement of future note-books, and thus he comes round at last to his own subject, Science, and to the business of securing allies for scientific works. *Making much of Russell that depends upon Sir David Murray, and by that means drawing Sir David, and by him and Sir Thomas Chaloner, in time, the Prince. Getting from Russell a collection of phainomena, of surgery, distillations, mineral trials, the setting on work my Lord of Northnd and Ralegh, and therefore Harriot, themselves being already inclined to experiments. Acquainting myself with Poe, as for my health, and by him learning the experiments which he hath of physic, and gaining entrance into the inner of some great persons. Seeing and trying whether the Archbishop of Canterbury may not be affected in it, being single and glorious and believing the sense, not desisting to draw in the Bishop Andrews,*[1] *being single, rich, and sickly, a professor to some experiments. . . . Query, of physicians to be gained, the likest is Paddy, Dr. Hammond. Query, of learned men beyond the seas to be made, and hearkening who they be that may be so inclined.* Then follow great plans of literary works, after which comes this note: *Laying for a place to command wits and pens, Westminster, Eton, Winchester, specially Trinity College in Cambridge, St. John's in Cambridge, Magdalene College in Oxford, and bespeaking this betimes with the King, my Lord Archbishop, my Lord Treasurer.* Then follow notes as to the proposed College of Science, its *order and discipline,* its travelling fellows, *vaults, furnaces, terraces*

---

[1] *Life,* Vol. iv. p. 63. Mr. Spedding says, 'The reading here is doubtful, but I think Launcelot Andrews must be meant. He was at this time Bishop of Chichester.'

for insulation; after which he passes into a Scheme of *Legitimate Investigation,* and proceeds, in accordance with the scheme, to investigate the nature of motion. Close upon this follow some notes on high politics, beginning with *the bringing of the King low by poverty and empty coffers,* and passing on to Bacon's favourite suggestion of a *Monarchy in the West* formed by Great Britain together with a civilized Ireland and the Low Countries annexed. Next come notes on Recusants, plans for building and landscape-gardening, *practising to be inward with my Lady Dorset per Champners ad utilit. testam.*—i.e., by means of Champners for testamentary purposes.[1] Then follow copious memorial notes of health and lists of his rents, jewels, debts, improvements. Then more notes about the Recusants, and a second edition of the notes against the Attorney, entitled *Hubbard's Disadvantage.* The entries conclude with a list of creditors and debts owing to them, preceded by a note of *Services on foot,* and another of *customs fit for me individually (custumæ aptæ ad individuum).* Our extracts shall conclude with these :—*To furnish my Lord of Suffolk with ornaments for public speeches. To make him think how he should be reverenced by a Lord Chancellor, if I were; prince-like . . . To have particular occasions, fit and grateful and continual, to maintain private speech with every the great persons, and sometimes drawing more than one of them together. Query, for credit; but so as to save time; and to this end not many things at once, but to draw in length . . . At*

---

[1] It is not necessary to suppose that Bacon hoped to derive any personal advantage from Lady Dorset any more than from the Archbishop of Canterbury and Bishop Andrews mentioned above, one as being *single and glorious,* and the other as *single and sickly.* But science might profit by legacies, and science was in Bacon's mind.

In Essay xxxiv. l. 98, Bacon expressly blames *fishing for testaments:* but there he is blaming *fishing* for one's own sake. Bacon would *fish* for the sake of science.

council-table chiefly to make good my Lord of Salisbury's motions and speeches, and for the rest sometimes one, sometimes another; chiefly his that is most earnest and in affection.

Is it possible to read these notes without feeling that they betoken a mind unique and extraordinary, worldly, it is true, but not after the common fashion of worldliness: say rather an unworldly mind of superhuman magnanimity, gradually becoming enslaved by the world, while professing to use the world as a mere tool? It was a maxim of Bacon in Science that one can only become master of Nature by first obeying Nature: and with fatal consequences Bacon transfers his aphorism from Science to Morality: he will place all the arts of worldliness at the feet of Truth, and will master them by first obeying them. But, as he himself asks in the Essays, *how can a man comprehend great matters that breaketh his mind to small observations?* And how could a man hope to be the discoverer of a new world of scientific discovery, or to inaugurate a new national policy, who had to break his mind to the observance of Cecil's cold suspicions, or Suffolk's pompous self-conceit, or the tedious bookishness of James? Admit that Bacon, in thus winding himself into the ways of influential men, was acting, or thought he was acting, for Science, or for the Nation, not for himself; yet in these degenerate arts and shifts what kind of apprenticeship was there for the task of a Prophet of Science, a founder of the Monarchy of the West? Nay more, was it not inevitable that this great mind, while bent on outwitting Mammon for the interests of Science, would gradually find itself outwitted, entangled, and enslaved?

It was inevitable: and the rest of Bacon's life contains little but the record of his gradual acquiescence in defeat and servitude. But at least, before we proceed further in that degrading history, we may reiterate with advantage that Bacon was no vulgar schemer or common miser. It is so easy to disbelieve all his protestations of desire for leisure, and of passionate allegiance to science, so natural, especially for coarse, sensual, malignant minds, to explain his conduct as the result of ambition, avarice, and hypocrisy; and such an explanation is so fatal to the right understanding of his nature, that we may, even at the risk of some repetition, be justified in briefly describing the standpoint from which Bacon was reviewing his fortunes in July, 1608.

He had early made up his mind that he was to lead the life of a philosopher, and that philosophers must not shrink from action. *Pragmatical men must be taught not to despise learning as unpractical;* they must be made to see that *learning is not like a lark which can mount and sing, and please itself and nothing else; but it partakes of the nature of a hawk, which can soar aloft and can also descend and strike upon its prey at leisure.*[1] It is a fault incident to learned men *that they fail sometimes in applying themselves to particular persons.*[2] Bacon blames *the tenderness and want of compliance in some of the most ancient and revered philosophers, who retired too easily from civil business that they might avoid indignities and perturbations, and live (as they thought) more pure and saint-like.*[3] By serving Mammon he will be better able, he thinks, to serve the cause of Truth. In seeking wealth and place, he is thinking, in part at least, of the favour that wealth and place will procure for the *Great Instauration. It is of no little importance to the dignity of literature that a man, naturally fitted rather for literature than for anything else, and borne by some destiny against the inclination of his genius into the business of active life, should have risen to such high and*

---

[1] *Works,* Vol. vi. p. 58.　　[2] Ib., Vol. iii. p. 279.　　[3] Ib., Vol. v. p. 10.

honourable appointments, under so wise a king. It is for this he serves Essex; for this he courts the rising Villiers; for this he cringes to the powerful Buckingham. When he plans in his Diary the *drawing in* of this lord or that bishop, it is always with a view to the advancement of learning. Avarice is a vice quite foreign to his nature. As a young man he is censured by his mother for his unthrifty habits and his prodigal indulgence to his servants. And his later life contains evidence of the same free expenditure and the same want of control over his household, but no indications at all of the deliberate accumulation of money for its own sake apart from the power it would give. In the *History of Henry VII.* no fault of that monarch is more keenly satirised than his greed for money, and the attraction exercised on him by the *glimmerings of a confiscation*.[1] Read in this light, the *testamentary* notes in the Diary are harmless: they simply show that Bacon was on the alert, as he was in the case of Sutton's bequest, to divert such legacies as he could from almsgiving, school-founding, and the like, to scientific purposes. His heart's desire is that he may save time and promote the truth by conciliating authority and disarming opposition. As the French in Italy found no need to fight, but only to chalk up quarters for their troops, so he, to quote his constant metaphor, hopes to find *chalked-up quarters* for his philosophy in the hearts of men. Such is the prize that he will gain by his worldliness. Thus will he hallow the name of the one True Logic by bowing in the house of Rimmon.

In justice to Bacon we must also repeat that his philosophy was in its nature social, and absolutely required companionship. The path of his science, he expressly tells us, *is not a way over which only one man can pass at a time*.[2] His science depends upon facts, and facts

[1] *Works*, Vol. vi. p. 150. [2] *Works*, Vol. iv. p. 102.

can only be obtained by observations, and observations, to be numerous, require numerous observers. *One must employ factors and merchants* for facts, he says,[1] and the mere work of compiling the Natural History, which was to form the Third Part of the Great Instauration, is described as *a work for a King, or Pope, or some College or Order.* It clearly necessitated co-operation on a large scale, and how could he obtain such co-operation better than by appealing to the titled and powerful among his countrymen? And how could he appeal to them with better chance of success than by making himself a name among statesmen, and a place among the counsellors of the realm? Thus, step by step, he was diverted from the purer ambition of his youth under the pretext of attaining the height of that ambition by a shorter path. More than once did he resolve to tear himself from politics and place-hunting, to *retire with two men to Cambridge,* or, at all events, to *put his ambition wholly upon his pen.* But circumstances (aided by his own restless craving for action) were too strong for him : his father's sudden death, his domestic necessities, his birth, training, and connections, and his power of grave weighty speech stamping him as a born servant of the State—everything seemed to conspire to tempt him from philosophy, and the temptation was too strong. Riches and honour, and the reputation of a statesman, these in themselves he might have resisted; but when they presented themselves under the mask of friends and servants of the Truth, as instruments to prepare the way for the Kingdom of Man over Nature, it was not in Bacon's power to hold out. It was Satan tempting as an angel of light.

And surely no story of unhappy wretches bartering away their immortal souls to the Evil One for a hollow pretence

---

[1] *Works,* Vol. iv. p. 252.

of present happiness, and afterwards beating themselves idly against the narrowing net that presses them towards the inevitable pit, is much sadder than the record of the retribution, artistic if ever retribution was, that befell the Traitor to Truth. Mammon bestowed his gifts, but they are found to be no gifts, and he takes full wages in return. Bacon wins the credit he desires to win *comparate to the Attorney*, and becomes Attorney in his place; but it is for the purpose of prosecuting St. John, torturing Peacham,[1] and holding up to posterity for ever the contrast between his courtier-like servility and Coke's manly independence. By making great people *think how they should be reverenced by a Lord Chancellor if I were*, he at last takes his seat on the woolsack: but it is to *reverence* indeed; to cringe, to work or be worked like a tool, in carrying out not his own but another's policy; to receive the orders of Villiers, and to fawn and grovel when the favourite is offended; to reverse illegally a just decision[2] upon the favourite's intercession; and finally to be degraded from his high post, without having introduced a single measure for the permanent benefit of the nation, but with the result of having tarnished the reputation of the bench and shaken men's confidence in humanity. It is pitiable to see the persistent advocate of external war helplessly lamenting his royal Master's pacific policy—*pray God we surfeit not of it;* protesting that *security*[3] *is an ill guard for a kingdom;* in due time penning a royal proclamation, in which he dilates on the advantages of peace; *as in our princely judgment we hold nothing more worthy of a Christian monarch than the conservation of peace at home and abroad;* and

---

[1] That Bacon approved of the torture of Peacham is implied by his recommending torture for Peacock in the words, *If it may not be done otherwise, it is fit Peacock be put to torture. He deserveth it as well as Peacham did. Life*, Vol. vii. p. 77.

[2] *Life*, Vol. vii. Appendix.   [3] i.e. Carelessness, unguardedness.

urging, as one of the advantages of the Spanish match, *that by the same conjunction there will be erected a tribunal or prætorian power to decide the controversies which may arise amongst the princes and estates of Christendom without effusion of Christian blood.*

Part of the retribution visited on Bacon seems to have been a blindness to the distinction between what is great and petty as well as between what is good and bad. Among other infatuations he appears to have conceived a genuine respect, if not admiration, for James I. The King was not quite the contemptible buffoon that he has been popularly supposed to be: but he was not the Solomon that he was supposed by Bacon.[1] The truth is, admiration for place and power had dazzled his intellect and confounded his judgment. His sanguine spirit tinged the new reign and his own prospects in it with the same false glow of hopefulness with which it tinged the realm of Science. James was to be a Solomon, Bacon was to be Solomon's chief counsellor and inspirer, and Villiers was the young and rising spirit, who would look up to Bacon as to a father and give the shape of action to the high visions of the philosophic statesman. The impending clouds between King and Commons were to be cleared away by the breezes of wholesome war; the nation was further to be pacified and contented by improved laws and institutions without detriment to the royal prerogative. Scotland was to be colonised, Ireland to be pacified and civilised, the Low Countries to be annexed. Such was Bacon's policy; and had he not been blinded by the close brightness of the throne he might have gone some way to the attainment of it. For the *peremptory royalist*, who was nevertheless repeatedly selected by the Commons as their representative, and *never one hour out of*

---

[1] *Without flattery I think your Majesty the best of Kings, and my noble Lord of Buckingham the best of persons favoured. Life*, Vol. vii. p. 78.

credit with the lower house, had advantages possessed by few for bridging the widening gulf between the Commons and the Crown.[1] As it was, he did nothing but harm to the royal cause by the 'new doctrine, but now broached,' in which he exaggerated the King's prerogative, and by his attempts to restrict and fetter, as far as in him lay, the independence of the judges.

Yet nothing at first could be less courtier-like and more sententiously parental than the tone in which Bacon lectures the young Villiers, just on the threshold of his career as favourite, upon the duties of his new life: *It is now time that you should refer your actions chiefly to the good of your sovereign and your country. It is the life of an ox or beast always to eat and never to exercise; but men are born (and especially Christian men) not to cram in their fortunes, but to exercise their virtues. . . . Above all, depend wholly (next to God) upon the King; and be ruled (as hitherto you have been) by his instructions, for that is best for yourself.*[2] But all this is mere waste paper, the romantic effusion of a dreamer, whose understanding is made by his will, and who has brought himself to this, that he can believe whatever is pleasant to believe. Compare the advice given the same year—*By no means be you persuaded to interfere yourself by word or letters in any cause depending, or like to be depending, in any court of justice*—with the actual practice of Buckingham and Bacon, the former continually recommending, and the latter (without one remonstrance on record) acknowledging recommendations of parties engaged in causes *depending or like to be depending.* It is not in the least

---

[1] *Life,* Vol. vi. p. 134. But Mr. Gardiner (*History of England from the Accession of James I.* &c., Vol. i. p. 181) is probably nearer the truth in saying, 'If James had been other than he was, the name of Bacon would have come down to us as great in politics as it is in science.' James being what he was, nothing could be done.

[2] *Life,* Vol. vi. p. 6.

surprising that Bacon failed to acquire the influence he ought over the royal favourite. The two men moved in different worlds; and Bacon was weighted, not only by his suppleness, his too easy temper, and his excessive desire to please, but also by the very force and height of his intellect. All the dreams of the study vanished when the philosopher entered the royal presence and was confronted with the practical needs of the moment, the intimidation of the judges, the disgracing of Coke, the upholding of benevolences and monopolies, and of the royal prerogative generally. Instead of Bacon's lifting up James to the heights of the philosophic world, James drew Bacon down to the royal world. But to work in that grosser atmosphere at those degenerate arts and shifts, which Bacon was wont to call *fiddling*, the author of the Instauratio Magna was not by nature fitted. The difference between him and Buckingham was so vast that one of two things was inevitable: either Buckingham must dictate to Bacon, or Bacon to Buckingham; for a natural consent of thought between the two was out of the question. Naturally, Bacon thought himself best qualified to dictate, and at first he did so. But when the *parental* tone had been bitterly resented by Buckingham and reproved by the King, it might have been supposed that Bacon's eyes would have been opened to his own insignificance and nothingness in all affairs of State, and that he might have perceived the worthlessness of office held under such conditions.

But it was not so. Mammon, it would seem, had 'been in his heart, deposed his intellect.' Beyond an occasional hint of vexation at the King's pacific policy we have no traces of irritation, no evidence that Bacon resented the King's misappreciation. The fact is, he had by this time so broken himself to the task of studying the humours of great people as the stepping-stone to higher objects, that he had drifted into the habit of acting as though he believed that such an obsequious parody of statesmanship was a fit goal for a great man's life. We have read above, Bacon's ironical description of the ideal Statesman of Selfishness, written in the days of his earlier and purer manhood, *how he is to make himself cunning rather in the humours and drifts of persons than in the nature of business and affairs. . . And ever rather let him take the side which is likeliest to be followed than that which is soundest and best.* And this is what Bacon had brought himself to do and to do naturally. It is precisely what he deliberately sets down in his Diary above: *At council table chiefly to make good my Lord of Salisbury's motions and speeches, and for the rest sometimes one, sometimes another; chiefly his that is most earnest and in affection.* When a nature so sanguine, so colossal in its plans and hopes, so indifferent to details, so dispassionately careless of individual interests, and so wholly devoted to a mere intellectual object, once begins to deviate from the path of conventional morality, it is not easy to predict where the deviations will end. Bacon began, no doubt, by determining not to be influenced on the bench by any recommendations of parties engaged in cases pending, except so far as he might show them some personal attention not affecting his legal decisions. But he must have known that this was seldom possible, and even where possible, it was not what was meant by the recommender. Little by little he extends his personal attentions, till at last he ventured in one case, that of Dr. Steward, to reverse his own just decision by a subsequent unjust decision, in which to the injustice of the judgment was added irregularity of procedure.[1]

---

[1] See *Life*, Vol. vii. p. 585 where Mr. Heath emphatically decides against Bacon. But I understand from Mr. Spedding that he demurs to this decision on the ground that 'modern Chancery lawyers know the modern rules of proceeding . . . . but I have no reason to think that they know what was

And in the same way, as regards the habit of receiving presents, there is no sufficient reason to doubt that he began by determining to receive none except from parties whose cases had been decided; but here again his indifference to detail, his habit of taking for granted the most favourable aspect of things, and perhaps his gradually increasing sense of the power of money, all combine to make him believe, against belief, in the probity of servants who were taking bribes before his eyes. To quote one example, a valuable cabinet is brought to his house. *I said to him that brought it, that I came to view it, and not to receive it; and gave commandment that it should be carried back, and was offended when I heard it was not.* A year and a half afterwards the cabinet is still in his possession, claimed by a creditor of the donor, and by the donor's request Bacon retains it, and is retaining it at the time when he is accused of corruption. Now, in many men such conduct would be undoubtedly and rightly considered a proof of dishonesty: and it is very easy to ridicule in an epigram any attempt to maintain that what in common men would have been dishonesty was not dishonesty in Bacon. But take all Bacon's antecedents into account, and it will not seem so ridiculous that he may have been honest; add also the clumsiness of such dishonesty, if it had really been dishonest, and Bacon's honesty may seem by no means improbable: consider, lastly, Bacon's utter and evident ignorance of any danger from charges about to be

the practice in James I.'s time, or what were the limits of the discretionary power reserved by a Lord Chancellor for exceptional cases. It is true that Mr. Heath quotes Bacon's own rules. But if they were rules made by himself, I do not know that they were binding for better or worse. When I lay down a rule for myself in dealing with my neighbours, if I find that on some occasion a rigorous adherence to it will cause mischief, I release myself from the obligation. So it may have been with Bacon in this case for anything I know.' Many admirers of Bacon will wish they could be satisfied with this argument.

brought against him, his unfeigned pleasure at the prospect of the meeting of that very Parliament which was to prove his ruin, and then, when the charges were stated, his astonishment, his tone of innocence, gradually exchanged for perplexity, for shame, for remorse—and I believe a careful student of Bacon's life will come to no other conclusion than the paradox arrived at by Mr. Spedding, that Bacon took money from suitors whose cases were before him, that he did this repeatedly, and yet that he did it without feeling that he was laying himself open to a charge of what in law would be called bribery, and without any consciousness that he had secrets to conceal of which the disclosure would be fatal to his reputation. In the notes prepared by him for an interview with the King there is a significant erasure, which seems to indicate the unsettled perplexity which, when he reviews his past conduct, makes him almost unable to say definitely what he has done and what he has not done. After stating the three degrees of bribery, and the first and most serious as being *of bargain or contract for reward to pervert justice pendente lite*, he thus meets the first: *for the first of them I take myself to be as innocent as any born upon St. Innocent's-day, in my heart.* Note the *in my heart;* as though he could answer for his heart but not for his actions. And that this is his meaning is borne out by the following sentence, written, but afterwards crossed out: *And yet perhaps, in some two or three of them, the proofs may stand pregnant to the contrary.* These words can scarcely bear any other meaning than this, that the writer is conscious of having acted in such a way that, although his heart has been kept pure and single, the world will never believe it, nor can be reasonably expected to believe it, in the face of the *pregnant proofs to the contrary*. Explain it how we may, it is certain that, in spite of all his confessions,

Bacon believed himself to be morally innocent, innocent *in his heart*. Preserved in cipher by his biographer, but not published, there has been discovered Bacon's own verdict on himself in these words : *I was the justest judge that was in England these fifty years, but it was the justest censure in Parliament that was these two hundred years.* Was this true? Probably not; but it was certainly true that he believed it to be true: and the explanation of it is to be looked for partly, no doubt, in his kindliness to inferiors and desire to conciliate superiors, doing the best for all alike, but above all in his unique nature, contemptuous of individual interests, and bent on benefiting mankind on a stupendous scale, conscious of noble ends and divine purposes ; conscious, in a word, of that grandiose kind of goodness to which in his magnificent style he gives the name of Philanthropia,[1] which would have made the Priest of the Kingdom of Man laugh to scorn the bare supposition that it was possible for him to be guilty of corruption. And this explains how it was that he retained his self-respect, even after his fall and to the very last. The gossips of the day were startled by his erect carriage and confident bearing: to them he seemed to have no feeling of his situation. 'Do what we will,' said the Prince of Wales, 'this man scorns to go out like a snuff.' Not indeed that the fallen Chancellor had not his moments of contrition ; not that he did not pour out his soul in bitter heartfelt penitence to the Mind of the Universe ; but the cause of his remorse and subject his penitence was not the receiving of presents from suitors, not the recollection of gifts of 50 gold buttons, or a cabinet, or 110 pounds of plate received *pendente lite*. All this was nothing, or at least not worth particularising, in his secret confession to the Searcher of Souls. He groans under the burden of a greater sin,

[1] *Essay* xiii., l. 3.

his neglect of his Mission, his treason to the Truth : *besides my innumerable sins I confess before Thee that I am debtor to Thee for the gracious talent of Thy gifts and graces, which I have neither put into a napkin, nor put it, as I ought, to exchangers, where it might have made best profit, but misspent it in things for which I was least fit, so as I may truly say my soul hath been a stranger in the course of my pilgrimage.*[1] It is the old text again, *multum incola.* With this Bacon's life begins, and with this it ends.

---

[1] *Life*, Vol. vii. p. 231. In 1605-6 (*Life*, Vol. iii. p. 253) he had made a similar confession that, in his alienation from his occupations, there had been *many errors which I do willingly acknowledge; and amongst the rest this great one that led the rest; that knowing myself by inward calling to be fitter to hold a book than to play a part, I have led my life in civil causes: for which I was not very fit by nature, and more unfit by the preoccupation of my mind.*

CHAPTER II.

BACON AS A PHILOSOPHER.

THE belief in a God, a *Mind of the Universe*, is at the root of Bacon's philosophy, and is the ground of his confidence in the human power of attaining truth. The study of nature is appointed men by God, who *hath set the world in the heart of men.* These words he interprets as *declaring not obscurely that God hath framed the mind of man as a glass capable of the image of the universal world (joying to receive the signature thereof), as the eye is of light.*[1] It is strange to see how Bacon, who blames Plato for intermingling theology with his philosophy, falls naturally himself into theological language when inculcating the study of nature. Non-religious in discoursing of conduct, when he touches on science he breathes the very spirit of an Evangelist. He speaks of *entering the Kingdom of Man* as Christian writers speak of entering the Kingdom of God; and in both cases the condition is the same—we must become as *little children.* The word of God, audible and legible in nature, is *that sound and language which went forth into all lands and did not incur the confusion of Babel: this should men study to be perfect in, and, becoming again as little children, condescend to take the alphabet of it into their own hands.*[2] As there is no concord between God and Mammon, so *there is a great difference between the*

[1] *Works*, Vol. iii. p. 220.   [2] *Works*, Vol. v. p. 132.

Idols of the human mind and the Ideas of the divine: as, in order to enter the kingdom of Heaven, we have to renounce the world, the flesh and the Devil, so, in order to enter the kingdom of Man, the Idols must be *renounced and put away with a fixed and solemn determination, and the understanding must be thoroughly freed and cleansed.*[1] The atomic theory, in Bacon's judgment, rather favours than assails the belief in the existence of a God; *for it is a thousand times more credible that four mutable elements and one immutable fifth essence, duly and eternally placed, need no God, than that an army of infinite small portions or seeds unplaced should have produced this order and beauty without a Divine Marshal;*[2] and again, *the wisdom of God shines out more brightly when nature does one thing, while Providence does quite another consequence, than if single schemes and natural motions were impressed with the stamp of Providence.*[3]

The rapturous language in which the Poets and Prophets of Israel described the wedlock that united Jehovah to his chosen people, is selected by Bacon as fittest to describe the future union between the Mind of Man and the Universe. *We have prepared,* he says, *the Bride chamber of the Mind and Universe,* speaking of the work he has achieved in the Advancement of Learning: and again, in the Essays, he declares that *the inquiry of Truth, which is the love-making or wooing of it; the knowledge of Truth, which is the presence of it; and the belief of Truth, which is the enjoying of it—is the sovereign good of human nature.*[4]

---

[1] It is true that Bacon generally uses the word *Idols,* without any reference to false gods, and merely as 'inania placita,' mere empty dogmas as opposed to divine ideas. But here the context indicates some tinge of the former meaning.

[2] *Essay* xvi. l. 15.

[3] *De Augmentis,* iii. 4, quoted in *Works,* Vol. i. p. 57

[4] *Essay* i. l. 37-41.

He seems to believe that in some happier original condition of Mankind, the Mind and Nature were once wedded, but are now divorced. He aims *at restoring to its perfect and original condition that commerce between the Mind of Man and the Nature of things which is more precious than anything on earth*,[1] and claims to have *established for ever lawful marriage between the empirical and the rational faculty, the unkind and ill-starred divorce and separation of which has thrown into confusion all the affairs of the human family.* We have here, not the prosaic realisable schemes of a low utilitarianism aiming at nothing more, as Lord Macaulay would have us believe, than the 'supply of our vulgar wants,' but rather the prophetic raptures of a Poet. Wordsworth himself can soar no higher, and (consciously or not) finds no words but Bacon's to describe the glorious fruit that shall spring from—

> — the discerning intellect of man
> When wedded to this goodly Universe.

Yet the great popular Essayist of our century sees no sense of Mission in Bacon, nothing that savours of the divine in Bacon's philosophy—nothing but the application of the reasoning powers to the comforts and conveniences of man. Lord Macaulay contrasts the utilitarian Bacon with Plato and Seneca, the enthusiasts for truth, as though the former took for his sole object that which the two latter utterly despised. Plato's good-humoured depreciation of astronomy, regarded as a mere auxiliary to agriculture and navigation, is placed in sharp antithesis to Bacon's practical preference of profitable pursuits. It cannot be denied that scattered through Bacon's works there may be found expressions that may appear, on a superficial view, to justify this contrast.

[1] *Works*, Vol. iv. p. 7.

Fruit unquestionably was the main object of Bacon's philosophy, and against a barren philosophy he wages implacable war. But Bacon's *fruit* means more than Lord Macaulay supposes, more than the mere 'supply of the vulgar wants of men': it includes the discovery of all the secret laws of nature, and its object is to make man the Lord of the World, wielding at his absolute command all the natural forces of the Universe. The attainment of such an object could not but bring with it some elevation of man's intellectual nature, some new and wider possibilities of moral development.

Bacon at all events would have disavowed Lord Macaulay's defence of him against his ancient rivals. The mere discovery of a few isolated truths—however conducive to man's comfort—was as contemptible to Bacon as to Seneca or Plato. He blames those who have been diverted from the philosophic path by the temptation of early unripe fruit, *the wandering inquiry . . . . that has sought experiments of Fruit and not of Light.*[1] It is true he avows that he is *not raising a capitol or pyramid for the pride of man.* But, on the other hand, neither is he building a shop What he is doing is, *laying a foundation in the human understanding for a holy temple after the model of the world.*[2] He deprecates the divorce between utility and truth. *Truth and utility*, he says, *are here the very same things, and works themselves are of greater value as pledges of truth than as contributing to the comforts of life*;[3] and again, *I care little about the mechanical arts themselves, only about those things which they contribute to the equipment of philosophy.*[4] In astronomy it is the same; *I want not predictions of eclipses*, he says, *but the truth.*[5] Plato could have said no more.

---

[1] *Works*, Vol. iv. p. 17.   [2] Ib. p. 110: see also p. 115.
[3] Ib. p. 107.   [4] Ib. p. 271.   [5] *Works*, Vol. v. p. 511.

An important part of Bacon's philosophy is negative and preventive. Like Machiavelli in morals, so Bacon in Science, will begin by describing what men do, before he comes to speak of what they ought to do. And, looking at the history of philosophy, he finds that men have erred, are erring, and are in danger of erring, through haste and indolence, through presumption and despair. The world is a volume of God, a kind of *Second Scripture;* and *as the words or terms of all languages in an immense variety are composed of a few simple letters, so all the actions and powers of things are formed by a few natures and original elements of simple motions.*[1] It follows therefore that the right method to study the volume is first to master the Alphabet, *the original elements of simple motions,* and then to proceed to the study of complex phenomena arising out of them. But men in their presumptuous haste suppose that they can jump at the meaning of Nature, just as boys will jump at the meaning of sentences without undergoing the preliminary labour of mastering the elements of the language: men put their own ideas into nature, as slovenly readers will impute their own meaning to their author. Upon such sciolists *Heraclitus gave a just censure, saying, Men sought wisdom in their own little worlds and not in the great and common world: for they disdain to spell, and so by degrees to read in the volume of God's works.* First therefore men must be taught to put away their own hastily conceived prejudices, and to look with simple eyes upon the *great and common world.* Nothing can be expected in the way of fruit till this is done: when this is done, the Mind and the Universe, at present divorced, will be for ever reunited.

Now of all the enemies that have contributed to the

---

[1] *Works.* Vol. v., p. 426.

divorce between the intellect and the world, *Authority* is the most formidable. Authority has substituted the *little world* of this or that philosopher for the *great and common world;* it has encouraged indolence and has suppressed inquiry. Authority therefore must be first pulled down from her throne before Truth can reign supreme in the realm of philosophy. But Authority is incarnate in Aristotle, and therefore against Aristotle Bacon wages incessant war, not so much as being Aristotle, but as representing the *ostentatious* Greek philosophy. *Ostentatious* is the epithet applied by Bacon to the philosophy of the great Greek writers, Plato, Aristotle, and the rest, to distinguish it from the quiet, philosophic study of nature practised by their predecessors, Anaxagoras, Heraclitus, and others. Even Socrates is *ostentatious.* Bacon speaks respectfully of *the old times before the Greeks, when natural science was perhaps more flourishing though it made less noise, not having yet passed into the pipes and trumpets of the Greeks;*[1] and declares that *that wisdom which we have derived principally from the Greeks is but like the boyhood of Knowledge; it can talk, but it cannot generate; for it is fruitful of controversies and barren of works.*[2] Time, he says, is like a river which brings down to us on its surface the light frivolities of the past, while solid discoveries—those of the Egyptians or of the older Greek philosophers, whose writings have been lost—have been allowed to sink into oblivion. People have been from time to time seduced from the true path of patient research by some *man of bold disposition, famous for methods and short ways, which people like.*[3] Such a one is Aristotle, who is also to be censured for his *boldness,* his *spirit of difference and contradictions*[4] springing from his self-will, and also because, *after the Ottoman fashion,* he thought

---

[1] *Works,* Vol. iv. p. 108.
[2] Ib. p. 15.
[3] Ib. p. 14.
[4] Ib. p. 344.

that he could not reign with safety unless he put all his brethren to death.[1]

Aristotle is also hateful to Bacon, not only as the representative of authority, but also as identified with the Logic of the Schools, in which deduction was everything and induction nothing. Besides subverting authority, it is therefore necessary to subvert the established Logic. To such lengths does Bacon carry his hostility to Logic and to the barren uses of the Syllogism, that he speaks sometimes of rejecting syllogistic Logic altogether. The deductive logicians are compared to spiders, spinning cobwebs out of their own entrails, whereas they ought rather to imitate the bees gathering the stores of the flowers before they use their art to transmute what they have collected into honey. Not that Bacon would have seriously rejected the syllogism—which can no more be rejected than reasoning itself—but he perceived, what will hardly be denied, that there is little use for anything more than the syllogisms of common sense in the investigations of Natural Science. The syllogism is useless till you have exactly defined your terms. But the more important problems of Natural Science mostly depend upon the definitions of terms. When you have obtained your adequate names or definitions of heat and light, for example, you have obtained in great measure what you want. So important were names, the right names, indicating the essential natures of the things named, that to Bacon there seemed a natural connection between Adam the namer, and Adam the ruler of creatures. When fallen man should be restored to his pristine blessedness, he would regain the power of ruling by regaining the power of naming: *whensoever he shall be able to call the creatures by their names he shall again command*

[1] *Works*, Vol. iv. p. 358.

them. Considering the absurd and harmful importance attached to the syllogism in the Middle Ages, we have probably no right to blame Bacon for the contempt he pours on deductive Logic, at all events when applied to Natural Science.

But besides these obstacles arising from authority, and from false methods encouraged by authority, Bacon lays great stress on others, on those preconceived shadowy notions which he called *Idols*—i.e., *images*—in opposition to the divine *ideas* or realities. Some of these are inherent in the human mind, as for example the general prejudice in favour of symmetry and order, or the prejudice that opens men's minds to instances favourable to their own opinion, and closes their eyes against unfavourable instances: such prejudices extend to the whole tribe of men, and may therefore be called *Idols of the Tribe*. Again, individual men, circumscribed within the narrow and dark limits of their individuality, as shaped by their country, their age, their own physical and mental peculiarities, find themselves as it were fettered in a cave, lighted by the fire of their own little world, and not by the sunlight of the great common world, so that, instead of discerning realities, they only see the shadows of realities, the shadows cast by their own fire on the surface of their own cave: such individual misconceptions or Idols may be called *Idols of the Cave*. Language is a third imposture, almost inherent in human nature, pretending to supply nothing but the expression of thoughts, but, under the mask of this pretence, tyrannizing over and moulding thoughts. It is the Idol of intercourse, deriving its influence from all meetings of men, and may therefore be called the *Idol of the Market-place*. Lastly, Authority itself, though not strictly speaking on the same footing as the other three Idols, as not being internal but rather external to the human mind, may nevertheless, on account of its baneful influence, be conveniently classed with the Idols. In the place of the unobtrusive worship of the Truth, Authority substitutes the mere fictions and theatrical stage-plays (for they are no better) of the *ostentatious philosophers*. It may therefore be called the *Idol of the Theatre*. These four Idols are to be solemnly renounced by all who desire to enter the Kingdom of Man over Nature.

Hitherto we have been dealing with what men do and ought not to do: now we pass to the question, what ought men to do? After a preliminary mapping out and partition of the provinces of knowledge, showing which are already in part or wholly subdued, and which remain to be subdued, the answer is given to this question as follows : Man is to obtain his kingdom over Nature by mastering her language so as to make her speak with it as man wills, and by obeying her laws so as to make her work his own will in accordance with her own laws. The laws of nature are to be ascertained by observation of particular instances ; instance after instance is to be brought in (or *induced*), and from the study of these particular instances we are to ascend to a general rule or law. This method, depending upon the bringing in, or *inducing*, of instances, is called *Induction :* but by the term induction Bacon does not mean *the old induction of which the logicians speak, which proceeds by simple enumeration*, and which he justly calls *a puerile thing*.[1] *To the immediate and proper perceptions of the Senses* he does not attach much weight.[2] He therefore seeks *to provide helps for the sense, substitutes to supply its deficiencies, rectifications to correct its errors;* and this he seeks to accomplish *not so much by instruments as by experiments*. One important characteristic, then, of the New Induction is experiment.

[1] *Works*, Vol. iv. p. 25. [2] Ib. p. 26.

But there is an art of conducting experiments. Some empirical philosophers are content to rest in Empiricism ; others ascend too hastily to first principles : both extremes must be avoided. Bacon therefore will teach this *Art of Experiments;* and the art shall be so completely taught in all the details of its precepts, that by means of it subordinate observers and experimenters shall be able to work in the right direction under the general control of a superintendent, who may be called the Architect. Now of this art of experiments the secret and basis is this, that *Cupid sprang out of the egg hatched by Night*, that all light arises out of darkness, all positive knowledge from negative knowledge : or, to quit metaphor, no phenomenon can have the cause of its presence ascertained till there have been observed a number of cases where the phenomenon is absent.

Commenting upon Bacon's analysis of Induction, Lord Macaulay complains that it is no more than 'an analysis of that which we are all doing from morning to night ;' and he proceeds to give a homely instance of it : 'A plain man finds his stomach out of order. He never heard Lord Bacon's name ; but he proceeds in the strictest conformity with the rules laid down in the second book of the *Novum Organum*, and satisfies himself that mincepies have done the mischief. "I ate mincepies on Monday and Wednesday, and I was kept awake by indigestion all night." This is the *comparentia ad intellectum instantiarum convenientium*. "I did not eat any on Tuesday and Friday, and I was quite well." This is the *comparentia instantiarum in proximo quæ natura data privantur*. "I ate very sparingly of them on Sunday, and was very slightly indisposed in the evening. But on Christmas-day I almost dined on them, and was so ill that I was in great danger." This is the *comparentia instantiarum secundum magis et minus*. "It cannot have been the brandy which I took with them: for I have drunk brandy daily for years without being the worse for it." This is the *rejectio naturarum*. Our invalid then proceeds to what is termed by Bacon the *Vindemiatio*, and pronounces that mincepies do not agree with him.' Lord Macaulay goes on to express his opinion that Bacon greatly overrated the utility of his method, and that the inductive process, like many other processes, is not likely to be better performed merely because men know how they perform it.

In answer to this it must be said, in the first place, that the Essayist has scarcely done justice to the strictness and elaborateness of the Baconian Induction, and to the necessity for such strictness, if it is to be worth anything; and, in the second place, that he has exaggerated the inductive activity of average people when he speaks of even such an induction as he describes as being 'what we are all doing from morning to night.' The Inductive process of Lord Macaulay's 'plain man' is far above the level of most 'plain men.': but, even as it is, it is far below the level of the Baconian Induction. If one is to follow up Lord Macaulay's illustration, other causes besides the brandy may have been at work to produce the indigestion which the invalid attributes to the mincepies—cucumber, for example, or salmon; or the dinner may have been badly cooked; or the invalid may have dined under the depressing influence of bad news, or in a hurry. Therefore it will be necessary for the Baconian inductor to perform two classes of quite distinct experiments. In the first of these he will continue to eat mincepies, but on each occasion will reject some one kind of food that might be suspected of having produced the indigestion: on Monday, for instance, he will dine as before, only no salmon; on Tuesday as before, only no cucumber; on Wednesday as before, only no brandy; and so on. If in each case he still feels indigestion after dinner, he will be led to the belief that salmon alone was not the cause of it, nor was cucumber, nor was brandy. But, although no one of these three things in itself may produce indigestion, the combination of any one with any other may. Therefore, continuing this class of experiments, he must, while always continuing to eat mincepies, discontinue the combination of those other three things taken two and two together: and then, if he still feels ill, he must admit that there is some other cause for his illness beside the combinations of these things in pairs. Lastly, although these three things taken singly and taken in pairs, do not disagree with him, yet taken all together, they may: he must therefore, while continuing to eat mincepies, discontinue the other three things, and then, if he still feels ill, he is led to infer that these three things have nothing to do with his illness: and by *an anticipation of the mind*, as Bacon called it, the experimenter may perhaps leap to the conclusion that the mincepies are the cause of his indigestion.

But it is but a leap, not a regular ascent. The Inductor is by no means certain yet that he has arrived at the real cause. For beside those three prominent claimants mentioned in the last paragraph, there may be a host of other latent antecedents, any one of which, or combination of which, may have made him ill. Therefore now he must try a second and quite distinct class of experiments, in each of which he must omit the mincepies. With this omission, he must dine in all respects, as far as possible, as he dined on the days when he was ill. To make sure that he is not omitting some latent antecedent, he must try several of these dinners: he must dine after walking home and after riding home, after good news and after bad news, in a hurry and at leisure, and with many other varying circumstances, but always omitting mincepies. This class of experiments is the Night's egg out of which Cupid is to spring. And now indeed, after several experiments of this second class, assimilating his dining in all respects to the dining on the days when he was ill, with the single exception that he eats no mincepies, if he finds that in no case does he suffer indigestion, this will be a strong proof that the mincepies were the cause : and, if he could be certain that he had reproduced all the antecedents of those invalid days—all, that is, except the mincepies—and yet no indigestion followed, then the proof would not be strong but certain. He would absolutely know that the mincepies, and nothing else, had caused his indigestion. And this positive knowledge would have proceeded out of negative knowledge. It would be light out of darkness, Cupid springing from Night's egg.

Now to maintain, as Lord Macaulay does, that 'plain men' reason in this way, and that there is nothing uncommon in this kind of Induction, is to assume a very high standard of intelligence indeed. True, as soon as the New Induction is described, we feel it to be natural and obvious. Like the spiteful friars crying down the discovery of Columbus, any one of us can make the egg stand on its end when Columbus has shown us the way. But if it be true that this complete kind of Induction has not been described by Aristotle, nor by later authors, then it seems hard to deny to Bacon the credit of having given shape and living force to the Logic of Common Sense, simply because it was the Logic at which Common Sense had been for many ages blindly aiming without coming very near the mark. Because Bacon and Aristotle use the same term 'Induction,' therefore it has been most unfairly assumed that Bacon has invented nothing new. But the two inductions are, for practical purposes, entirely different. The Old Induction was content with observation, the New encourages experiment; the Old Induction *by Enumeration* is notoriously as a rule useless, sometimes misleading; the New Induction often leads easily right, and, if cautiously and scientifically used, cannot lead wrong; the Old encouraged indolence and servile deference to authority, the New stimulates independent thought and research; the two methods differ in nature, differ in results: why then should they be called the same, in defiance of Bacon's protest that they are entirely different? But, in fact, to accuse the rules of the New Induction of being old, as old as the existence of the human mind, is the highest compliment that its author could desire, and amounts in reality to no more than saying with him, *Certainly they are quite new, totally new in their very kind, and yet they are copied from a very ancient model, even the world itself and the nature of things.*[1]

Another consideration never to be lost sight of in speaking of Bacon's system, is that he did not live to complete it. Before speaking of his *Prerogative Instances* it may be well to mention, as a hint of the incompleteness of his system, that out of the nine following sections of his subject only one is discussed by him. *I propose*, he says, *to treat in the first place of Prerogative Instances.* The discussion of these alone constitutes a treatise: but he goes on to mention—and the titles are worth setting down (though there is no space to explain or comment on them) simply to show the elaborateness of the system as it was intended to be—2nd, *Supports of Induction;* 3rd, the *Rectification of Induction;* 4th, of *Varying the Investigation according to the nature of the subject;* 5th, of *Prerogative Natures* with respect to Investigation, or

[1] *Works*, Vol. iv. p. 11

of what should be inquired first and what last; 6th, of the *Limits of Investigation,* or a Synopsis of all the Natures in the Universe; 7th, of the *Application to Practice,* or of things in their relation to Man; 8th, of *Preparations for Investigations;* 9th, of the *Ascending and Descending Scale of Axioms.* Of all these titles none but the *Prerogative Instances* are discussed, and these alone take up three-quarters of the Second Book of the *Novum Organum.* Had Bacon lived to complete the other Sections, he might perhaps have shown still better cause for calling his Induction *new.*

By *Prerogative Instances* Bacon means those instances that are entitled to priority of consideration. Obviously, in the search after causes, much will depend upon a judicious selection of the phenomena that should first be studied. Into this question Bacon enters with great care, and gives twenty-seven names of classes of *Prerogative Instances.* For example, *Solitary Instances* are of great importance: these are instances that exhibit the nature under consideration in subjects having nothing in common except that nature. Thus, suppose you are investigating the nature of colour itself by investigating it in various subjects, in flowers, stones, metals, woods, prisms, crystals, and dews. Prisms, crystals, and dews have nothing in common with flowers, stones, and metals, except that all are coloured, *from which,* says Bacon, *we easily gather that colour is nothing more than a modification of the image of light received upon the object, resulting in the former case from the different degrees of incidence, in the latter from the various textures and configurations of the body.*[1] Of such instances, he says, that *it is clear that they make the way short, and accelerate and strengthen the process of exclusion, so that a few of them are as good as many.* Again, another important or Prerogative Instance is a *Migratory Instance,* where the nature in question is seen

[1] *Works,* Vol. iv. p. 156.

just beginning or just vanishing. Others again are called *Striking Instances*, where the nature is seen unmistakably and strikingly manifested. Then there are *Ultimate Instances*, where the nature is seen in an extreme form, as expansiveness is seen in the explosion of gunpowder. There are also the *Instances of the Finger-post* (commonly known as *Instantiæ Crucis*, or *Crucial Instances*), which are described as follows: *When in the investigation of any nature the understanding is so balanced as to be uncertain to which of two or more natures the cause of the nature in question should be assigned, Instances of the Finger-post shew the union of one of the natures with the nature in question to be sure and indissoluble, of the other to be varied and separable.* With no less quaint, picturesque names, and with the same care and amplitude, Bacon discusses the whole of the twenty-seven classes of Prerogative Instances.

A brief illustration of Bacon's whole method may now be given. We have, suppose, to investigate the nature of heat. We shall have done this then, and only then, when we have ascertained not only the efficient causes that produce heat in this or that concrete body, but also the ultimate Cause, or *Form*, or *Law*,[1] that produces heat in all bodies. We must begin by making a table of instances where heat is found, each instance containing different circumstances or antecedents—e.g. sun-rays, fire, living bodies, &c. This must be done without bias; we must take each case impartially, whether it be for or against our preconceived notions. This first table will be the table *Essentiæ et Præsentiæ*—i.e. *of Existence and Presence.* Next, we must make a second table of instances, where sun-rays, fire, living bodies, &c., are

---

[1] *Eam autem legem ejusque paragraphos Formarum nomine intelligimus.* Bacon recognises that *Forms* and *Laws* do not give existence; but still the *Law* is *the basis of knowledge as well as of action. Works,* Vol. i. p. 226.

found without heat. This is the table of *Departure* or *Absence in the Corresponding Case* (*Absentiæ et Declinationis in proximo*.) Then a third table must be made of *Degrees* (*Graduum*), where the instances of heat are arranged according to the greater or less degree in which heat is found. On these three *Tables of Appearance* (*Comparentiæ*), the Induction must work.

Great importance is attached to these Tables, constituting as they do a kind of prepared Natural History. In Bacon's time a Natural History meant often nothing but a collection of *Lusus Naturæ*, a chaotic mass of monstrosities and inexplicable wonders, the more inexplicable and wonderful, the better. On such ill-digested histories of Nature, even where they were accurate and trustworthy, Bacon set little store. They bewildered and distracted as much as they helped. They were like the unprepared stores of the ants : heaped together just as they came to hand without the transforming touch of art : but the pupils of the New Logic are to be bees, gathering stores from many sources, but transmuting and preparing them for their special object with the aid of reason. Well-arranged facts are even more important than the rule of Interpretation, than Induction itself : for in truth Induction has been already at work in preparing the *Three Tables of Appearance*. It is all-important, if we are to do justice to Bacon against the attacks of modern assailants, to remember that he himself declares that men, with a sufficient supply of facts, *would be able, by the native genius and force of the mind, to fall into my form of interpretation*.[1] Indeed, although no safe conclusion can yet be attained, yet the laborious worker in the Vineyard of Logic may be allowed as it were the premature luxury of a *First*

[1] *Works*, Vol. iv. p. 115.

Vintage (*Vindemiatio Prima*) extracted directly from the Three Tables. It is a kind of *Licence to the roving Intellect* (*Permissio Intellectus*), or it may be called an *Anticipation of the Mind* (*Anticipatio Mentis*)—what we should call now-a-days a working hypothesis. But afterwards, on these Tables of sufficient facts, the New Induction is to work, and it is to work by the *Method of Exclusions*. That is to say, having limited the number of possible causes of heat, we can try a variety of experiments with each of these possible causes as antecedents; and wherever heat is absent, we shall know that it is not caused by that antecedent. That antecedent having been rejected, we can reject others in turn till we have rejected all but the actual efficient cause.

For a time we are to be content with efficient causes, and with the Science that deals with them, Physics. But ultimately we are to proceed from them to higher causes or Laws, and the Science that deals with these is Metaphysics. Metaphysics in the old sense of the term— i.e. supernatural nature—there will be henceforth none, no monstrosities, no anomalies in nature:[1] but, in Bacon's sense, Metaphysics will be *a branch or descendant of Natural Science*,[2] the Science next above Physics, teaching us not only that heat is a mode of motion, but also leading us on to see the nature of motion in itself, and showing us how motion ramifies into its different offshoots, such as generation, corruption, heat, light, and the rest—a Science that *supposeth in nature a reason, understanding, and platform, and that handleth Final Causes*.

Lastly, Bacon's sense of the unity and simplicity of things leads him still further upward to see above Physics and above Metaphysics a Science that is the highest of

---

[1] *Life*, Vol. vii. p. 377.   [2] *Works*, Vol. iii. p. 353.

all, parent and stem of all sciences, a science whose axioms are equally true in Mathematics, in Logic, in Medicine, in Politics. Some of the axioms of this highest Philosophy, or *Prima Philosophia*, are given by him. Thus the axiom that *the nature of everything is best seen in its smallest portions*, serves Democritus in Physics, and Aristotle in Politics. *Things are preserved from destruction by bringing them back to their first principles*, is a rule that holds good both in Physics and in Politics. The rule, *if equals be added to unequals the wholes will be unequal*, is a rule of mathematics; but it is also an axiom of justice. Other axioms of the *Prima Philosophia* are—*things move violently to their place, but easily in their place; putrefaction is more contagious before than after maturity* (true both in Physics and in Morals); *a discord ending immediately in a concord sets off the harmony* (true no less in Ethics than in Music). The authority of Heraclitus is alleged to prove the affinity between the rules of nature and the rules of policy; and it is in politics more especially that Bacon gives the reins to this Philosophy of imagination. *The knowledge of making the government of the world a mirror for the government of a State is,* according to Bacon, *a wisdom almost lost;* and the *Prima Philosophia* has originated some of the pithiest and most suggestive sentences in the Essays: *As the births of living creatures at first are ill shapen, so are all innovations which are the births of Time: All things that have affinity with the heavens* (and therefore kings) *move upon the centre of another which they benefit: It is a secret both in nature and in state that it is safer to change many things than one.* We are to imitate Time, *which innovateth greatly, but quietly, and by degrees scarce to be perceived,* and we are to remember that *Time moveth so round that a froward retention of custom is as turbulent a thing as an innovation*

It will appear almost incredible to modern readers that Bacon should have contemplated the possibility of ever constructing a genuine Science dealing with maxims so general. It may seem a very suggestive aspect of things, but no science. Yet unquestionably Bacon expected that it would eventually prove its claim to be called a Science. Illustrating it by application to the attraction of iron towards the loadstone, he says that the *Prima Philosophia* will not touch the mere physical phenomenon, but, handling Similitude and Diversity, it will assign the cause why diversity should encourage union. The similarity or analogy between different sciences is, according to Bacon, not accidental; it is as natural and as inevitable as the resemblance between the rippling surface of the sea, the ripple-marked clouds in the sky, the rippling lines on the sea-sand, and the hilly ripples of a sea-shaped undulating land—all of which are but Nature's footprints as she treads in one fashion on her various elements: for *these are not only similitudes, as men of narrow observation may conceive them to be, but the same footsteps of nature, treading or printing upon several subjects or matters.* After so distinct a statement, it is clear that no sketch of Bacon's philosophy can afford to pass by that which he himself evidently regarded as the apex of his pyramid. Yet Dr. Fischer[1] is no doubt right in saying that here 'the mind of Bacon extends beyond his method.' The analogies of Bacon are often singularly suggestive, opening up to the view long avenues of truth, where before one saw nothing but a tangled forest; but they cannot be called legitimate parts of his system. The general analogy traced by him between the organs of sense and reflecting bodies, for example, between the eye and the mirror, or between the ear and the echoing roof; the similitude between the bright fil-

[1] *Francis of Verulam*, p. 139.

trations that issue in gems, and the other bright filtrations that exude in beautiful colours, formed by the juices of birds filtered delicately through quills; the comparison between roots and earth-tending branches, between fins and feet, teeth and beak, these and many others, as often false as true, are frequently, even when false, extremely suggestive. But however suggestive, they are not inductive, and therefore not Baconian. In one sense they may be indeed said to be characteristic of Bacon, for they are the results of his personal character, that mind not *keen and steady*, but *lofty and discursive*, that glance not truly philosophic, but poetic, which will find similitudes everywhere, in heaven and earth. We have seen that Bacon laid special stress upon his possessing *a mind versatile enough for that most important object, the recognition of similitudes*. It is this versatility that is the parent of *Prima Philosophia*, and there are many reasons why we should be thankful for it. The Essays gain more from it than the scientific works lose. And although it must always be regarded as an excrescence on his philosophy—at least in the incomplete form in which that philosophy is handed down to us—it is part and parcel of himself. Baconian it is not; but it is pre-eminently Bacon's.

Passing from the *Prima Philosophia*, we are led to ask what is the weak point in Bacon's system? The system, as we have found, ascertains Causes by ascertaining what Antecedents are not Causes, and by continuing to exclude Antecedent after Antecedent, till at last none is left but the Antecedent Cause. The weak point is this, the impossibility of ascertaining that the Exclusion has been complete. There is always a possibility that some fictitious and apparent cause may conceal behind itself the real and latent cause so cunningly, that no experiment may detect the latter. And therefore we can hardly acquit Bacon of exaggeration when he speaks of the *abso-*

lute certainty attainable by his method. Yet we are bound to recollect that he himself was aware of the danger inherent in the method of Exclusion. Hence he supplements Exclusion with *Helps to Induction, Rectifications of Induction*, and the other seven auxiliaries mentioned above on page lxxviii. Possibly his system thus elaborated might have approximated more closely to certainty than the system as we have it, incomplete. Yet few will deny that here we have the heel of our Achilles. Bacon's faith in the simplicity of Nature, which enables him to force his way invulnerable through a host of obstacles, leaves him vulnerable here. He seems to have thought that everything, gold for instance, contains but some six or seven qualities, and that, when these qualities had once been mastered, the thing in question could be constructed; and therefore the right course would be to investigate not gold, but the qualities of gold. Now to say that no one thing should be investigated in itself is reasonable, and to have said that gold would be profitably investigated in company with other metals would have been also reasonable; but to say that the surest way to make gold is to know the Causes of its natures, viz., *greatness of weight, closeness of parts, fixation, pliantness or softness, immunity from rust, colour or tincture of yellow*, together with the axioms that concern these causes—this advice is at all events not in conformity with the method that has been practically adopted by progressive sciences. Quite naïve is the confidence with which Bacon adds, *If a man can make a metal that has all these properties, let men dispute as they please whether it be gold or no.* So certain is he that he has exhausted all the essential qualities of gold.

It would not be difficult to show that here, as in the *Prima Philosophia*, he is inconsistent with himself. As in morality, so in philosophy, he has laid down rules that he himself does not obey. His *lofty and discursive spirit* will not bear in mind its own warning that *the human understanding is of its own nature prone to suppose the existence of more order and regularity in the world than it finds.* Quite against his own system, for example, is the assumption that *everything tangible that we are acquainted with contains an invisible and intangible spirit, which it works and clothes as with a garment,*[1] and that *we must inquire what amount of spirit there is in every body, what of tangible essence.*[2] There are many other instances of similar erroneous assumptions. That he should assume (in the absence of such testimony to the contrary as is apparent to the senses unaided by instruments or experiments) that the moon's rays give no warmth, and that iron does not expand with heat, is unphilosophical but excusable. But the same high grandiose nature that renders him indifferent to petty moral details, renders him also culpably careless about many scientific details, and allowed him to rest in ignorance of many important scientific discoveries made by his contemporaries or predecessors, and lying ready to his hand.

Lord Macaulay speaks in admiration of the versatility of Bacon's mind, as equally well adapted for exploring the heights of philosophy or for the minute inspection of the pettiest detail. But he has been imposed on by Bacon's parade of detail. Aware of his deficiency, Bacon is always on his guard against it, always striving to make himself what he was not by nature—*an exact man:* and, in his efforts to be exact, ostentatiously accumulating details in writing, and often very trifling details, he has imposed on the Essayist,

---

[1] *Works*, Vol. iv. p. 195 ; and again Vol. v. p. 224, *Let it be admitted as is most certain.*
[2] *Works*, Vol. iv. p. 125

whose forte was not science. Mr. Ellis has pointed out instances of Bacon's inexactness or ignorance, and, as collected by Mr. Spedding, they make a heavy list. At the time when Bacon wrote the *De Augmentis*, 'he appears to have been utterly ignorant of the discoveries which had been made by Keppler's calculations. Though he complained in 1623 of the want of compendious methods for facilitating arithmetical computations, especially with regard to the doctrine of series, and fully recognised the importance of them as an aid to physical inquiries, he does not say a word about Napier's logarithms, which had been published only nine years before, and reprinted more than once in the interval. He complained that no considerable advance had been made in Geometry beyond Euclid, without taking any notice of what had been done by Archimedes. He saw the importance of determining accurately the specific gravities of different substances, and himself attempted to form a table of them by a rude process of his own, without knowing of the more scientific though still imperfect methods previously employed by Archimedes, Ghetaldus, and Porta. . . . . He observes that a ball of one pound weight will fall nearly as fast through the air as a ball of two, without alluding to the theory of the acceleration of falling bodies, which had been made by Galileo more than thirty years before. He proposes an inquiry with regard to the lever—namely, whether in a balance with arms of different lengths but equal weight the distance from the fulcrum has any effect upon the inclination—though the theory of the lever was as well understood in his own time as it is now. In making an experiment of his own to ascertain the cause of the motion of a windmill, he overlooks an obvious circumstance which makes the experiment inconclusive, and an equally obvious variation of the same experiment, which would have shown him that his theory was false.

He speaks of the poles of the earth as fixed in a manner which seems to imply that he was not acquainted with the precession of the equinoxes, and, in another place, of the north pole being above, and the south pole below, as a reason why in our hemisphere the north winds predominate over the south.' After this we shall not be surprised to find a practical man like William Harvey speaking very lightly of Bacon as a scientific philosopher. 'He writes philosophy,' says Harvey, 'like a Lord Chancellor.'[1]

But practical scientific men, though unimpeachable judges of the accuracy of scientific details, may perhaps be by no means the best critics of large schemes of scientific discovery. A successful discoverer, one to whom nature and long experience have given a knack of hitting on the right experiment and deducing from it its right lesson, one whose native genius stands him in the place of a technical *Filum Labyrinthi* or *Interpretatio Naturæ* —is the man of all men most likely to see in the New Induction but a mere paper-philosophy. He has never used it, he says; his discoveries have never been made in that way; and consequently it is useless. But, in fact, he has used it, or has used his abridgment of it, without knowing it. If he is indeed a scientific man, worthy of the name, and not a mere stumbler upon truth —like the beasts, the gods of the Egyptians, coming upon medicinal plants by chance—he has *renounced* his *Idols*, he has collected and arranged his *sufficient facts*, his *Three Tables of Appearance*, he has selected his *Prerogative Instances*, he has employed the *New Induction*, and has worked by the *Method of Exclusions*. Only he has done it all by the light of Nature. What then? Is Bacon to have less credit because he set forth the

---

[1] Quoted, *Works*, Vol. iii. p. 515.

method that is dictated by nature, the method that must be consciously or unconsciously pursued by every successful investigator? Bacon himself, at all events, counted it no discredit that he owed his method to Nature. *The Interpretation*, he says, *is the true and natural process of the mind when all obstacles are removed;* and again, *we do not consider the art of Interpretation indispensable or perfect as though nothing could be done without it.*[1] He does not deny that improvement may be made, in his particular investigations on his method; *On the contrary, I that regard the human mind not only in its own faculties, but in its connection with things, must needs hold that the art of discovery may advance as discoveries advance.*[2] The discoverer who so ungratefully decries Bacon's system is really claimed by the philosopher as an adherent, as one of those unconscious pupils who are *able by the native and genuine force of the mind, without any other art, to fall into my form of interpretation.*[2]

'But,' it may be asked, 'if the great discoverers of scientific truth have not employed, and do not see their way to employing, the elaborate technicalities of Bacon's method, why should they be grateful? Would not discoveries have gone on just as well without Bacon's aid?' Probably not quite so well. Probably Bacon has done much to raise the general level of scientific thought; and in this general rise the great scientific discoverers have, though unconsciously, shared. Rules of harmony may be useless, directly, for Mozarts and Mendelssohns: but the statement of such rules must have been beneficial to music as a whole, and, indirectly, to them. The standard of science throughout the world has been raised by the *Novum Organum*. Put aside the details of its complicated machinery as useless, yet the spirit of it

---

[1] *Works*, Vol. i. p. 84.   [2] *Works*, Vol. iv. p. 115.

must be confessed to diffuse in all readers the love of Truth, and the sense of Law; and these two make up the very atmosphere of Science.

And even for this complicated machinery excuse may be found in the special aspect in which Bacon regarded the work of research. It was to be social work. There was to be a college of truth-seekers of different grades, such as are described in the *New Atlantis*;[1] there were to be *Pioneers, Compilers, Lamps, Inventors,* and *Interpreters of Nature.* Such a college Bacon seems to have regarded as an attainable object, if he could but interest the King sufficiently in it. On Eton or Westminster, St. John's College, Cambridge, or Magdalene College, Oxford, he cast wistful eyes, seeing in them the College of Truth-seekers almost made to his hand. But now, if there was to be such a college in fact and not in dream-land, it became necessary to lay down rules to guide the different grades of Truth-seekers. It seemed to Bacon that this could be done so minutely as to dispense with individual judgment. *Our method of discovering knowledge,* he says, *is of such a kind that it leaves very little to keenness and strength of intellect, but almost levels all intellects and abilities.* The Architect might dispense with his rules, but the bricklayer and mason would need them. In the freer and fuller interchange of thought in modern times, in which the scientific men of Europe now recognise that they are not working each by himself, but that one discoverer helps on another; in the recognition that now no one man can take *all science to be his province,* but that the different provinces and departments of science must be assigned to several different workers—there is something of the spirit of Bacon's College. How far it might be possible to do more than this, how far men

---

[1] *Works,* Vol. iii. p. 164.

of ordinary ability might, as subordinate investigators, conduct experiments in Bacon's method in such a way as to be practically useful to the Architectural genius of some supervising Interpreter of Nature—this is an experiment, as far as I know, never yet systematically tried. Possibly, even under such circumstances, many details of Bacon's machinery might be found unnecessary and hampering. But, at all events, Bacon's technicalities ought not to be condemned by those who have not understood their purpose : and they will not be authoritatively and finally condemned till the experiment for which they were intended has been fairly tried and authoritatively pronounced a failure.

But it is for his neglect of the astronomical discoveries of his age that Bacon has been most severely censured. Unquestionably, Bacon knew little of mathematics, and did not quite see, or at least sufficiently realise, that a mathematician can dispense with induction ; with a sheet of paper and pen he can observe the peculiarities, and experiment upon the peculiarities of ellipses and hyperbolas as certainly and far more easily than by watching the planets or comets moving in their celestial ellipses and hyperbolas. And not seeing this, as a mathematician-in-grain would have seen it, he was rather prejudiced against a science that seemed to be daring to progress without the aid of his *New Induction.* He wishes therefore to see set on foot a *History of celestial bodies pure and simple, and without any infusion of dogmas . . . a history, in short, setting forth a simple narrative of the facts, just as if nothing had been settled by the arts of astronomy and geology, and only experiments and observations had been accurately collected and described with perspicuity.* [1] Such a History, especially if containing such facts as Bacon himself laid stress upon, giving one as a specimen,

[1] *Works,* Vol. v. p. 510.

would have been of little or no value; and Bacon cannot escape blame for his neglect of the discoveries of the mathematician. But he has been blamed by many who have not in the least understood why Bacon was so suspicious of astronomy. For, in fact, there was something highly creditable to him as a philosopher in the reason he himself alleges for suspecting *the new carmen who drive the earth about*—as he styles the new astronomers. It is his sense of the law and unity of Nature that inspires him with distrust, and makes him hold aloof. 'For why,' he asked, 'should celestial bodies move in ellipses, and terrestrial bodies not? Whence this divorce between earth and heaven? Newton had not yet arisen, to connect the motions of the planets with the fall of the apple, and thus bind heaven and earth together in the unity of one simple law of attraction. Consequently the new discoveries, true though they might be, seemed to Bacon propped upon unsound hypotheses, upon the old arbitrary, fictitious, and disorderly distinctions between things celestial and terrestrial. Though Bacon hoped for some results from his History, yet he looked still more hopefully to another source; and Newton himself might have agreed with him here: *I rest that hope much more upon observation of the common passions and desires of matter in both globes. For these supposed divorces between ethereal and sublunary things seem to me but figments, superstitions mixed with rashness: seeing that it is most certain that very many effects, as of expansion, contraction, impression, cession, collection into masses, attraction, repulsion, assimilation, union, and the like, have place not only here with us, but also in the heights of the heaven and the depths of the earth.*

On the whole, we cannot accept the truth of Harvey's epigram that Bacon 'wrote about science like a Lord Chancellor.' At least we cannot accept it as it stands.

That he sometimes experimented like a Lord Chancellor, or that he sometimes wrote on scientific details like a Lord Chancellor—either of these statements we might accept. But neither inadequate experiments, nor errors in scientific detail, should induce us to ignore the genuine service that he wrought for scientific Truth. To break down for ever the authority of the School Philosophy ; to reveal the inherent infirmities and the pitfalls that beset the human mind in its journey towards knowledge ; to hold up to deserved contempt the barrenness of the unaided Syllogism and the old puerile Induction ; to trace and formulate (though perhaps with excessive detail and with too sanguine expectations) the natural steps of the rightly-guided mind, and to give to each step substance and a name—this in itself was no mean achievement, but it is not the largest debt we owe to Bacon. No man who has ever been touched with the spirit of the *Novum Organum* can easily relapse into the belief that the world is a collection of accidents, or that its ways are past finding out. To have imbued and permeated mankind with a sense of the divine order and oneness of the Universe and of its adaptation to the human mind ; to have turned men's thoughts to science as to a divine pursuit, sanctioned by Him who hath *set the world in the heart of men*, and worthy to be called the study of the Second Scripture of God ; to have proclaimed in undying words that all men shall learn that volume of God's works if they will but condescend to spell before they read ; that all may be admitted into the Kingdom of Man over Nature by becoming as little children, and by learning to obey Nature that they may command her, and to understand her language that they may compel her to speak it—this Gospel to have proclaimed, and thus to have prepared the way for the scientific redemption of mankind, entitles Bacon to claim something more than that he 'wrote about science like a Lord Chancellor'—say rather, like a Priest, like a Prophet of Science, whose Mission he himself describes as being *to prepare and adorn the bride chamber of the Mind and the Universe.*

More than once in the course of this chapter it has been necessary to point out that Bacon's philosophic system is incomplete, not even half finished; and one can scarcely quit the subject without regretting that Bacon's deviation into the busy paths of office cut short his labours in philosophy. It has been suggested, indeed, that we have no cause to deplore Bacon's preference of politics. It is admitted that Bacon himself mourned in after-life over his misspent talents; but it is said that 'if Bacon had carried out his early threat and retired with a couple of men to Cambridge, and spent his life in exploring the one true path by which man might attain to be master of Nature, and followed it out far enough to find (as he must have done) that it led to impassable places—and had at the same time seen from his retirement the political condition of the country going from bad to worse for want of better advice and more faithful service, would he not in like manner have accused himself of having misspent his talents in things for which he was less fit than he had fancied, and forsaken a vocation in which he might have helped to save a country from a civil war?'

But the answer seems to be first that, even though the 'life with two men at Cambridge' had been a blank of disappointment, yet even that blank would have been better than such a life of political action as Bacon was condemned to lead. He contributed nothing of the 'better advice' or 'faithful service' that might have averted the coming civil war. He did worse than nothing. He degraded himself, he injured his country and posterity by tarnishing the honourable traditions of the Bench; he lowered morality and shook the faith of human kind in human nature by making himself an ever-memorable warning of the compatibility of greatness and weakness. Surely, rather than this it would have been preferable even to have done nothing with two men at Cambridge. But, in the next place, it is almost a matter of certainty that his abstention from politics would have resulted in a large increase of literary and scientific work. If we turn to the records of his life, we shall find that the periods when he is free from office are those in which his pen is most active. In 1603, for example, at the time when he desires *to meddle as little as he can in the King's causes*, he writes the *First Book of the Advancement of Learning;* but, as business increases, his pen becomes more idle, and from the time he was appointed Attorney-General to the year after his being appointed Lord Chancellor—1613-1619—he publishes nothing whatever. On the other hand, after his disgrace and enforced retirement in 1621, work after work issues from his pen—the History of Henry VII., the *Historia Ventorum*, with five similar Histories. The *De Augmentis* is published in 1623, and the *New Atlantis* is written in 1624. If Bacon had remained Lord Chancellor till his death we should never have had the *New Atlantis:* and we are probably right in adding, if Bacon had never been Lord Chancellor we should have had the *New Atlantis* complete, and many works beside. Grant that a persistent working out of his system would have led Bacon in time to 'impassable places': yet surely that would have been a consummation not to be deplored. An active and versatile mind like Bacon's following his philosophy into impassable places, and forced either to retrace his steps and to mark out the impassable places for posterity, or else to add modifications, qualifications, and supplements to his philosophy, would surely have left some memorial of its labours worthy of the attention of posterity. Independently of their scientific value, his works might have been valuable in a literary aspect. On the whole, we must admit that it would have been better alike for Bacon and for posterity that he should have lost his way in the impassable places of science than in the impassable places of morality. To have had even the *New Atlantis* complete, much more the *Instauratio Magna*, we could well have spared the *Confession and humble submission of me the Lord Chancellor.*

CHAPTER III.

BACON AS A THEOLOGIAN AND ECCLESIASTICAL POLITICIAN.

BACON'S theology is far less theological than his science. Perfectly orthodox, definite, and precise, it seems in gaining definiteness to have lost vitality. In his anxiety to prove that Religion need not dread any encroachments from Science, he comes near divorcing Faith and Reason. Faith cannot be jostled by Reason, he urges, for they move in different spheres. If they do come into collision, Reason must give way : we must believe in the mysteries of the Faith, even though it be against the *reluctation* of Reason. The principles of Religion ought no more to be discussed than the rules of chess. What inferences are to be deduced from these principles—this may be handled by reason ; but not the principles themselves. Here and there Bacon speaks as though moral science might be the servant and handmaid of Religion; but that the progress of our knowledge of the works of the Creator, revealing more and more of order and development, should add to new knowledge of His will as the ages pass on, does not seem to have occurred to him : nor does he speak with any hopefulness or sanguineness of any revelation to be anticipated from the growing history of mankind, and from the experiences of the household and the State, purified century by century. Yet this is what we might have expected from him as the natural completion of his method. No one delighted more to repeat that God had *set the world in the heart of men* that men might search it out. Now from 'the world' to exclude men, while including irrational creatures, ought to have seemed a paradox. Men therefore, as well as beasts and stones, ought to have seemed to be intended to be mirrors of God's nature. Yet Bacon did not see that anything new might be learned of the Divine Image from its reflection on humanity. His low views of human nature stood in his way here. *All human things are full,* he says, *of ingratitude and treachery.* For the purpose of guarding oneself against evil, and of training and strengthening the human mind, it might be worth while to study human nature, partly in the writers on moral philosophy, but especially (and here he is truly wise) in the poets and historians. Such knowledge is useful for the *Art of Advancement.* But that by studying the brother whom we have seen, we may expect to learn anything of Him whom we have not seen—this is not taught in Bacon's theology.

It is evident that Bacon has no enthusiasm for formal theology. He states tersely but precisely the propositions generally received by Christians; but he appears to state them, rather to clear them out of the way, than for the purpose of basing on them any practical results. With a characteristic sanguineness unhappily not justified by facts, he regards as one of the present circumstances favourable to Science, *the consumption of all that can ever be said in controversies of religion, which have so much diverted men from other sciences.* Weary of the petty ecclesiastical differences that distracted the English Church, he desires nothing better than some general convention to restore concord to the State, and to save future waste of precious time that might be devoted to Truth. For such a purpose the best plan will be, he thinks, to lay down certain first principles that shall be above discussion. As these cannot be deduced from Nature by Reason, they must come from some other source; and he sees no other source but the Scriptures. Not being subject to induction and experiment, such first principles or aphorisms must needs be independent of Reason. To discuss them is like discussing the rules of a game, which admit of rejection or acceptance, but of discussion never. Bacon sees a singular advantage in that the Christian religion *excludeth and interdicteth human reason, whether by interpretation or anticipation, from examining or discussing of the mysteries and principles of faith.*[1] For he adds, *if any man shall think by view and inquiry into these sensible and material things, to attain to any light for the revealing of the nature or will of God, he shall dangerously abuse himself.*[2] What nature is, as compared with the vain imaginations of men's minds, that the Bible is, as compared with the empty inventions of mankind. The heavens are said to declare God's glory, but they do not declare His will. Under the appearance of magnifying the Scriptures, Bacon gives dangerous encouragement to the practice of deducing from them anything that any one chooses to put into them. The literal sense, it is true, is *as it were the main stream or river, but the moral sense chiefly, and sometimes the allegorical or typical, are they whereof the church hath most use; not that I wish men to be bold in allegories or light in allusions; but that I do much condemn that interpretation of the Scripture which is only after the manner as men use to interpret a profane book.*[3]

But irrepressibly sometimes peeps out the love of scientific truth veiled under this deference to religion and to the Scriptures. Science is unclean, and must not venture to touch her purer sister; but Bacon's fear is not so much that Religion may be defiled as lest Science should be

[1] *Works*, Vol. iii. p. 251.   [2] Ib. p. 218.   [3] Ib. 487.

consumed in the fiery arms of the spiritual embrace. He is alarmed and anxious lest Science should seek support in the Bible instead of in the Sacred Scripture of Nature. No depreciation of his dear pursuit is too strong to prevent so terrible a miscarriage as this. To seek philosophy in divinity is to seek the dead among the living, to hope to find *the pots or lavers* in the Holiest place of all. In his anxiety to avoid such a danger he sometimes ventures on language more consonant than most of his sayings on the Scriptures with the thoughts of modern times. The Scriptures, he suggests, are probably fitted to our limited and imperfect understandings, just as the form of the key is fitted to the ward of the lock. Hence, if the Bible illustrates its spiritual truths by human imagery, we need not take the illustration for absolute truth, any more than an illustration in common conversation from a basilisk or unicorn should be taken as a token that the speaker believes that unicorns and basilisks have a real existence.

Yet we should be wrong in assuming that Bacon was a hypocrite, or that (as we read of Galileo and others) he was consciously paying an affected deference to religion with the mere purpose of preventing opposition to his beloved science. He had a firm belief in a Mind of the Universe, and in Love as the highest of the divine attributes, and as the saving characteristic of humanity, without which *men are no better than a sort of vermin*.[1] But with much of the petty polemics and ecclesiastical squabbles of the day he had no sympathy; and, if he was at all interested in them, it was as a politician, not as a theologian. Like a large number of modern Christians, he did not disbelieve in any of the complicated dogmas that make up modern Christianity; but, on the

---

[1] *Essay* xiii. l. 8.

other hand, he did not believe in them in the highest sense of the word *belief.* They were not necessary to him; they were not part of his spiritual frame, but hung loosely on him, and he did not move easily in them. And therefore, when he comes to write familiarly in the Essays about daily conduct, and such matters as *come home to the hearts and bosoms of men*, he finds no place for his formal theology. He writes like a philosopher, or like a courtier, or like a statesman, but rarely or never like an orthodox Anglican. And even in the *Advancement of Learning*, where he is compelled to speak formally and precisely, there is something significant in the insuppressible earnestness with which the philosophic and real self of the writer occasionally forces its way out; as when he warns theologians against a *course of artificial divinity*, and tells them that, *as for perfection or completeness in divinity, it is not to be sought*.[1] And the mainspring of the Christian faith is touched when he emphatically declares that, *if a man's mind be truly inflamed with charity, it doth work him suddenly into greater perfection than all the doctrine of morality can do.*

But still it is as a politician and a statesman that Bacon is most interested in religion. Religion is a prop to good government; and Bacon no doubt appreciated the saying of Machiavelli, that 'those princes and commonwealths who would keep their governments entire and incorrupt, are above all things to have a care of religion and its ceremonies, and preserve them in due veneration; for in the whole world there is not a greater sign of imminent ruin than when God and his worship are despised.'[2] Schisms are the precursors of sedition, and, as such, not to be overlooked by statesmen.

[1] *Works*, Vol. iii. p. 484.
[2] *Discourses* i. 12. This and the following extracts are taken from the English translation published in London in 1680.

But Bacon is very far from taking the purely passionless, mechanical, and external view that Machiavelli takes of religion. In Machiavelli's eyes religion is a mere political machinery, and has no other interest. As for its truth or falsehood, that is not the statesman's concern. That a well-founded religion in Machiavelli's State need not be true, appears from the following proposition: 'A Prince or Commonwealth ought most accurately to regard that his religion be well-founded, and then his government will last, for there is no surer way to keep that good and united. Whatever therefore occurs that may any way be extended to the advantage and reputation of the religion which they desire to establish (how uncertain or frivolous soever it may seem to themselves), yet by all means it is to be propagated and encouraged; and the wiser the prince, the more sure it is to be done. This course having been observed by wise men, has produced the opinion of miracles, which are celebrated even in those religions which are false. For, let their original be as idle as they please, a wise prince will be sure to set them forward, and the Prince's authority recommends them to everybody else.' However Bacon in practical politics or State trials may occasionally condescend to recommend a *false fame*, yet it is not in this spirit that he thinks or writes on religion. Machiavelli writes as a sceptic and an alien from the Church, Bacon as a religious man and a loyal member of a National Church. To Machiavelli religion seemed no friend to Italy, rather a foe: to Bacon religion seemed associated with a great national uprising against foreign domination, and unity of religion appeared essential at home, if England was to be great abroad.

It must be admitted that Machiavelli himself could not have felt a much greater contempt than Bacon felt for the pettiness of some of the points of the ecclesiastical discussions of the time, and the pettiness in the manner of discussing them. But there is nothing cynical in his grave and weighty censure of this pettiness. *Thus much*, he says, *we all know and confess that they be not of the highest nature ... we contend about ceremonies and things indifferent.* He gladly passes from these to dwell on the magnitude of the truths received by all, and on the importance of marking out the broad boundaries of *the league amongst Christians that is penned by our Saviour, 'he that is not against us is with us;'* remembering that *the ancient and true bonds of Unity are one faith, one baptism, and not one ceremony, one policy.*[1] Very similar is the tenour of the following passage at the end of the Ninth Book of the *De Augmentis: It is of extreme importance to the peace of the Church that the Christian covenant ordained by our Saviour be properly and clearly explained in these two heads, which appear somewhat discordant; whereof the one lays down 'he that is not with us is against us,' and the other, 'he that is not against us is with us.' For the bonds of Christian communion are set down, 'One Lord, one Faith, one Baptism;' not 'one Ceremony, one Opinion;'* after which he sets down, as a deficiency in theology, a treatise on *the Degrees of Unity in the Church.* This way of viewing Religion grows on him with years; and in the Essays of 1625 he still harps on the necessity of *soundly and plainly expounding the two cross clauses in the league of Christianity penned by our Saviour himself.* Not without a touch of bitter sadness he adds, *This is a thing may seem to many trivial and done already; but if it were done less partially it would be embraced more generally.* There is nothing ignoble nor unworthy in the engrossing interest this side of religion had for Bacon. He views it as a Christian, but as

[1] *Life*, Vol. i. p. 75, *On the Controversies of the Church*, written in 1589.

an English Christian, seeing danger and imminent sedition for England in the lowering and gathering clouds of ecclesiastical discord. It is not without significance that the title of *Religion*, given to the Essay in 1612, gives place in 1625 to *the Unity of Religion*. To Bacon disunion in religion implied a disunited England, a helpless prey to foreign despotism and foreign superstition.

Between the two contending parties in the Church, the Reformers or Puritans and the Conservatives or High Churchmen, Bacon arbitrates with a grave impartiality. He censures both sides for the unchristian and uncharitable temper of their polemics, and points out the inconsistency of both in declaring matters that a few years ago were by both sides left open and unessential, to be now essential and vital. The Puritans, he says, objected at first to nothing but a few superstitious ceremonies, abuses in patronage, and the like: from this they rose to an assault upon Episcopacy, and other institutions of the Church; and now, lastly, *they are advanced to define of an only and perpetual form of policy in the Church, which (without consideration of possibility or foresight of peril and perturbation of the Church and State) must be erected and planted by the magistrate*;[1] while an extreme section maintain that this must be done at once by the people, *without attending of the establishment of authority, and in the meantime they refuse to communicate with us, reputing us to have no church.* On the other hand, the High Churchmen, he says, were once content to call many ceremonies indifferent, and to acknowledge many imperfections in the church; afterwards they grew *stiffly to hold that nothing was to be innovated (partly because it needed not, partly because it would make a breach upon the rest). Thence (exasperate through contentions)* they

---

[1] *Life*, Vol. i. p. 86.

are fallen to a direct condemnation of the contrary part, as of a sect. Yea, and some indiscreet persons have been bold, in open preaching, to use dishonourable and derogative speech, and censure of the churches abroad; and that so far, as some of our men (as I have heard) ordained in foreign parts, have been pronounced to be no lawful ministers.[1]

The good of the nation is, in Bacon's opinion, to be the basis upon which such *indifferent* matters are to be decided. The question is not what is best, but what is best for England. Not that he admits that the foreign Reformed churches are superior to the Church of England in their constitution; but even if they are, he blames *the partial* (i.e. biassed) *affectation and imitation of foreign churches... Our church is not now to plant. It is settled and established. It may be, in civil States, a republic is a better policy than a kingdom; yet God forbid that lawful kingdoms should be tied to innovate and make alterations.* And to the same drift he writes in 1603: *I could never find but that God hath left the like liberty to the Church government as He hath done to the civil government, to be varied according to time, and place, and accidents, which nevertheless His high and divine providence doth order and dispose.*[2] So far, he is against the Puritans. He further blames their indiscriminate censure of the virtuous men of past or present times who may not happen to agree with them, their captiousness and blind fanaticism, their want of sobriety and thoughtfulness, the vague generality of their preaching, and their occasionally forced interpretations of the Scriptures. But against the High Churchmen he has no less to urge. They have been unbrotherly, suspicious, hard, oppressive, too ready to use bad names, too swift to receive accusations, too

[1] *Life*, vol. i. p. 87.   [2] Ib. Vol. iii. p. 107

strait in examinations and inquisitions, in swearing men to blanks and generalities, a thing captious and strainable. They think to silence their opponents by forbidding them to preach; but, *in such great scarcity of preachers, this is to punish the people, and not them. Instead of fixing both eyes on the supposed evil done by these preachers, ought they not (I mean the bishops) to keep one eye open upon the good that these men do?* And when he comes to speak further in detail of the petty molestations and oppressions to which tender spirits had been subjected, a noble spirit of indignation bursts out in the protest, *Ira viri non operatur justitiam Dei—The wrath of man worketh not the righteousness of God.*

On the whole, Bacon's verdict leans clearly to the side of the Puritans. Some may find an explanation of this in Bacon's predilections, and in a puritanical spirit inherited by him from his mother. But this is hardly necessary or probable. Bacon's religious ways by no means satisfied his mother. He was far too remiss for her in the performance of his religious duties, and she finds herself obliged to warn her son Anthony against his brother's general laxity in these matters. Nor is Bacon's love of fervid and powerful preaching sufficient to account for his preference of the Puritan claims, though he unquestionably did respect some of the abler preachers on that side, and even had a good word to say for the inhibited practice of *prophesying*. But the one sufficient explanation is found in the nature of the dispute, and in his views as a statesman. Here was the great English nation, but newly freed from Roman domination, raised up by Providence to be a bulwark against the despotism of superstition, the natural centre and refuge of all the smaller Protestant States—yet unhappily divided against itself upon points indifferent and trifling, such as the use of gown or surplice, use or disuse of the ring in marriage, the use of music in worship, the rite of confirmation, the use of the word Priest or Minister, the use of the General Absolution, and the like. In some of these matters the Puritans seemed to Bacon to have reason on their side: but even in others, since the one party held them to be superstitious while the other party could not maintain them to be essential, it seemed to him that they fell *within the compass of the Apostle's rule, which is that the stronger do descend unto the weaker.* Nor was it an unimportant consideration that to incline to the side of the Puritans, and to assimilate the Church of England to the Reformed churches abroad, seemed likely to be a means of increasing England's political influence; thus might the Church help the State in founding that great Protestant Monarchy of the West which was one of Bacon's constant dreams. For the purpose of gaining an enforced uniformity in such petty matters, to break up the English nation into two hostile religious camps, seemed to Bacon, and must have seemed to many others, not only *unbrotherly*, but also a grave political error.

Church reform, quite apart from the polemics of the day, seemed to Bacon a natural and desirable thing. That the Church should continue for fifty years in all respects unaltered, so far from seeming to him cause for congratulation, rather gave ground for the gravest apprehension. Time, as his master Machiavelli had taught him, bringeth ever new good and new evil, and is always innovating, so that nothing can remain as it was, except by innovations made to suit the innovations of time. And he continues, putting a question that may well be repeated in modern times, *I would only ask why the Civil State should be purged and restored by good and wholesome laws, made every third or fourth year in parliaments assembled, devising remedies as fast as time breedeth mischiefs, and contrariwise the Ecclesiastical State should still continue upon the dregs of time, and receive no alteration now for these five-and-forty years and more? If any man shall object that, if the like intermission had been used in civil cases also, the error had not been great, surely the wisdom of the kingdom hath been otherwise in experience for three hundred years' space at the least. But if it be said to me that there is a difference between civil causes and ecclesiastical, they may as well tell me that churches and chapels need no reparations, though houses and castles do: whereas commonly, to speak truth, dilapidations of the inward and spiritual edification of the Church of God are in all times as great as the outward and material.*[1] To the bishops themselves he appeals in the year 1589 to take up the task of Church reform. *To my lords the bishops, I say that it is hard for them to avoid blame (in the opinion of an indifferent person) in standing so precisely upon altering nothing. Leges novis legibus non recreatæ acescunt: laws not refreshed with new laws wax sour. Qui mala non permutat in bonis non perseverat: without change of the ill, a man cannot continue the good. To take away abuses, supplanteth not good orders, but establisheth them. Morosa moris retentio res turbulenta est æque ac novitas: a contentious retaining of custom is a turbulent thing, as well as innovation. . . . We have heard of no offers of the bishops of bills in parliament. . . . I pray God to inspire the bishops with a fervent love and care for the people, and that they may not so much urge things in controversy as things out of controversy, which all men confess to be gracious and good.*[2]

In later days Bacon had become less hopeful or less desirous of Church reform; and among the *Means of procuring Unity*, described in the Essay of 1625,[3] Reform finds no place. The Essay on Superstition may indeed be quoted as warning us against *over-great reverence of*

---

[1] *Life*, Vol. iii. p. 105.   [2] *Life*, Vol. i. p. 87.
[3] *Essay* iii. Mr. Gardiner (Vol. ii. p. 258) thinks that Bacon in later years objected to change because, if it had come at all then, it would have come from the High Churchmen.

traditions which cannot but load the Church; and as reminding us that, *as whole meat corrupteth to little worms, so good forms and orders corrupt into a number of petty observances;* but, more closely viewed, this Essay exhibits conservative tendencies. For whereas in 1612 it ends with a warning against conservatism, in 1625 it is made to end with a warning against excessive reform. And indeed throughout the Essays there are to be found few or no enforcements of Bacon's favourite maxim that in Church as well as in State *a contentious retaining of custom is a turbulent thing.* In the impossibility of securing any popular changes in the Church so as to create a real unity, it seemed best to secure the appearance of unity by rousing a fear common to all, and by putting prominently forward the danger threatening England from Roman superstition, as the great cause why the nation should rally round the National Church. It is probable that Bacon also foresaw the reluctance of the King to any effectual reform, the impossibility of satisfying either party in the Church, and the unpopularity awaiting the Reformer, whoever he might be.[1] We have seen above that he deprecated the waste of time and energy over theological disputes: he had gladly believed that the material for such controversies had been now quite exhausted, so that Science might secure her share of attention. With these feelings, it is not surprising that as Bacon, out of deference to the King, gave up his dreams of war and colonisation, and an aggressive Protestant Policy, so also he dropped his advocacy of Church reform. It was so much easier to let the Church alone than to sow the *seeds of her future amplitude and greatness.*

There is certainly a noticeable increase in the bitter-

[1] Mr. Gardiner (*History from the Accession* &c., Vol. i. p. 183) thinks Bacon may have slightly alienated the King at first by his proposals for the pacification of the Church, which 'were too statesmanlike for James.'

ness with which Bacon speaks of the Church of Rome. In 1589 he is able to censure those of the Puritan party who *think it the true touch-stone to try what is good and holy by measuring what is more or less opposite to the institutions of the Church of Rome. . . . It is very meet that men be aware how they be abused by this opinion, and that they know that it is a consideration of much greater wisdom and sobriety to be well advised whether, in the general demolition of the Church of Rome, there were not (as men's actions are imperfect) some good purged with the bad, rather than to purge the Church, as they pretend, every day anew.* Not again in later years can Bacon say a word for the Roman Church. The Essay on *Religion*, in 1612, is nothing but a protest against the crimes perpetrated in the name of the Roman Superstition; and even in the ampler and graver Essay of 1625, on the *Unity of Religion*, Bacon can suggest no means for procuring Unity except the *damning and sending to hell for ever those facts and opinions that tend to the support of such crimes* as Rome had encouraged. It is true that in the Essay on *Superstition* he finds space for a few additional censures on the Puritanical *superstition in avoiding superstition*. But all words that might be construed into approval of the Church of Rome, all warnings against excessive recoil from Rome, are carefully avoided. Compare the passage quoted above with the following passage written in 1625; the same thought is expressed, but *Superstition* is substituted for *Rome*, lest Rome should seem to be approved : *There is a superstition in avoiding superstitions, when men think to do best if they go furthest from the superstition formerly received. Therefore care would be had that (as it fareth in ill purgings) the good be not taken away with the bad; which commonly is done when the people is the reformer.*[1]

[1] *Essay* xvii. ll. 50-55.

The genuine and intense hatred felt by Bacon for Romanism is well illustrated by the letter he wrote to Toby Matthew on hearing that the latter had been converted to the Church of Rome. Toby Matthew was his best friend, the sharer of his literary secrets, devoted to him in adversity no less than in prosperity. It was to Matthew's request that we owe the Essay on Friendship, which was written as a memorial of their intimacy. If Bacon could not trust this man, he could trust no one. Yet so closely connected was Romanism, in Bacon's mind, with treason, so certain did it seem that superstition must be followed by sedition, so logical and inevitable that the loyal servant of the Pope must become disloyal to his country, that Bacon (1607-8) writes in the tone of one who can see no hope for the preservation of his friend's honour and loyalty save in the supernatural providence of God, who alone understands the inexplicable perversities of mankind : *I myself am out of doubt that you have been miserably abused when you were first seduced; but that which I take in compassion others may take in severity. I pray God, that understandeth us all better than we understand one another, contain you (even as I hope He will) at the least within the bounds of loyalty to his Majesty, and natural piety towards your country. And I entreat you much sometimes to meditate upon the extreme effects of superstition in this last Powder Treason, fit to be tabled and pictured in the chambers of meditation as another hell above the ground, and well justifying the censure of the heathen that superstition is worse than atheism; by how much 'it is less evil to have no opinion of God at all than such as is impious towards his divine majesty and goodness.' Good Mr. Matthew, receive yourself from these courses of perdition.* The words near the end of the extract, in inverted commas, are almost identical with the opening lines of the Essay on Superstition published in 1612; and while they reveal to us the profound and lasting dread of Rome caused by the Gunpowder Plot, they also show how completely Bacon identified the great Babylon with all the evils of distorted religion. What Duessa is in the Faery Queene, that is Rome in Bacon's policy. Wherever in the Essays he writes the word 'Superstition,' we may take it for granted that he is thinking of Rome.

Hence Bacon went heart and soul with the laws against recusants, and was an unflinching advocate of Elizabeth's policy towards them. He justified such laws, as he would have justified a war against the Turks, not because they were Turks, but because Turks were the natural enemies of Christendom. He admits that *we may not propagate religion by wars or by sanguinary persecutions to force consciences, except it be in cases of overt scandal, blasphemy, or intermixture of practice against the State.* But then all English members of the Roman Church seemed to Bacon pledged by their religion to *practice against the State.* He would probably have found no fault with Italians professing the Roman faith, nor with Frenchmen or Spaniards, whose governments and nations were not committed to war with Rome. But with Englishmen it was different. All nations had their national church assigned to them by Providence in accordance with their political circumstances; and to England Providence had assigned a church fitted for her external relations no less than her internal condition, a church that represented the political as well as the moral and religious freedom of the people. To this church therefore every lover of England owed loyal allegiance, not so much for what the church was, as for what the church represented.

For Elizabeth therefore Bacon stands forth as an eulogist, not an apologist. It was not the Queen, he says, that persecuted; it was Rome that brought persecution on itself. Up to the twenty-third year of her reign she sheltered the recusants with *a gracious connivancy. But,* he continues, *just then the ambitious and vast design of Spain for the subjugation of the kingdom came gradually to light. Of this, a principal part was the raising up within the bowels of the realm of a disaffected and revolutionary party which should join with the invading enemy, and the hope of this lay in our religious dissensions. . . . . And, as the mischief increased, the origin of it being traced to the seminary priests, who were bred in foreign parts . . . there was no remedy for it but that men of this class should be prohibited, upon pain of death, from coming into the kingdom at all.* King James was for dealing with the recusants more mildly. *Pœna ad paucos—punishment for few,* was his motto. But it is by no means clear that Bacon approved of the change. In the same passage of the Diary in which he records the King's wish, he notes that *it was inquired what priests were in jail in every circuit, and reported scarce half a dozen in all, which showeth no watch or search.* Lord Salisbury hints in council that the Pope's object may be, by driving the King to the use of harsh measures, to set the nation at discord, and so to make England a prey to foreign conquest. But to this, says Bacon, the Archbishop replied that, by that argument, 'the more furiously the Pope proceeds, the more remiss are we to be,' to which Bacon adds a mark of emphatic approval, *Quod nota—mark this.*

To the last Bacon seems to have retained his belief in repressive measures and his hatred of Roman superstition. In his Essay on Custom and Education, published in 1612, he has a passage retained in the Edition of 1625, in which he bitterly complains that Machiavelli, when recommending the employment of professed and hardened murderers for the purposes of assassination, was not aware how far Superstition can make up for deficiency in hardness of heart and in experience of crime. *Machiavel knew not of a Friar Clement, nor a Ravaillac, nor a Jauregny, nor a Baltazar Gerard. Yet his rule holdeth still that nature, nor the engagement of words, are not so forcible as custom. Only Superstition is now so well advanced that men of the first blood are as firm as butchers by occupation.*[1] Bacon's whole nature revolted from such crimes, perpetrated in such a cause, not merely because they were crimes, but also because they were anomalies, breaking all expected order, dislocating the machinery of government, and making all premeditated policy futile. And if he was wrong in supposing that a religion could be permanently kept down by moderately repressive laws, that at least was an error that could only be detected by experiment. His contemporaries believed it to be no error: and to this day some great men share their belief. Nor was Bacon's theology so pure and spiritual as to render it a matter of surprise that on this point he was no wiser than others.

[1] *Essay* xxxix. ll. 12-19.

CHAPTER IV

BACON AS A POLITICIAN.

In civil, as in ecclesiastical policy, Bacon had one main object, the preservation of the national unity. What was his ideal form of government there is little evidence to determine. He speaks, it is true, with some contempt of *a monarchy where there is no nobility*, associating it with the hated name of Turks, and calling it a *pure and absolute tyranny*.[1] Elsewhere he admits that a republic may be (not is) a better form of government than a kingdom. But with such abstract questions as these he is not concerned: they are idle in comparison with practical politics. God has appointed different forms of government, signiories, kingdoms, republics, and the like. In different forms of government different policies are needed, and England, being what it is, requires an English policy. Bacon is not writing (as Machiavelli writes) a disinterested and passionless treatise upon mechanical politics (as one may write on the game of chess), giving rules by which a would-be despot may acquire power, and retain power, whether rightly or wrongly. He writes as an English Statesman, recognising, as essential parts of England, King, Lords, Commons, and Clergy, and having for his object the preservation or harmonious development of all members of the body politic in England.

[1] *Essay* xiv. l. 2

Bacon therefore was not an upholder of despotism, nor did he—at least consciously and deliberately—desire to aggrandise the Crown to the detriment of the other Estates of the realm. If he did so occasionally in practice, it was at all events against his theory and his own personal nature. It was like his moral slips and failures—an exception, not the rule. Against any such aggrandisement, destructive of the symmetry of the English Constitution, his own *Prima Philosophia* protested. England was a kingdom, and a kingdom with nobles and commons is like the starry skies in which the *Primum Mobile* moves all things, while yet each planet has also its private and separate motion; or again, the King is a heavenly body, and as such must, like the sun, *move round some centre which it benefits.* And, to stoop from *Prima Philosophia* to facts and probabilities, it would be difficult to show that Bacon—whatever may have been his conduct on one or two occasions—systematically attempted to make the King independent of Parliament.

On the contrary, of all the King's servants no one was more earnest and sanguine in recommending and almost obtruding Parliaments, even at times when such recommendations seemed sure to be distasteful to the King. No number of failures could make Bacon disbelieve in the utility and fitness of frequent convening of Parliaments. If they failed, it was always, he thought, because they were not treated rightly. The very Parliament that caused his fall was summoned with his goodwill, and in accordance with his repeated advice. For to Bacon the Parliament seemed to be the natural Council for the Crown, appointed by that Providence which had shaped the national growth. It was to be a Council; not a shop, where the King was to barter away chips and rags of his royal prerogative for his people's money. Such mercenary notions were no less inexpedient than undignified. Everything that suggested such notions was to be carefully avoided: the very word *supply* was objectionable to Bacon on account of its undignified associations; it was better to speak of the King's need of *treasure*. The right theory of Parliament was that all estates of the realm, Clergy, Lords, and Commons, should be summoned at often recurring periods by the Sovereign, in order to hear and discuss his gracious plans and propositions for the welfare of the realm, and themselves to suggest plans and propositions of their own. We have seen how Bacon blames the Bishops for having *no bills to offer in Parliament;* and he himself in the Commons went almost out of his way sometimes to interlace the chaffering and haggling between Crown and people with *bills for the public service*. In the course of the Parliamentary discussions it would naturally occur, he said, that some honest and independent member would move a contribution to be made to the King's treasure: but such matters of routine, affecting the Crown particularly, ought not to take precedence of the common interests of the realm. The imperial dictum, *what touches us ourself shall be last served*, was to be the model and pattern for the royal dealings with Parliament: the King ought not to put himself before his Subjects. Still less ought questions of supply to be fought about, or made favours of, by any royal pleadings, or by gifts that were but transparent veils of bribes.

Here, as elsewhere, it will be both interesting and useful to compare Machiavelli's views with Bacon's; and on this point they seem to be at variance. Looking back to the old strifes and compromises between Patricians and Plebeians in the Roman Republic, Machiavelli sees nothing to be regretted or dreaded (except by superficial people) in the 'tumultuations' of the different orders of the Roman people. The excitement, the concourse, the violent language, and even occasionally the outbreak into violent action—all this was but the natural friction between class and class, between interest and interest; and, if not essential, it was at least useful for the production of good laws. The stir of the forum was the best practical debate: such was Machiavelli's opinion. But Machiavelli was writing of a republic, Bacon of a kingdom. The disorder that was admissible and perhaps useful for the former, was intolerable in the latter. A kingdom, let us remember, is to Bacon a model of heaven: and how can conflict and friction be allowable in a system where there is established one only source of motion, the *Primum Mobile*, to which all other motions must be subordinate? Conflict and strife may be fit for the atomic chaos, not for the cosmic order shaped by the Mind of the Universe.[1]

Outside as well as inside the council-hall there was a place and work for each estate of the realm. *A great and potent nobility addeth majesty to a monarch, but diminisheth power; and putteth life and spirit into the people, but presseth their fortune.* Bacon does not join in Machiavelli's sweeping condemnation of gentlemen. 'I call those gentlemen,' says the Italian, 'who live idly and plentifully upon their estates without any care or employment; and they are very pernicious wherever they are.'[2] That might be true in the Italian republics, but was not true, in Bacon's judgment, as respects the English kingdom. In a kingdom a little idleness seemed

[1] Mr. Gardiner (Vol. ii. p. 117) well brings out Bacon's dread of 'an incoherent mass' of patriotic legislators, such as might have been looked for in a supreme House of Commons.

[2] *Discourses*, Book ii. chap. 55. Elsewhere, however, he regrets the exclusion of the element of the nobility by the predominance of the commercial element in Florence, as tending to military weakness.

advantageous to the military spirit, and, provided they were not so numerous as to impoverish the nation, gentlemen were an advantage. *Out of all question, the splendour and magnificence and great retinues and hospitality of noblemen and gentlemen, received into custom, doth much conduce unto martial greatness:*[1] and again, *Kings that have able men of their nobility shall find ease in employing them, and a better slide into their business; for people naturally bend to them, as born in some sort to command.*[2] Besides, the nobility form a kind of breakwater, sheltering the King from sudden storms of popular fury. A monarchy without nobility is an institution unworthy of civilised Europe, and fit for none but Turks.

As for the middle classes, that is, the merchants and yeomen, their use and function is still more obvious. The merchants are the conducting veins that keep up the circulation of the body of the realm. The yeomen are the staple of the national armies. Both are to be cherished. Conversion of arable land to pasturage by rich landowners must be so limited that the class of yeomen may not be too much diminished; for the infantry are the nerves and sinews of an army, and the infantry are supplied by the yeomen. For the same reason States must *take heed how their nobility and gentlemen do multiply too fast*, for that changes the English yeoman into the French serf: *it maketh the common subject to grow to be a peasant and base swain driven out of heart, and, in effect, but the gentleman's labourer.*[3] For this reason also, the nation must not be too heavily taxed, not only because taxes may restrict production and trade, but also because it cannot be *that a people overlaid with taxes should ever become valiant and martial.*[4]

[1] *Essay* xxix. l. 135.
[2] *Essay* xiv. l. 49.
[3] *Essay* xxix. l. 105.
[4] Ib. l. 91.

It will have been apparent by this time what is the basis upon which Bacon's national policy is mainly founded. It is the army. War is regarded by him as essential to national life. The line of Æschylus embodying the blessing pronounced by Athene upon her chosen people, may be taken as the text of Bacon's political discourses :—

> Let there be foreign wars, not scantly coming.

No body, writes Bacon in the Essays, *can be healthful without exercise, neither natural body nor politic: and certainly to a kingdom or an estate a just and honourable war is the true exercise. A civil war indeed is like the heat of a fever; but a foreign war is like the heat of exercise, and serveth to keep the body in health; for in a slothful peace both courages will effeminate and manners corrupt.*[1]

Here again Machiavelli and Bacon differ, but here again they differ more in appearance than in reality. To the Italian, sick with the sight of foreign mercenaries playing at war with one another through the cities and dukedoms of his distracted country, and fattening on her miseries, war seemed less praiseworthy than to Bacon, and he especially reprobates the professed soldier : 'for he will never be thought a good man who takes upon him an employment by which, if he would reap any profit at any time, he is obliged to be false and rapacious and cruel.' But Bacon, to whom a soldier means not a hireling but an Englishman in arms for his country, speaks even of a professed soldier with favour : *The following by certain estates of men answerable to that which a great person himself professeth (as of soldiers to him that hath been employed in the wars and the like), hath ever been a thing*

---

[1] *Essay* xxix. l. 260.

civil and well taken even in monarchies. Bacon's love of war, or rather his sense of the necessity of war for England, pervades all his speeches and treaties, and influences all his policy. Speaking in 1606-7[1] of the apprehended influx of Scots into England, and deriding the danger of over population, after mentioning as one remedy at hand *that desolate and wasted kingdom of Ireland, which doth as it were continually call unto us for our colonies and plantations,* he adds, *or to take the worst effect, look into all stories, you shall find the remedy none other than some honourable war for the enlargement of their borders which find themselves bent upon foreign parts; which inconvenience in a valorous and warlike nation I know not whether I should term an inconvenience or no; for the saying is most true, though in another sense, 'omne solum forti patria.' And certainly (Mr. Speaker) I hope I may speak it without offence that, if we did hold ourselves worthy whensoever just cause should be given, either to recover our ancient rights or to revenge our late wrongs, or to attain the honour of our ancestors, or to enlarge the patrimony of our posterity, we would never in this manner forget the considerations of amplitude and greatness, and fall at variance about profit and reckonings, fitter a great deal for private persons than for Parliaments and Kingdoms.* No passage that I know of, expresses that multiplicity in unity, that identity of object amid diversity of agents and means, which was to characterize Bacon's ideal English nation, so aptly as the well-known extract from the council scene in Henry V :—

> *Exeter*—For government, though high and low and lower,
> Put into parts, doth keep in one consent,
> Congreeing in a full and natural close
> Like music.

---

[1] *Life*, Vol. iii. p. 314.

Canterbury—Therefore doth heaven divide
    The state of man in divers functions,
    Setting endeavour in continual motion,
    To which is fixed, as an aim or butt,
    Obedience : for so work the honey-bees,
    Creatures that by a rule in nature teach
    The act of order to a peopled kingdom.
    They have a king and officers of sorts,
    Where some, like magistrates, correct at home ;
    Others, like merchants, venture trade abroad ;
    Others, like soldiers, armed in their stings
    Make boot upon the summer's velvet buds,
    Which pillage they with merry march bring home
    To the tent royal of their Emperor.

And with Bacon, as with Henry's councillors, the natural sequel to such a description of a well-ordered kingdom appeared to be a summons to war ; 'therefore to France, my liege.'

Bacon then was not enamoured of despotism ; it was a form of government that he despised, as fit for none but Turks. If he upheld the royal prerogative, he upheld it (in theory at least) only as part of the body politic, only as he would have upheld the rights of the Nobility or the Commons. In practice, no doubt, he went further than this. His closeness to the throne, his dependence upon court favour, his eagerness for office, his suppleness of temper, and his undoubted respect for James and desire to retain the royal esteem, biassed him unduly to the side of the crown. But he certainly had no desire to mine the liberties of England, or prepare the way for a despotism. As well might it be said that the Liberal party at that time deliberately desired to bring about a democracy. In the ample debatable ground that lay between the royal prerogative and the people's rights, there were many points over which both honest lawyers and wise politicians might well contend. If both parties claimed the disputed territory, and both insisted on a definite line of demarcation, it was important that neither side should gain so complete a victory as to shift the balance of power. Now the Crown had suffered, and was clearly likely to suffer more and more, from want of means. Even under the economical Elizabeth, subsidies had increased in frequency and amount, and yet had been found barely sufficient for the purposes of her parsimonious government. Moreover she had recently given up one source of profit, in surrendering the disputed monopolies. In these circumstances it was becoming a serious question whether the control of the purse by the House of Commons might not gradually subordinate and weaken the royal power so far as ultimately to dislocate the machinery of government. To us this danger seems visionary, or rather it seems not visionary, but not a danger. But to those who, like Bacon, regarded the royal power as the *Primum Mobile* of the political system, the danger must have seemed very serious indeed.[1] The late Queen who was, in Bacon's eyes, a pattern of administrative ability by her dignity, her tact, and her timely concessions, had preserved her prerogative unimpaired. But there seemed a danger lest James might be less successful, might barter away his prerogative piece by piece for temporary relief in the shape of subsidies, thus dangerously revolutionizing the constitution of the country. To the King himself Bacon plainly hints the impolicy of his conduct: he entreats his Majesty *not to descend below himself;* reminds him pretty plainly of his promise not to make long speeches to the House; and, while he suggests a systematic partition and assignment of the revenue to its different objects, he urges him at the same time not to be afraid of his debts, but to be confident that all will be well if the King will but assume the fitting

[1] See note on page cxix.

tone of a Prince, the voice of a *Common Parent*. Bacon has no faith in any of the wretched expedients by which Cecil had hoped to render the Crown so wealthy as to be independent of the Commons. Such independence was not to be thought of; King and Parliament ought to be inseparable, 'high and low and lower congreeing in a full and natural close.' But then, on the other hand, recognition of the rights of the Commons did not prevent recognition of the Royal Prerogative. The time was a critical one; a struggle between Crown and People seemed in the nature of things inevitable. If a treaty was to be arranged between the two contending powers, it was of importance that the Crown should come to the conference without impairing by its own action the advantage secured to it by the precedents of antiquity.

It was not therefore as a mere courtier, still less as an enemy to the liberties of England, that Bacon, in sharp opposition to Coke, stood forward, as he himself says, in the character of *a peremptory royalist*,[1] magnifying to the utmost the royal privileges. In the very passage where he assumes this title, he prides himself on *never having been for a single hour out of favour with the lower House.* Yet to such extent did he afterwards carry his advocacy, that his contemporaries spoke in wonder of 'the new doctrine but now broached'[2] by the Lord Chancellor, when he 'took occasion to enlarge himself much upon the prerogative . . . saying further (whatsoever some unlearned lawyers might prattle to the contrary) that it was the accomplishment and perfection of the common law.' *Above all*, such are his instructions to the judges, *you ought to maintain the King's prerogative;* and again, *the King's prerogative is law, the principal part of law.* Judges are reminded that they are planets, while the

[1] *Life*, Vol. iv. p. 280. [2] Ib. Vol vi. p. 118.

King is *Primum Mobile,* that first and highest motion which all the planets or great persons of a kingdom are to obey, *carried swiftly by the highest motions and softly by their own motion. Do as the planets do,* says the Lord Chancellor to the judges, *move always and be carried with the motion of your first mover, which is your Sovereign.* The same deference inspires the Essay on Judicature, wherein the judges are instructed to *remember that Salomon's throne was supported by lions on both sides; let them be lions, but yet lions under the throne, being circumspect that they do not check or oppose any points of sovereignty.*[1] James himself is reminded of his participation in the celestial nature : *If you are heavenly, you must have influence* (i.e. the astral stream supposed to flow down on mortals from the heavenly bodies). He is addressed by Bacon as one able to make of him *a vessel of honour or dishonour. Reverence is that wherewith princes are girt from God,* and no misgovernment can divest them of their sovereignty ; *howsoever Henry IV.'s act by a secret providence of God prevailed, yet it was but an usurpation.*[2] There are few modern Englishmen that will not rather sympathize with the sturdy opposition of Coke, who stoutly refused to give an official opinion to the Crown on the merits of a case not yet brought before him, than with the courtly and convenient compliance of Bacon, however it may have been based upon *Prima Philosophia* and dictated by high policy. But it is at least something to feel that Bacon's political conduct does not oblige us to regard him either as a hypocrite or as a covert and deliberate enemy to the liberties of England.

As regards internal policy, Bacon went with his own times against the experience of later times in advocating

---

[1] *Essay* xvi. l. 137.   [2] *Life*, Vol. v. p. 145.

what we should now call an excess of the interfering, fostering, or paternal element in government. As remedies for the discontent arising from poverty, he recommends not only the *opening*, but also the *balancing* of trade, and the *cherishing* of manufactures. For example, a company of merchants is to receive a charter for the exportation of cloths, but only on condition of their being dyed and dressed in England, so as to keep that trade in English hands.[1] Furthermore, laws are to be made for *the banishing of idleness, the repressing of waste, the improvement and husbanding of the soil, the regulating of prices of things vendible, the moderation of taxes and tributes, and the like*.[2] Wealth is to be diffused; for *money is like muck, not good except it be spread.* This is to be done, chiefly by suppressing, *or at the least keeping a straight hand upon the devouring trades of usury, engrossing, great pasturages, and the like*.[3] To govern a country by splitting it into factions is folly; nevertheless the Commons ought so far to be maintained and attached to the Crown that, if ever the giants, or nobles, assail Jupiter, there may be a ready ally for the sovereign in the multitude, Briareus with the hundred hands. Moderate liberty is to be allowed for griefs and discontentments, lest the *wound bleed inwards*. The higher nobles are to be kept at a distance, but not to be depressed. The *second nobles*, or gentry, are to be encouraged, for they are a counterpoise to the high nobility: besides, *being the most immediate in authority with the common people, they do best temper popular commotions*.[4] Merchants are to be left untaxed as far as possible; for what one gains directly by taxing them, one loses indirectly in the diminution of the wealth of the realm. The King is to beware of med-

[1] *Life,* Vol. v. p. 171.
[2] *Essay* xv. ll. 120-6.
[3] Ib. xv. l. 155.
[4] Ib. xv. l. 155.

dling with the religion, customs, or means of life of the Commons. Bacon sees, as Machiavelli saw, that it is not the occasional acts of despotic outrage that alienate the subjects from the Prince; it is the ever-present galling restrictions that worry the tradesman in his shop, the farmer at his plough, or all men in their households; these are the seeds of revolutions and the ruins of States. Give the Commons assurance in these matters, and there will be no danger from them. As for *men of war*, or professed soldiers, they are not to remain too long together, nor to be trained in too large masses, nor ought they to receive pay; but unpaid military bands, trained in small numbers and at different places, are *things of defence and no danger*. To the continuous training of the English militia, even in times of peace, Machiavelli attributed their immediate superiority over the trained soldiers of France; and Bacon not only recommends the training of militia, but would also in some measure subordinate even the industrial pursuits of the kingdom to the purposes of war. *Above all*, he says, *for empire or greatness it importeth most that a nation do profess arms as their principal honour, study, and occupation.* For this purpose agriculture must be encouraged, rather than *sedentary and within-door arts and delicate manufactures, which have in their nature a contrariety to a military disposition.* Military reasons are also given for encouraging naturalization: colonies also are regarded as subserving military ends. Thus, partly by including new subjects, partly by establishing *plantations* (not at hazard, nor in knots of private adventurers, nor for base, present and mechanical profit, but systematically, as public enterprises, after the manner of the Greeks or Romans, and for the ultimate benefit of the whole empire) the *Great State* that is to be, is *not so much to grow upon the world, as rather the world is to grow upon the State: that is the sure way of greatness.*

It is noteworthy how naturally, from the internal politics of Bacon's *Great State*, one is led back again to external and military policy. War, we have seen, was in Bacon's judgment the legitimate exercise for every nation. But further, it seemed to him the special need of England in those days. In his Preface to the *Interpretation of Nature*, he speaks of civil wars as a danger impending upon Europe. In his Diary he twice makes mention of the *inclination of the times to popularity*, and of the disposition to popular Estates *creeping on the ground* in many countries. The growing differences between Crown and Commons in England must have seemed to threaten that his own country would be first exposed to this visitation. Naturally therefore, in order to avert the fever of civil war, he turns to his favourite remedy, external war. In his notes on Policy, entered in his Diary during the year 1608, his first entry refers to *the bringing the King low by poverty and empty coffers*.[1] Then (after prophetically glancing at the prospect of *revolt or trouble first in Scotland; for, till that be, no danger of English discontent: in doubt of a war from thence*, and after a few other matters of detail) he makes the following note, *Persuade the King in glory—Aurea condet sæcula*. The meaning of these words is clear enough: Bacon is to divert the King's mind from petty internal disputes to a great and grand policy; the King is to *found a golden age* for England. A few lines further bring us to the secret of this golden age: *the fairest, without disorder or peril, is the general persuading to king and people, and course of infusing everywhere the foundation in this isle of a Monarchy in the West, as an apt seat, state, people for it; so civilising Ireland, further colonising the wilds of Scotland, annexing the Low Countries.*

[1] *Life*, Vol. iv. p. 73

Introduction

Video solem orientem in Occidente—I see the sun rising in the West. Such are the words in which Bacon proclaims to the King his vision of the great Western Monarchy that was to be, the champion of liberty and the bulwark against Roman superstition. It is the vision of Spenser, the ideal England of Shakspeare and of Milton. No one of these great poets shrank from war, or dreamed that England could fulfil her destiny, or even maintain her position without conflict. The island of Gloriana was pledged to perpetual war against Duessa: England's breed of heroes was to be 'famous and feared,' and the English nation was to be, as it always had been—

> An old and haughty nation proud in arms.

If therefore Bacon erred in advocating a warlike policy for England, he erred in company with no mean names. It is possible that he was not in error. A policy that Spenser, Shakspeare, Bacon, and Milton concurred in feeling to be accordant with the national character— most modern Englishmen will be slow to impugn. At least it may be remembered that the war he advocated was of no ignoble kind, not a war for mere aggrandisement, not for mere glory, but for Liberty and Truth. Here again Bacon would quote an axiom of *Prima Philosophia* in defence of his policy: *Things move violently to their place, but easily in their place.* When therefore England had assumed her rightful place as Head of the Great Protestant Confederacy in Europe, then she might more easily: till then, it could not be but that she must *move violently.*

In later days Bacon was driven from his grand warlike policy. Servants must suit their policy to their masters, and Bacon served a master who shrank from war even more than he clung to peace. Accordingly, we shall find the versatile pen of the former advocate of war now inditing royal discourses on the advantages of peace; suggesting, for example, as one of the advantages of the Spanish match, that it may result in the establishment of a tribunal of arbitration powerful enough to put down wars in Europe. But not even in those degenerate days can Bacon bring himself to give up all thoughts of war. War against the Turks was still possible; and in his later years he resorts to this as his last hope, in his *Dialogue on a Holy War*, discussing its possibility and lawfulness. The treatise is incomplete, and from its nature gives expression to various opinions; but there is little doubt that the decision of the completed Dialogue would have been for war against the Turks, not as the enemies of the Church but as the enemies of Christendom.[1] To the last therefore Bacon upheld a policy of war.

Such then was Bacon as a politician, no less grand and lofty in theory, no less supple and compliant in practice, than Bacon as a philosopher. None will refuse to his theoretical policy the merit of grandeur and consistency. His proposed *annexing of the Low Countries* might have engaged England in unnecessary quarrels: but it might, under a different Sovereign, have facilitated an understanding between the Crown and the people, and might have spared England a civil war. But, as we have seen above, the sanguine self-deception and excessive flexibility of his nature rendered his theoretical policy of no practical importance. With perfect ease and without the slightest sense of degradation, he could turn his lofty but versatile and discursive mind from the high dreams of *the Monarchy in the West* to the prosecution of a

---

[1] *Works*, Vol. vii. p. 24. Bacon antedated by some centuries the great event that even now we are only anticipating. *There cannot but ensue*, he says, *a dissolution in the state of the Turk, whereof the time seemeth to approach.*

patriot who dared to attack Benevolences, from the *golden age* of James I. to the disgracing of an independent judge, and the torturing of a wretched schoolmaster for 'practising to have infatuated the King's judgment by sorcery,' and while pluming himself upon his zeal for one who is, *without flattery, the best of Kings*, he can add a modest hope that *for my honest and true intentions to state and justice, and my love to my master, I am not the worst of Chancellors.*[1]

Turn to the *Antitheta* on Truth,[2] and you will there find two opposite propositions, the one favouring a life of philosophic study, the other a life of active politics. There can be no doubt to which side the writer inclined. The defence of politics runs thus, *God cares for the Universe; do you care for your country.* A narrow sentiment utterly unworthy of, and unlike, the character of him who described himself as *born for the service of mankind.* But of philosophy he writes, *How blessed it is to have the orb of the mind concentric with the orb of the Universe.* Here speaks Bacon himself, from his own heart, exactly describing the pursuit for which he was best fitted, and in which he would have attained the highest happiness. This saying can hardly fail to recall to our minds the very similar epigram written by Goldsmith upon the great statesman—

> Who, born for the Universe, narrowed his mind,
> And to party gave up what was meant for mankind.

Burke's epigram applies also to Bacon. He too, no less than Burke, was 'born for the Universe'; and, though he has bequeathed to the Universe rich and enduring legacies, yet he too 'narrowed his mind,' first from the wide expanse of philosophy to the narrower limits of national politics, and then again from that comparatively

---

[1] *Life*, Vol. vii. p. 78.   [2] See *Essays*, Vol. ii. p. 107.

ample space to the hampering restraints of a petty place-hunting and time-serving, unworthy of the name of statesmanship, 'giving up' to the defence of the Royal Prerogative and to the service of the English Solomon all that was meant for England, and much that was 'meant for mankind.'

CHAPTER V.

BACON AS A MORALIST.

BACON'S moral teaching is greatly influenced by two teachers, Plutarch (taken as the type of the historians of Greece and Rome) and Machiavelli. From the last chapter it will be seen that the morality of his foreign policy differs little from that of the ancients. Nor will this be a matter for surprise; for, until this century, Christian morality has exercised little influence upon the intercourse of nations. Bacon seems to have followed Machiavelli in believing that a State might act towards other States without regard to the rules that regulate the relations of individuals. In part this feeling—which is shared by many in modern times—may be accounted for by the absence of any rules for foreign policy in the New Testament. Christians have, too often, gladly adopted the belief that they may do as they like, provided what they like to do is not expressly forbidden in the Scriptures: and naturally the Scriptures, or at least the Christian Scriptures, say very little or nothing about the rules of intercourse between nations. In the absence of any Christian code, Plutarch and Livy have supplied Rules to most Christian statesmen, among others to Bacon. A nation therefore that is to be *great*, has the example of Rome held up to it for imitation. A State is not indeed **to make** war without pretext; but, on the other hand, it is to be *ready and prest* for a quarrel, and *not to stand too nicely upon occasions of war*. And as we have seen above, so far from being an evil to be avoided or a remedy not to be resorted to but in the last extremity, war is regarded by Bacon as the natural exercise for every healthy nation.

The influence of the ancient morality on Bacon is well illustrated by his treatment of duelling—a habit common in Christian nations, and very uncommon, or rather unheard of, in Greece and Rome. Irrespective of the condemnation pronounced on it by the ancient morality, duelling was in itself and in its consequences hateful and abominable in Bacon's eyes. Not bold himself, he despises and dreads boldness for its vulgar successes, and because, though it is *a child of ignorance and baseness, far inferior to other parts, nevertheless it doth fascinate and bind hand and foot those that are either shallow in judgment or weak in courage, which are the greatest part*.[1] Further, the scientific side of Bacon's nature, rejoicing in law and order, was repelled by lawlessness in every shape. When therefore boldness and lawlessness combined to encourage a habit so injurious to the military efficiency of the nation as duelling, Bacon has no words to express his contempt for it, a contempt that was doubtless increased by his own passionless disposition, and by his low sense of human moral nature and its petty squabbles, coupled with his high sense of the greatness of the human intellect and its grand mission. But all these causes of aversion together, even when combined with the horror felt for duelling by the King—who, to use his own words, saw himself royally attended every morning, but did not know how many of his train would be alive by sunset—scarcely affected him so much as the feeling

---

[1] *Essay* xii. l. 16.

that Greece and Rome were the true models for all time in matters of warfare, and that the Greeks and Romans did not fight duels. *A man's life,* he says, *is not to be trifled away; it is to be offered up and sacrificed to honourable services, public merits, good causes, and noble adventures.*[1] This none will dispute : but there is something not English and not practical in the philosophic contempt with which Bacon can despise reproaches, insults, and even blows. *As for words of reproach and contumely (whereof the lie was esteemed none), it is not credible (but that the orations themselves are extant) what extreme and exquisite reproaches were tossed up and down in the Senate of Rome and the places of assembly and the like in Græcia, and yet no man took himself fouled by them, but took them for breath and the style of an enemy, and either despised them or returned them; but no blood spilt about them. So of every touch or light blow of the person, they are not in themselves considerable, save that they have got upon them the stamp of a disgrace, which maketh these light things pass for great matters.* This is of a piece with his Essay on Anger. As a virtue, Anger is not recognised by Bacon, and with the Teutonic or Northern sense of honour he has no sympathy.

But it is through Machiavelli most of all, that we arrive at a clear understanding of Bacon's moral system. For, however Bacon may disavow his master and rebel against some of the blunt and logical Machiavellian dicta, yet Machiavelli was unquestionably Bacon's guide, if not in theoretical, at all events in practical morality. Protests and recalcitrations are not wanting in Bacon's more formal and artificial treatises, such as the passage in which he maintains that it is necessary for men *to be fully imbued with pious and moral knowledge before they*

[1] *Life,* Vol. iv. p. 406.

take any part in politics: but the morality of the Essays, which are eminently practical, and intended as the Author says to come into the *business and bosoms of men*—is the pure and simple morality of Machiavelli. The new art of 'policy' had superseded the old reign of force, and Machiavelli was the recognised master of the mysteries of policy. It fell in with Bacon's nature readily to admit that in politics, no less than in science, *knowledge is power;* and the politician must base action on knowledge. But knowledge in politics seemed to mean knowledge of men, and that, not knowledge of what men ought to be, but of men as men are. Moreover, the dangers besetting a politician arise, not from the virtues, but from the vices and weaknesses of men. These therefore it seemed that the politician must take as his special study—human weaknesses and human vices; and what man was likely to know these so well as the historian and politician who had sounded all the depths of Italian villainy? Some men might find fault with Machiavelli for undertaking so odious a task as that of describing the dark side of human nature : not so Bacon. As in science a man must take things as they are, not as though they were what he would like them to be ; so in politics the scientific politician must take men as they are, ignoring none of their faults, however inconvenient and disagreeable ; *so that we are much beholden to Machiavelli and other writers of that class, who openly and unfeignedly declare and describe what men do and not what they ought to do . . . . for, without this, virtue is open and unfenced.*[1]

In one respect the morality of Bacon is inferior to that of Machiavelli. The latter is writing for States and Commonwealths, not for individuals ; or, if for individuals, for individuals regarded as Princes, as public

---

[1] *Works*, Vol. v. p. 17.

characters. Now, as we have seen above, States and individuals are regarded as dwelling in different spheres of morality : consequently Machiavelli's morality is entirely unaffected by Christianity. On the morality of individuals or private morality he rarely touches, except to deplore the general treachery, falsehood, self-seeking, and insubordination of modern times as compared with the truthfulness, the religious reverence, the unselfish patriotism, and the strict discipline of the old Roman Republic. Clearly, had Machiavelli written on the morality of an Italian citizen, he would not have written as he wrote for his Italian *prince*. Princes are above laws, and have no conscience (or rarely can afford to have one); but citizens are on a different footing. In justice to Machiavelli, we are to remember that, when he speaks of right or wrong, of 'cruelty,' for example, 'well or ill applied,' he has in his mind either a State or a ruler who is bound to act like a State, and whose mind is to be so full of his duty towards his country that he can spare no time to think of his duty towards himself or towards individuals. Now the rules that Machiavelli has laid down for Princes and Commonwealths Bacon transfers to private life, or tries to transfer, not always successfully. The panoply of the Machiavellian morality is sometimes too massive and weighty, and hampers the free English nature. It is the simple shepherd boy unable to move easily in the royal armour which he has not proved. The native English sense of the power of truth and righteousness will at times rebel against and discard the rigid logic of the morality of selfishness. The divine power of goodness betrays the student of Machiavellian policy at times into language not strictly Machiavellian. But, in spite of these righteous inconsistencies, it is scarcely possible to read the *Discourses* and the *Essays* together without feeling that the latter stand on the lower level of morality.

Machiavelli delineates with an unflinching hand the *Art of Advancement* for an Empire or a Prince; Bacon applies these rules to the mere vulgar object of *Advancement in Life* for individuals, but applies them neither thoroughly nor consistently. Machiavelli has always in the background of his *Prince* the hopes of a redeemed and united Italy; in the background of the Essays there is nothing but Self.

Through Machiavelli we shall arrive at so clear an understanding of the relation between Bacon's morality and Bacon's religion, that it is quite worth while to spend a few moments in considering the attitude of the Author of the *Discourses* towards the Christianity of his time. Both Christianity and Papacy seem to Machiavelli responsible for much evil. The Italian patriot has a keen sense of the evils brought upon 'poor Italy' by the Papal Court, 'by the corruption of which Italy has lost all its religion and all its devotion ... so that we Italians have this obligation to the Church and its ministers, that by their means we are become heathenish and irreligious.' But it is not the Papal Court alone that is to blame. Christianity itself, or at all events the current form of Christianity, is accused of encouraging effeminacy, of alienating the choice spirits of the age from active political duties, of giving prominence to the wicked and unscrupulous, and of unfitting the whole nation for military service. 'In our religion the meek and humble, and such as devote themselves to the contemplation of divine things, are esteemed more happy than the greatest tyrant and the greatest conqueror upon earth; and the *summum bonum* which the others placed in the greatness of the mind, the strength of the body, and whatever else contributed to make men active, we have determined to consist in humility and abjection and contempt of the world; and if our religion requires any fortitude, it is rather to enable us to suffer than to act. So that it seems to me this way of living, so contrary to the ancients, has rendered the Christians more weak and effeminate, and left them as a prey to those who are more wicked and may order them as they believe; the most part thinking of Paradise than of preferment, and of enduring rather than revenging of injuries, as if heaven was to be won rather by idleness than by arms.' Justly wroth with 'the poor and pusillanimous people more given to their ease than to anything that was great,' he indignantly declares that 'if the Christian religion allows us to defend and exalt our country, it allows us certainly to love it and honour it, and prepare ourselves so as we may be able to defend it.'[1]

In this earnest protest against the parody of Christianity afforded by the religious life of his day many sincere Christians will heartily concur with Machiavelli. But his inferences are more open to objection when he proceeds to discuss the source whence men are to expect the Redemption of Italy. Goodness being, as he says, 'ineffectual,' force, mechanical force is the only hope of salvation: not brute force, it is true, but force directed and controlled by reason: still, for all that, force. Force has ruled the world in past ages: so at least it seems to him as he turns the pages of history. The flash of the armour of the Roman legions dazzles his eyes to the purer brightness of the Star of Israel. Even the history of the Chosen People, as read by the light of Roman history, presents itself to him in strange distortions. 'The Scripture shows us that those of the Prophets whose arms were in their hands and had power to compel, succeeded better in the reformation which they designed, whereas those who came only with exhortation and good language suffered martyrdom and banishment

[1] *Discourses* ii. 2.

.... as in our day it happened to Friar Jerome Savonarola, who ruined himself by his new institutions as soon as the people of Florence began to desert him. For he had no means to confirm those who had been of his opinion, nor to constrain such as dissented.' What then must that Prince do who desires a prosperous reign ? He must take the ways of the world.[1] 'Those ways are cruel and contrary, not only to all civil, but to Christian and indeed human conversation ; for which reason they are to be rejected by everybody : for certainly 'tis better to remain a private person than to make oneself king by the calamity and destruction of one's people. Nevertheless, he who neglects to take the first good way, if he will preserve himself, must make use of the bad ; for though many Princes take a middle way betwixt both, yet they find it extreme, difficult, and dangerous. For being neither good nor bad, they are neither feared nor beloved, and so, unlikely to prosper.' And, as 'the first good way' is very seldom adopted, the conclusion at which Machiavelli at last arrives, and which embodies the practical morality of Bacon's Essays, is expressed in these memorable words : 'The present manner of living is so different from the way that ought to be taken, that he who neglects what is done to follow what ought to be done, will sooner learn how to ruin than how to preserve himself. For a tender man and one that desires to be honest in everything, must needs run a great hazard among so many of a contrary principle. Wherefore it is necessary for a Prince that is willing to subsist, to harden himself and learn to be good or otherwise, according to the exigence of his affairs.'[2] This is a summary of Machiavelli's morality for Princes, and what Machiavelli meant for Princes Bacon transfers to individuals.

[1] *Discourses* i. 26.   [2] The *Prince*, xv.

It is true that, as we have said, Bacon seldom speaks out quite so straightforwardly as this. The Machiavellian thoroughness somewhat repels him, and drives him into inconsistency. He even censures his teacher for teaching *Evil Arts*. We must remember, he says, that *all virtue is most rewarded, and all wickedness most punished in itself.* To be freed from all the restraints of virtue may open a short straight path to fortune : *but it is in life as it is in ways ; the shortest way is commonly the foulest and muddiest, and surely the fairer way is not much about.* Such maxims as these of Machiavelli that, 'the surest way is to waive all moderation, and either to caress or extinguish ;' or again, 'when the injury extends to blood, threatening is very dangerous and much more so than downright execution ; for when a man is killed, he is past thinking of revenge, and those who are alive will quickly forget him ; but when a man is threatened and finds himself under a necessity of suffering, or doing something extraordinary, he becomes immediately dangerous'[1]—are revolting to Bacon's sense of goodness and pity. He will have none of Machiavelli's *Evil Arts* of 'cruelty well applied.' But yet he is too well aware of the fatal disadvantages besetting 'a tender man, and one that desires to be honest in everything.' Therefore he will go some way, though he cannot go all lengths, with his teacher. A man is above all things—so much Bacon admits—*not to show himself disarmed and exposed to scorn and injury by too much goodness and sweetness of nature.*[2] A little dissimulation is almost necessary to secrecy, simulation must be allowed where there is no remedy : and, *though some persons of weaker judgment, and perhaps too scrupulous morality, may disapprove of it,* yet the *Art of Ostentation,* or showing oneself off to

[1] *Discourses* iii. 6.   [2] *Works,* Vol. v. p. 69.

the best advantage, is not to be despised. He will not imitate Machiavelli in recommending Evil Arts, but these are none : these he calls *Good Arts*. It is no Evil Art, for example, but mere praiseworthy prudence, in the matter of friendship, to bear in mind *that ancient precept of Bias, not construed to any point of perfidiousness, but only to caution and moderation. Love as if you were sometime to hate, and hate as if you were sometime to love. For it utterly betrays and destroys all utility for men to embark themselves too far in unfortunate friendships, troublesome and turbulent quarrels, and foolish and childish jealousies and emulations.* Bacon then, as well as Machiavelli, is aware of the necessity that 'one must harden oneself if one is to subsist.' In his Essays on Conduct he holds up no ideal of life : he is even less of an idealist here than in his formal treatises ; for he is writing things *of a nature whereof a man shall find much in experience, little in books.* The Volume of Essays is what Bacon called the *Architect of Fortune, or the Knowledge of Advancement in Life*, set forth in a shape fit to *come home to men's business and bosoms.*

I have as vast contemplative ends as I have moderate civil ends : so Bacon wrote in his youth. In his later life he might, with as great or greater truth, have contrasted his vast contemplative ends with his moderate moral ends. Very melancholy is the contrast between his unflagging hopes of the intellectual Kingdom of Man and the dreary hopelessness with which he regards old age. To believe him, human life is a lesson in evil, and men are the worse for having lived : with such a deliberate sadness does he prefer youth to age. *To be serious*, he says, *youth has modesty and a sense of shame, old age is somewhat hardened; a young man has kindness and mercy, an old man has become pitiless and callous; youth has a praiseworthy emulation, old age ill-natured envy; youth*

*is inclined to religion and devotion by reason of its fervency
and inexperience of evil, in old age piety cools through
the lukewarmness of charity and long intercourse with
evil, together with the difficulty of believing; a young
man's wishes are vehement, an old man's moderate;
youth is fickle and unstable, old age more grave and constant;
youth is liberal, generous, and philanthropic, old
age is covetous, wise for itself, and self-seeking; youth is
confident and hopeful, old age diffident and distrustful; a
young man is easy and obliging, an old man churlish and
peevish; youth is frank and sincere, old age cautious and
reserved; youth desires great things, old age regards
those that are necessary; a young man thinks well of the
present, an old man prefers the past; a young man
reverences his superiors, an old man finds out their faults.*[1]
In his Essays the same verdict is more generally but no
less distinctly pronounced: *Age doth profit rather in the
powers of understanding than in the virtues of the will
and affections;*[2] and again, though here less emphatically,
*for the moral part perhaps youth will have the preeminence,
as age hath for the politic.*[3] A confession of
this kind strikes at the root of the hopes of moral improvement.
It is as though the general had despaired
of the Republic before going forth to fight her battles.
It is not thus that the victories of Science have been
won.

The secret of the Christian morality is the creed expressed
by Shakspeare, that—

> There is a soul of goodness in things evil
> If one had power to distil it out.

But Bacon had not this faith, and therefore not this
power. He had not realised, inherent in men's hearts,
the divine faculty of calling out goodness in the bad by

---

[1] *Works*, Vol. v. p. 320.   [2] *Essay* xlii. l. 54.   [3] *Essay* xlii. l. 47.

believing that goodness is there, and that no bad man is altogether bad. With his would-be scientific eye he looked on things as they were, not as they ought to be, and what he saw was, in his own words, *all things full of treachery and ingratitude.* Nay, he did not do humanity even the justice to look at it scientifically : for his glance was too superficial to give him scientific insight. Much that is noble in humanity was ignored by him because it was not on the surface. Just as, in physical science, he pronounces that the moon's light gives no warmth because he cannot feel it, and that heated iron has no expansion because he cannot see it ; so, in morals, he ignores the purifying influence of age, and trials, and the love of wife and children, and the death of friends and parents, because he himself has not experienced this influence. Being himself cold and unimpassioned (except in scientific matters) and unsympathetic, and in a word so devoted to the interests of mankind at large that he had no time to think of individuals—he was too short-sighted to discern in others those purifying results of which he was not conscious in himself. Hence it was that he showed himself inferior to Aristotle in allowing himself to be imposed upon by the superficial goodness of childhood and youth— those raw and unripe virtues which can only be called virtues by hopeful anticipation. In his own life he had realised the hardening and corrupting effects of the politics of his time upon his developed manhood ; and he speaks from experience when he prefers youth to old age. He had not to look back, as many have, upon a youth dissolute or wasted, but upon early days of high hopes, pure ambitions, and unremitting labours. To him old age had brought no amendment of past errors, no exemption from excesses or frivolities ; but it had trifled away the faculties and preparations of his youth, diverted him from the work for which he was fit to a work for which he was unfit, and, in return for this, it had dulled his conscience and taught him nothing but how to 'harden himself in order to subsist.'

Therefore, however much he may laud Truth and Goodness, he lauds them as ideals, and as ideals to which not only none can approximate, but also none must endeavour to approach too close if they wish to study Advancement in Life. Of all virtues and dignities of the mind, Goodness, he admits, *is the greatest, being the character of the Deity; and without it man is a busy, mischievous, wretched thing, no better than a kind of vermin.* But, on the other hand, *extreme lovers of their country or masters were never fortunate, neither can they be.* In the same way, *clear and round dealing is the honour of man's nature;* but, on the other hand, *no man can be secret except he give himself a little scope of dissimulation.* As for politicians, in them, tortuosity and deceit, and indeed envy and malignity, are almost matters of necessity: *such* (envious) *dispositions are the very errors of human nature, and yet they are the fittest timber to make great Politiques of, like to knee-timber that is good for ships, that are ordained to be tossed, but not for building houses that shall stand firm.* It is true that he adds that *it is the weaker sort of politics that are the great dissemblers;* and he shows at times a high moral and intellectual contempt for the *small wares* of cunning politicians. *Nothing,* he says, *doth more hurt in a State than that cunning men pass for wise.* But, in his Essay on Truth, he is obliged to admit that *mixture of falsehood is like alloy in coin of gold and silver, which may make the metal work the better,* though the metal is debased by it. And in practice Bacon found it necessary to use this *alloy.*

Pity therefore is the most prominent feeling in Bacon's views of mankind—a pity that never degenerates into scorn or contempt, but never quite rises into love. He is no Timon; he has no quarrel against mankind; he does not accuse them of any great crimes or foul innate depravities—simply of weakness, folly, and ignorance, resulting in general inability to resist the temptations of selfishness. *There is in human nature generally more of the fool than of the wise.*[1] Yet from this folly there inevitably issues immorality: *pity in the common people, if it run in a strong stream, doth ever cast up scandal and envy.*[2] At the best, the morality of the masses must be very low; most people *understand not many excellent virtues; the lowest virtues draw praise from them; the middle virtues work in them astonishment or admiration; but of the highest virtues they have no sense or perceiving at all.* Towards such poor creatures anger is out of place. Like the Wise Man in the New Atlantis, who *had an aspect as though he pitied men,* so Bacon pities men partly for their physical and bodily pains, partly for their intellectual blindness, but partly also for their meannesses, their spiteful ways, their envious jealousies, their petty and unprofitable selfishness. But he pities their morality, without much hope of amendment. For their physical and intellectual bondage he has his remedies, can hold out hopes of a complete Redemption offered by his Gospel of the Kingdom of Man; but to cure our moral diseases, he refers us almost exclusively to religion; and unfortunately religion is carefully excluded from the treatise *that is to pass into the business and bosoms of men.* The *Unity of Religion,* as a subject of political interest, has, it is true, a whole Essay devoted to it; but Religion, as a practical influence on conduct, is scarcely mentioned. Even Atheism is regarded rather as an intellectual and political, than as a moral disadvantage: it

---

[1] *Essay* xii. l. 12.
[2] *Works,* Vol. vi. p. 203; *Life,* Vol. iii. p. 137.

destroys magnanimity and the raising of man's nature, we are told ; and then the Romans are held up as a specimen to show how political greatness can be furthered by devoutness in religion. In the *De Augmentis* there are several passages that plainly recognise Christian love as a powerful reforming influence; but such passages are rarely to be found in the Essays. Nowhere is the hopelessness of pity more prominent than in the Essays on Anger and on Revenge. Anger, according to Bacon, is an irremediable baseness of human nature. To seek to extinguish it is a mere folly, a boast or *bravery of the Stoics*. It is natural and incurable, but still a baseness, a thing to be pitied in others, and to be ashamed of in oneself. That in certain circumstances it is right to be angry, and that anger in these circumstances is a virtue, a just tribute payable to one's faith in human goodness, does not seem to have occurred to Bacon. Men are born, he thinks, to be selfish, sometimes born to be malevolent. What then? They cannot help themselves, and why should a man be angry with them for what they cannot help? *Why*, he asks, *should I be angry with a man for loving himself better than me? And if any man should do wrong merely out of ill nature, why yet it is but like the thorn or briar, which prick and scratch because they can do no other? ... What would men have? Do they not think they will have their own ends, and be truer to themselves than to them?* And with the same leniency with which he judges others he judges himself. To be a little ostentatious, a little cunning, and a little selfish ; to scatter a *false fame*, so that it may *slide* for politic ends, to gain credit easily by gaining it at the expense of rivals; to study the ways and weaknesses of one's neighbours, so as to use them for one's own purposes—all these are venial faults, say rather not faults at all, but *Good Arts*, commendable in men who desire to avoid the base and useless life of contemplation foolishly preferred by Aristotle, and who have resolved to make themselves the *Architects of their own Fortunes* by learning the science of *Advancement in Life*.

Surely Montaigne is wiser in obeying his instinct as a French gentleman, than Bacon in following his Seven Precepts of the Architect of Fortune. Montaigne, as well as Bacon, has a strong sense of the imperfections of humanity, and of the apparent necessity of meeting falsehood with falsehood in politics; but let others bow in the house of Rimmon, he will not. 'In matters of policy,' he says, 'some functions are not only base, but faulty; vices find therein a seat, and employ themselves in the stitching up of our frame, as poisons for the preservation of our health. If they become excusable, because we have need of them, and that common necessity effaceth their true property, let us resign the acting of this part to hardy citizens, who stick not to sacrifice their honours and consciences, as these of old their lives, for their country's avail and safety. We that are more weak had best assume tasks of more ease and less hazard. The commonwealth requireth some to betray, some to lie, and some to massacre: leave we that commission to people more obedient and more pliable.'[1]

Of the reform and amendment of human nature Bacon treats in the *De Augmentis*.[2] He there deals with the Culture of the Mind, mapping out the subject into three departments. First, the *different characters of natures and dispositions*; second, the *knowledge touching the affections and perturbations*; third, the *remedies or cures*. Under the third head, *custom* and *habit* come prominently forward; and precepts are given for the formation of habits. Mention is also made of a different kind of culture, con-

---

[1] Florio's *Montaigne*, p. 476.   [2] *Works*, Vol. v. p. 29.

sisting of the cherishing of the good hours of the mind, and the obliteration of the bad. Here Religion steps in, and the discussion ends with that remedy which is of all others the most *compendious, noble and effectual*, which is, the *electing and propounding unto a man's self good and virtuous ends of his life and actions, such as may be in a reasonable sort within his compass to attain*. This remedy is the only natural one, for it alone works as Nature works, making the whole man grow in all his parts, whereas the hand of art makes the statue grow limb by limb. To take an instance, applying ourselves to virtue by the method of habit we improve ourselves, say in temperance, but not in fortitude; or in fortitude, but not in justice : but applying ourselves to Goodness as the object of life, we grow in all our faculties together, in every virtue that goodness suggests. Above all other religions the Christian faith, he says, imprints upon men's souls this Goodness or Charity, which includes all other virtues, and is so good a teacher, that *if a man's mind be truly inflamed with charity it raises him to greater perfection than all the doctrines of morality can do*. Of all virtues Charity alone admits of no excess; for *by aspiring to a similitude of God in goodness or love, neither angel nor man ever transgressed or shall transgress*.

In the Essays[1] we find the same praise of Charity or Goodness, but not the same power attributed to it. Cautions are given against the *errors of an habit so excellent*, for an excess of goodness may be a man's ruin in this evil world. The love of self, Bacon reminds us, is made by divinity the pattern of the love of our neighbour, and he warns us against sacrificing the former to the latter : *beware how in making the portraiture thou*

---

[1] *Essay* xiii. l. 33.

breakest the pattern.[1] But the power of Custom as a moral agent is repeatedly and emphatically recognised, as well as the powerlessness of mere force, or of doctrine and discourse. Both in the Essays and in the *De Augmentis* too little importance is attached to the influence of great leaders of thought upon the common people. Even in the *De Augmentis*, where religion is touched upon, it is not recognised that the motive force of Christianity is of the nature of an allegiance, a loyal and loving devotion towards a Leader; and in the Essays, as we have seen, Religion is scarcely recognised as an influence upon conduct, except in the form of Superstition, where it is bitterly assailed as the great enemy of nations. We may look also in vain through the Essays for any recognition that the purity of family life is the only permanent basis for national greatness. Love is, in his pages, nothing but the *child of folly*, to be kept at a distance, and, if it cannot be wholly excluded, at least to be *severed wholly from serious affairs and from actions of life*. Friendly love, it is true, *perfecteth mankind;* but of *nuptial love* he can say no more than that it *maketh mankind*. As for the hopes and fears of a second life they are as completely absent from these pages as they are from the Pentateuch. Even the sceptical, philosophic Hamlet cannot talk of death without the thought of the dreams that may come after it : but of all such thoughts, and all their influence on mankind, Bacon has no more to say than that the contemplation of death as a passage to another existence is *holy and religious*. After this preliminary tribute to convention, Bacon passes into himself again, and has nothing to utter on death that might not have been written by Plutarch, or Seneca, or even Pliny. The

[1] *Essay* xiii. l. 44.

same sharp contrast between Bacon using the conventional language of religion and Bacon speaking in his own person, is noticeable in his Preface to the *History of Life and Death*, where almost in the same breath he speaks of the preservation of life as a subject of preeminent importance, and yet apologizes for undertaking so slight a task on the plea that, *although we Christians ever aspire and pant after the land of promise, yet meanwhile it will be a mark of God's favour if, in our pilgrimage through the wilderness of this world, these our shoes and garments (I mean our frail bodies) are as little worn out as possible.* And again, a few lines further on, *though the life of man is only a mass and accumulation of sins and sorrows, and they who aspire to eternity set little value on life, yet even we Christians should not despise the continuance of works of charity.* There is no evidence to prove, but much to disprove, that Bacon *set little value on life*, or that he considered life as being only *a mass and accumulation of sins and sorrows*. When he was dangerously ill, we know that he was very glad to recover. But it would not be fair to infer that he was a hypocrite. If he was, ninety-nine out of a hundred Christians are hypocrites now. But these passages have been brought forward not to show that he was insincere (which he was not), but to show that no stress must be laid upon set and formal religious expressions used by Bacon in accordance with conventional thought. All the tributes paid to religion, all the direct and laboured recognitions of its power and utility, that can be strung together out of his formal and elaborate compositions on lofty philosophic theories, cannot outweigh the indirect evidence of neglect and indifference that is derived from the conspicuous absence of religion recognised as a motive power in this little volume that was to *come into the business and bosoms of men.*

Yet, in a vague way, both Machiavelli and Bacon do discern a certain regenerating influence, that of the many on the one; the spirit of self-sacrifice developed among individuals working together in bodies for common objects. More than once Machiavelli speaks as though a commonwealth were not only superior to a Prince in wisdom and constancy, but also endowed with some supernatural power of engendering virtue. Give him but a well-governed commonwealth, and all virtue seems to him 'not difficult to be introduced.' In answer to the question, 'What are those things that you would introduce according to the example of our ancestors?' the reply made by Machiavelli is, 'to honour and reward virtue; not to despise poverty; to value order and discipline of war; to constrain citizens to love one another; to live without factions; to postpone all private interest to the public welfare; and several other things that may be easily accommodate with our times. And these things are not difficult to be introduced, provided it be done deliberately and by right means, because in these the truth is so manifest and apparent that the commonest capacity may apprehend it;'[1] thus speaks Machiavelli, having in his mind the small Greek cities of antiquity, and contemplating the erection of other similar cities in Italy, little republics where each citizen might preserve his own individuality as judge and counsellor, and yet in the common contest against surrounding enemies the whole mass might be one, man bound to man by ties almost as strong as those of the ideal Christian Church. But Bacon has before him a different prospect. Writing, as he always writes on politics, with England in his mind, and perceiving that great kingdoms, though they may preserve, cannot en-

---

[1] *Art of War*, Book i. Machiavelli speaks in the person of *Fabritio*, a character in the dialogue.

gender, that social spirit of self-sacrifice which thrives on neighbourhood, he turns elsewhere for the school of custom. He sees it dimly in some smaller societies or corporations. He could wish to see such institutions as the Monastic orders, now perverted to superstitious ends, turned to their lawful end, the introduction of Goodness, the 'constraining' of citizens to love one another. *Collegiate custom* is to be a great reforming influence; for *if the force of custom simple and separate be great, the force of custom copulate and conjoined is far greater. For there, example teacheth, company comforteth, emulation quickeneth, glory raiseth; so as, in such places, the force of custom is in its exaltation. Certainly the great multiplication of virtues upon human nature resteth upon societies well ordained and disciplined. For commonwealths and good governments do nourish virtue grown, but do not much mend the seeds. But the misery is that the most effectual means are now applied to the ends least to be desired.* [1]

It is to be regretted that Bacon has not entered more into detail as to the places and the means by which *Collegiate Custom* might be brought to bear upon men. In schools, if anywhere, such custom is *in its exaltation*; yet of schools the Essays contain no mention. Indeed, Bacon seems to have attached little importance to the sowing of the educational seed broad-cast through England as it had been sown in Scotland. Writing on the bequest of Sutton, which originated Charterhouse School, he says that Grammar-schools are too numerous already, and no more are needed. In part, his indifference to schools may have arisen from his dislike of the narrow and barren routine of the school-learning of those days; but it would be quite characteristic of that indiffer-

---

[1] *Essay* xxxix. l. 53.

ence to details which we have recognised as part of his nature, that with his gaze fixed on the loftier secrets of science, he should have no eyes for the petty matters of children and childish training. He looks to men and to the training of men, and to endowed Professors at the Universities, and to immediate fruit from the tree of Science. But, if he had not chosen to draw the line so sharply between religion and conduct, he, with his broad and unbiassed views of church government, might have found ready to his hands a grand instrument for *Collegiate Custom* in the Christian congregation utilised for the purposes of philanthropic action. Such colleges furnish us our nearest approach to the corporate action of the old Greek cities, and, without some such supplement, the influence of the nation is insufficient for the development of the individual.

Both Bacon and Machiavelli seem to me to prove that the ablest men must work under great disadvantages in endeavouring to teach morality without reference to Christianity. Both try to work like practical men, like men of science, taking men as they are, and facts as they are, observing everything, ignoring nothing : but, in spite of all their efforts, both are eminently unscientific and unpractical. They leave out of account a thousand latent things; they ignore the subtler side of human nature ; they are ignorant of the rudiments of the passions ; they have not even learned the meaning of love, which is the alphabet of morality. Hence both teacher and pupil underrate the difficulties of the problem before them. Men are regarded by them as machines, and we have found Machiavelli actually speaking of '*constraining* citizens to love one another.' Both are far too scientific to encourage aspirations, or to hold up ideals. If they cannot attain the best, they will not strive after it, nor trouble themselves with the thought of it, but they will aim at the best possible, at 'things easy to be introduced,' says the Teacher : or, as the Pupil puts it somewhat less confidently, at *good and virtuous ends, such as may be in a reasonable sort within a man's compass to attain.* To aim at the unattainable, and to make success consist in failures more and more approximating to successes—this was not a course that commended itself to either of these mechanical moralists. Machiavelli holds up by way of warning the failures of Savonarola, who ruined himself by his new institutions, and perished because he would not resort to violence to enforce them; and Bacon also censures those too scrupulous persons who dislike the arts of morigeration and ostentation, and who prefer to lead retired lives rather than study the Architect of Fortune : yet Savonarola did more than Machiavelli for Italian morality and therefore for Italian freedom ; and, if we could see into the invisible causes of national greatness, if we could but weigh, for example, the influence of Bacon's life and character upon the court of James the First ; could we trace the influence of the supple, versatile, dissimulating and simulating Chancellor upon the plastic mind of the young Prince who afterwards rent England asunder by his falseness, we might not find it impossible to believe that England owes less to Bacon than to Sir Thomas More.

Yet for the Universe he was, and will always remain, a colossal benefactor. His influence on the search after Truth may be more easily felt than described ; but it will never cease to be felt as long as the *De Augmentis* and the *Novum Organum* continue to inspire their readers with their sublime hopes and aspirations. The Universe cannot—must not, in justice to Truth—ignore the moral defects of its benefactor; but it will learn to recognise beneath them, a childlike hopefulness and simplicity rendering him happily blind to difficulties as well as unhappily blind to inconvenient distinctions; a genuine kindliness to inferiors; a desire to think well of superiors; towards all a vast, serene, yet pitying philanthropy; and, lastly, a high unselfish and deliberate purpose, long adhered to in spite of many temptations, left for a time but never utterly deserted, and in the end returned to, after a chastening retribution, with such a heartfelt penitence that, in spite of all shortcomings, the human heart is drawn towards him rightly or wrongly as towards a man not only great, but also, in a manner, good.

ESSAYS
OR
COVNSELS
CIVIL AND
MORAL,
OF
FRANCIS LORD *VERULAM*,
VISCOUNT St. ALBAN.

Newly enlarged.

LONDON,
Printed by IOHN HAVILAND for
HANNA BARRET, and RICHARD
WHITAKER, and are to be sold
at the sign of the Kings head in
Pauls Church-yard. 1625.

To

The Right Honourable my very good Lord: the DUKE OF BUCKINGHAM *his Grace, Lord High Admiral of England.*

EXCELLENT LORD,

SALOMON says, *A good name is as a precious ointment;* and I assure myself such will your Grace's name be with posterity. For your fortune and merit both have been eminent, and you have planted things like to last. I do now publish my Essays, which, of all my works, have been most current, for that, as it seems, they come home to men's business and bosoms. I have enlarged them both in number and weight, so that they are indeed a new work. I thought it therefore agreeable to my affection and obligation to your Grace, to prefix your name before them both in English and in Latin. For I do conceive that the Latin Volume of them (being in the universal language) may last as long as books last. My Instauration I dedicated to the King; my History of Henry the Seventh (which I have now also translated into Latin) and my portions of Natural History, to the Prince; and these I dedicate to your Grace, being of the best fruits that, by the good increase which God gives to my pen and labours, I could yield. God lead your Grace by the hand.

Your Grace's most obliged and faithful servant,

Fr. ST. ALBAN.

The Table

Numbers marked * refer to the pages in the second volume.

	PAGE			PAGE
Of Truth	1	18	Of Travel	60
Of Death	4	19	Of Empire	63
Of Unity in Religion	7	20	Of Counsel	69
Of Revenge	12	21	Of Delays	75
Of Adversity	14	22	Of Cunning	77
Of Simulation and Dissimulation	16	23	Of Wisdom for a Man's Self	82
Of Parents and Children	20	24	Of Innovations	84
		25	Of Dispatch	86
Of Marriage and Single Life	22	26	Of Seeming Wise	89
		27	Of Friendship	91
Of Envy	25	28	Of Expense	99
Of Love	31	29	Of the true Greatness of Kingdoms and Estates	102
Of Great Place	34			
Of Boldness	38			
Of Goodness, and Goodness of Nature	41	30	Of Regiment of Health	1*
		31	Of Suspicion	4*
Of Nobility	44	32	Of Discourse	6*
Of Seditions and Troubles	46	33	Of Plantations	10*
		34	Of Riches	14*
Of Atheism	54	35	Of Prophecies	18*
Of Superstition	58	36	Of Ambition	22*

The Table

		PAGE			PAGE
37	Of Masks and Triumphs	25*	49	Of Suitors	68*
38	Of Nature in Men	28*	50	Of Studies	72*
39	Of Custom and Education	31*	51	Of Faction	75*
40	Of Fortune	34*	52	Of Ceremonies and Respects	78*
41	Of Usury	37*	53	Of Praise	81*
42	Of Youth and Age	42*	54	Of Vain-Glory	84*
43	Of Beauty	45*	55	Of Honour and Reputation	87*
44	Of Deformity	47*	56	Of Judicature	91*
45	Of Building	49*	57	Of Anger	96*
46	Of Gardens	54*	58	Of Vicissitudes of Things	99*
47	Of Negotiating	62*			
48	Of Followers and Friends	65*			

Of Fame, a fragment.

ESSAYS

ESSAYS

I

Of Truth

WHAT is Truth? said jesting Pilate; and would not stay for an answer. Certainly there be that delight in giddiness, and count it a bondage to fix a belief; affecting free-will in thinking, as well as in acting. And, though the sects of philosophers of that kind be gone, yet there remain certain discoursing wits which are of the same veins; though there be not so much blood in them as was in those of the ancients. But it is not only the difficulty and labour which men take in finding out of truth—nor, again, that, when it is found, it imposeth upon men's thoughts—that doth bring lies in favour; but a natural though corrupt love of the lie itself. One of the later school of the Grecians examineth the matter, and is at a stand to think what should be in it, that men should love lies, where neither they make for pleasure, as with poets, nor with advantage, as with the merchant, but for the lie's sake. But I cannot tell: this same truth is a naked and open daylight, that doth not show the masques and mummeries, and triumphs of the world, half so stately and daintily as candle-lights. Truth may perhaps come to the price of a pearl, that sheweth best by day; but it will not rise to the price of a diamond or carbuncle that sheweth best in varied lights. A mixture of a lie doth ever add pleasure. Doth any man doubt, that if there were taken out of men's minds vain opinions, flattering hopes, false valuations, imaginations as one would, and the like, but it would leave the minds of a number of men poor shrunken things, full of melancholy and indisposition, and unpleasing to themselves? One of the fathers, in great severity, called poesy <u>vinum dæmonum</u>, because it filleth the imagination, and yet it is but with the shadow of a lie. But it is not the lie that passeth through the mind, but the lie that sinketh in and settleth in it, that doth the hurt such as we spake of before. But howsoever these things are thus in men's depraved judgments and affections, yet truth, which only doth judge itself, teacheth that the inquiry of truth (which is the love-making, or wooing of it) the knowledge of truth (which is the presence of it) and the belief of truth (which is the enjoying of it) is the sovereign good of human nature. The first <u>creature</u> of God, in the works of the days, was the light of the sense; the last was the light of reason; and his Sabbath work, ever since, is the illumination of his spirit. First he breathed light upon the face of the matter, or chaos; then he breathed light into the face of man; and <u>still</u> he breatheth and inspireth light into the face of his chosen. The poet, that beautified the sect that was otherwise inferior to the rest, saith yet excellently well, *It is a pleasure to stand upon the shore, and to see ships tost upon the sea; a pleasure to stand in the window of a castle, and to see the battle, and the adventures thereof below; but no pleasure is comparable to the standing upon the vantage ground of truth* (a hill not to be <u>commanded</u>, and where the air is always clear and serene), *and to see the errors, and wanderings,* and mists, and tempests, in the vale below; so always that this prospect be with pity, and not with swelling or pride. Certainly it is heaven upon earth to have a man's mind move in charity, rest in providence, and turn upon the poles of truth.

To pass from theological and philosophical truth to the truth of civil business, it will be acknowledged, even by those that practise it not, that clear and round dealing is the honour of man's nature, and that mixture of falsehood is like alloy in coin of gold and silver, which may make the metal work the better, but it embaseth it. For these winding and crooked courses are the goings of the serpent, which goeth basely upon the belly, and not upon the feet. There is no vice that doth so cover a man with shame as to be found false and perfidious; and therefore Montaigne saith prettily, when he inquired the reason why the word of the lie should be such a disgrace and such an odious charge—saith he *If it be well weighed, to say that a man lieth, is as much as to say that he is brave towards God, and a coward towards man; for a lie faces God, and shrinks from man.* Surely the wickedness of falsehood and breach of faith cannot possibly be so highly expressed as in that it shall be the last peal to call the judgments of God upon the generations of men: it being foretold, that when Christ cometh, *He shall not find faith upon the earth.*

II

Of Death

MEN fear death as children fear to go in the dark; and as that natural fear in children is increased with tales, so is the other. Certainly, the contemplation of death, as *the wages of sin* and passage to another world, is holy and religious; but the fear of it, as a tribute due unto nature, is weak. Yet in religious meditations there is sometimes mixture of vanity and of superstition. You shall read in some of the friars' books of mortification, that a man should think with himself what the pain is, if he have but his finger's end pressed or tortured, and thereby imagine what the pains of death are when the whole body is corrupted and dissolved; when many times death passeth with less pain than the torture of a limb. For the most vital parts are not the quickest of sense: and by him that spake only as a philosopher and natural man, it was well said, *Pompa mortis magis terret quam mors ipsa.* Groans, and convulsions, and a discoloured face, and friends weeping, and blacks, and obsequies, and the like, shew death terrible.

It is worthy the observing, that there is no passion in

the mind of man so weak, but it mates and masters the fear of death: and therefore Death is no such terrible enemy when a man hath so many attendants about him that can win the combat of him. Revenge triumphs over death; love slights it; honour aspireth to it; grief flieth to it; fear preoccupateth it; nay, we read, after Otho the Emperor had slain himself, pity (which is the tenderest of affections) provoked many to die out of mere compassion to their sovereign, and as the truest sort of followers. Nay, Seneca adds niceness and satiety: *Cogita quamdiu eadem feceris; mori velle, non tantum fortis, aut miser, sed etiam fastidiosus potest.* A man would die, though he were neither valiant nor miserable, only upon a weariness to do the same thing so oft over and over. It is no less worthy to observe, how little alteration in good spirits the approaches of death make; for they appear to be the same men up to the last instant. Augustus Cæsar died in a compliment: *Livia, conjugii nostri memor vive, et vale.* Tiberius in dissimulation, as Tacitus saith of him, *Jam Tiberium vires et corpus, non dissimulatio, deserebant.* Vespasian in a jest, sitting upon the stool, *Ut puto Deus fio.* Galba with a sentence, *Feri, si ex re sit populi Romani,* holding forth his neck. Septimius Severus in dispatch, *Adeste, si quid mihi restat agendum.* And the like.

Certainly the Stoics bestowed too much cost upon death, and by their great preparations made it appear more fearful. Better saith he *Qui finem vitæ extremum inter munera ponat Naturæ.* It is as natural to die as to be born: and to a little infant, perhaps, the one is as painful as the other. He that dies in an earnest pursuit, is like one that is wounded in hot blood: who, for the time, scarce feels the hurt; and therefore a mind fixed and bent upon somewhat that is good doth avert the dolours of death. But, above all, believe it, the sweetest canticle is, *Nunc dimittis*, when a man hath obtained worthy ends and expectations. Death hath this also, that it openeth the gate to good fame, and extinguisheth envy:

—*Extinctus amabitur idem.*

III

Of Unity in Religion

RELIGION being the chief band of human society, it is a happy thing when itself is well contained within the true band of unity. The quarrels and divisions about religion were evils unknown to the heathen. The reason was, because the religion of the heathen consisted rather in rites and ceremonies than in any constant belief. For you may imagine what kind of faith theirs was, when the chief doctors and fathers of their church were the poets. But the true God had this attribute that he is a jealous God; and therefore his worship and religion will endure no mixture nor partner. We shall therefore speak a few words concerning the Unity of the Church; what are the Fruits thereof; what the Bounds; and what the Means.

The Fruits of Unity (next unto the well-pleasing of God which is all in all) are two; the one towards those that are without the Church, the other towards those that are within. For the former; it is certain, that heresies and schisms are of all others the greatest scandals, yea, more than corruption of manners. For as in the natural body a wound or solution of continuity is worse than a corrupt humour, so in the spiritual. So that nothing doth so much keep men out of the Church,

and drive men out of the Church, as breach of unity.
And, therefore, whensoever it cometh to that pass that one saith, *Ecce in deserto*, another saith, *Ecce in penetralibus*,—that is, when some men seek Christ in the conventicles of heretics, and others in an outward face of a Church—that voice had need continually to sound in men's ears, *Nolite exire*. The Doctor of the Gentiles (the propriety of whose vocation drew him to have a special care of those without) saith, *If a heathen come in, and hear you speak with several tongues, will he not say that you are mad?* And certainly it is little better when atheists and profane persons do hear of so many discordant and contrary opinions in religion; it doth avert them from the Church, and maketh them *to sit down in the chair of the scorners*. It is but a light thing to be vouched in so serious a matter, but yet it expresseth well the deformity; there is a Master of scoffing, that in his catalogue of books of a feigned library, sets down this title of a book, *The Morris Dance of Heretics*. For, indeed, every sect of them have a diverse posture, or cringe, by themselves; which cannot but move derision in worldlings and depraved politics, who are apt to contemn holy things.

As for the Fruit towards those that are within, it is peace, which containeth infinite blessings. It establisheth faith; it kindleth charity; the outward peace of the Church distilleth into peace of conscience, and it turneth the labours of writing and reading controversies into treatises of mortification and devotion.

Concerning the Bounds of Unity, the true placing of them importeth exceedingly. There appear to be two extremes; for to certain zelants all speech of pacification is odious. *Is it peace, Jehu? What hast thou to do with peace? turn thee behind me.* Peace is not the matter, but following and party. Contrariwise, certain Laodiceans and lukewarm persons think they may accommodate points of religion by middle ways, and taking part of both, and witty reconcilements, as if they would make an arbitrement between God and man. Both these extremes are to be avoided; which will be done if the league of Christians, penned by our Saviour Himself, were in the two cross clauses thereof soundly and plainly expounded: *He that is not with us is against us*; and again, *He that is not against us is with us*; that is, if the points fundamental, and of substance in religion, were truly discerned and distinguished from points not merely of faith, but of opinion, order, or good intention. This is a thing may seem to many a matter trivial, and done already; but if it were done less partially, it would be embraced more generally.

Of this I may give only this advice, according to my small model. Men ought to take heed of rending God's Church by two kinds of controversies. The one is, when the matter of the point controverted is too small and light, not worth the heat and strife about it, kindled only by contradiction. For, as it is noted by one of the fathers, *Christ's coat indeed had no seam, but the Church's vesture was of divers colours;* whereupon he saith, *In veste varietas sit, scissura non sit*; they be two things, Unity and Uniformity. The other is, when the matter of the point controverted is great, but it is driven to an over-great subtilty and obscurity, so that it becometh a thing rather ingenious than substantial. A man that is of judgment and understanding shall sometimes hear ignorant men differ, and know well within himself that those which so differ mean one thing, and yet they themselves would never agree. And if it come so to pass in that distance of judgment which is between man and man, shall we not think that God above, that knows the heart, doth not discern that frail men, in some of their contradictions, intend the same thing, and accepteth of both? The nature of such controversies is excellently expressed by St. Paul in the warning and precept that he giveth concerning the same, *Devita profanas vocum novitates et oppositiones falsi nominis scientiæ.* Men create oppositions which are not, and put them into new terms so fixed as, whereas the meaning ought to govern the term, the term in effect governeth the meaning. There be also two false Peaces, or Unities, the one, when the peace is grounded but upon an implicit ignorance (for all colours will agree in the dark); the other when it is pieced up upon a direct admission of contraries in fundamental points. For truth and falsehood in such things are like the iron and clay in the toes of Nebuchadnezzar's image: they may cleave but they will not incorporate.

Concerning the Means of procuring Unity, men must beware, that in the procuring or muniting of religious unity, they do not dissolve and deface the laws of charity and of human society. There be two swords amongst Christians, the spiritual and the temporal, and both have their due office and place in the maintenance of religion. But we may not take up the third sword, which is Mahomet's sword, or like unto it—that is, to propagate religion by wars, or by sanguinary persecutions to force consciences (except it be in cases of overt scandal, blasphemy, or intermixture of practice against the state), much less to nourish seditions, to authorise conspiracies and rebellions, to put the sword into the people's hands, and the like, tending to the subversion of all government, which is the ordinance of God. For this is but to dash the first table against the second; and so to consider men as Christians, as we forget that they are men. Lucretius the poet, when he beheld the act of Agamemnon, that could endure the sacrificing of his own daughter, exclaimed :—

Tantum religio potuit suadere malorum.

What would he have said, if he had known of the massacre in France, or the powder treason of England? He would have been seven times more Epicure and atheist than he was. For as the temporal sword is to be drawn with great circumspection in cases of religion, so it is a thing monstrous to put it into the hands of the common people. Let that be left to the Anabaptists and other furies. It was a great blasphemy when the devil said, *I will ascend and be like the Highest*; but it is greater blasphemy to personate God, and bring him in saying, *I will descend and be like the prince of darkness.* And what is it better, to make the cause of religion to descend to the cruel and execrable actions of murdering princes, butchery of people, and subversion of states and governments? Surely this is to bring down the Holy Ghost, instead of the likeness of a dove, in the shape of a vulture or raven; and to set out of the bark of a Christian Church a flag of a bark of pirates and assassins. Therefore it is most necessary that the Church by doctrine and decree, princes by their sword, and all learnings—both Christian and moral—as by their Mercury rod, do damn and send to hell for ever those facts and opinions tending to the support of the same, as hath been already in good part done. Surely in councils concerning religion, that counsel of the Apostle would be prefixed, *Ira hominis non implet justitiam Dei.* And it was a notable observation of a wise father and no less ingenuously confessed, that *those which held and persuaded pressure of consciences, were commonly interessed therein themselves for their own ends.*

IV
Of Revenge

REVENGE is a kind of wild justice, which the more man's nature runs to, the more ought law to weed it out. For as for the first wrong, it does but offend the law; but the revenge of that wrong putteth the law out of office. Cer-
5 tainly, in taking revenge, a man is but even with his enemy, but in passing it over, he is superior; for it is a prince's part to pardon: and Salomon, I am sure, saith, *It is the glory of a man to pass by an offence.*

That which is past is gone and irrevocable, and
10 wise men have enough to do with things present and to come; therefore they do but trifle with themselves, that labour in past matters. There is no man doth a wrong for the wrong's sake, but thereby to purchase himself profit, or pleasure, or honour, or the like; therefore why
15 should I be angry with a man for loving himself better than me? And if any man should do wrong, merely out of ill-nature, why, yet it is but like the thorn or briar, which prick and scratch, because they can do no other.

The most tolerable sort of revenge is for those wrongs
20 which there is no law to remedy: but then, let a man

take heed the revenge be such as there is no law to punish; else a man's enemy is still beforehand, and it is two for one.

Some, when they take revenge, are desirous the party should know whence it cometh. This is the more generous. For the delight seemeth to be not so much in doing the hurt, as in making the party repent. But base and crafty cowards are like the arrow that flieth in the dark.

Cosmus, Duke of Florence, had a desperate saying against perfidious or neglecting friends, as if those wrongs were unpardonable. *You shall read* (saith he) *that we are commanded to forgive our enemies; but you never read that we are commanded to forgive our friends.* But yet the spirit of Job was in a better tune: *Shall we* (saith he) *take good at God's hands, and not be content to take evil also?* And so of friends in a proportion. This is certain, that a man that studieth revenge keeps his own wounds green, which otherwise would heal and do well. Public revenges are for the most part fortunate; as that for the death of Cæsar; for the death of Pertinax; for the death of Henry the Third of France; and many more. But in private revenges it is not so. Nay rather, vindicative persons live the life of witches, who, as they are mischievous, so end they infortunate.

V

Of Adversity

It was an high speech of Seneca (after the manner of the Stoics), that *the good things which belong to Prosperity are to be wished, but the good things that belong to Adversity are to be admired. Bona rerum secundarum optabilia, adversarum mirabilia.* Certainly, if miracles be the command over nature, they appear most in Adversity. It is yet a higher speech of his than the other (much too high for a heathen), *It is true greatness to have in one the frailty of a man, and the security of a God. Vere magnum, habere fragilitatem hominis, securitatem Dei.* This would have done better in poesy, where transcendencies are more allowed; and the poets, indeed, have been busy with it. For it is in effect the thing which is figured in that strange fiction of the ancient poets, which seemeth not to be without mystery, nay, and to have some approach to the state of a Christian: that *Hercules, when he went to unbind Prometheus* (by whom human nature is represented), *sailed the length of the great ocean in an earthen pot or pitcher*; lively describing Christian resolution, that saileth in the frail bark of the flesh thorough the waves of the world.

Of Adversity

But to speak in a mean. The virtue of Prosperity is temperance; the virtue of Adversity is fortitude: which in morals is the more heroical virtue. Prosperity is the blessing of the Old Testament; adversity is the blessing of the New: which carrieth the greater benediction, and the clearer revelation of God's favour. Yet even in the Old Testament, if you listen to David's harp, you shall hear as many hearse like airs as carols; and the pencil of the Holy Ghost hath laboured more in describing the afflictions of Job than the felicities of Solomon. Prosperity is not without many fears and distastes; and Adversity is not without comforts and hopes. We see in needleworks and embroideries, it is more pleasing to have a lively work upon a sad and solemn ground, than to have a dark and melancholy work upon a lightsome ground. Judge, therefore, of the pleasure of the heart by the pleasure of the eye. Certainly virtue is like precious odours, most fragrant when they are incensed or crushed; for prosperity doth best discover vice, but adversity doth best discover virtue.

VI
Of Simulation and Dissimulation

DISSIMULATION is but a faint kind of policy, or wisdom. For it asketh a strong wit and a strong heart to know when to tell truth, and to do it. Therefore it is the weaker sort of politicians that are the greatest dissemblers.

Tacitus saith, *Livia sorted well with the arts of her husband and dissimulation of her son* ; attributing arts of policy to Augustus, and dissimulation to Tiberius. And again, when Mucianus encourageth Vespasian to take arms against Vitellius, he saith, *We rise not against the piercing judgment of Augustus, nor the extreme caution or closeness of Tiberius.* These properties of arts or policy, and dissimulation and closeness, are indeed habits and faculties several, and to be distinguished. For if a man have that penetration of judgment as he can discern what things are to be laid open, and what to be secreted, and what to be shewed at half-lights, and to whom and when (which indeed are arts of state, and arts of life, as Tacitus well calleth them), to him a habit of dissimulation is a hindrance and a poorness. But if a man cannot obtain to that judgment, then it is left to him generally to be close, and a dissembler. For where a man cannot choose or vary in particulars, there it is good to take the safest and wariest way in general, like the going softly by one that cannot well see. Certainly the ablest men that ever were have had all an openness and frankness of dealing, and a name of certainty and veracity. But then they were like horses well managed; for they could tell passing well when to stop or turn : and at such times when they thought the case indeed required dissimulation, if then they used it, it came to pass that the former opinion, spread abroad, of their good faith and clearness of dealing, made them almost invisible.

There be three degrees of this hiding and veiling of a man's self : the first, Closeness, Reservation, and Secrecy, —when a man leaveth himself without observation, or, without hold to be taken, what he is; the second, Dissimulation, in the negative,—when a man lets fall signs and arguments that he is not that he is ; and the third, Simulation, in the affirmative,—when a man industriously and expressly feigns and pretends to be that he is not.

For the first of these, Secrecy ; it is indeed the virtue of a confessor. And assuredly the secret man heareth many confessions; for who will open himself to a blab or a babbler? But if a man be thought secret, it inviteth discovery, as the more close air sucketh in the more open. And, as in confession the revealing is not for worldly use, but for the ease of a man's heart, so, secret men come to the knowledge of many things in that kind, while men rather discharge their minds than impart their minds. In few words, mysteries are due to Secrecy. Besides (to say truth) nakedness is uncomely as well in mind as in body ; and it addeth no small reverence to men's manners and actions, if they be not altogether open. As for talkers, and futile persons, they are com-

monly vain and credulous withal. For he that talketh
what he knoweth, will also talk what he knoweth not.
Therefore set it down, that *an habit of secrecy is both
politic and moral*. And in this part it is good that a
man's face give his tongue leave to speak. For the dis·
covery of a man's self, by the tracts of his countenance,
is a great weakness and betraying; by how much it is
many times more marked and believed than a man's
words.

For the second, which is Dissimulation, it followeth
many times upon Secrecy, by a necessity. So that he
that will be secret, must be a dissembler in some degree.
For men are too cunning to suffer a man to keep an indifferent carriage between both, and to be secret, without
swaying the balance on either side. They will so beset
a man with questions, and draw him on, and pick it out
of him, that, without an absurd silence, he must show an
inclination one way; or if he do not, they will gather as
much by his silence as by his speech. As for equivoca-
tions, or oraculous speeches, they cannot hold out long.
So that no man can be secret, except he give himself a
little scope of dissimulation; which is, as it were, but the
skirts or train of secrecy.

But for the third degree, which is Simulation and
false profession, that I hold more culpable, and less
politic; except it be in great and rare matters. And,
therefore, a general custom of Simulation (which is this
last degree) is a vice rising either of a natural falseness,
or fearfulness, or of a mind that hath some main faults,
which because a man must needs disguise, it maketh him
practise simulation in other things, lest his hand should
be out of ure.

The great advantages of Simulation and Dissimulation are three. First, to lay asleep opposition, and to
surprise; for where a man's intentions are published, it

is an alarum to call up all that are against them. The second is, to reserve to a man's self a fair retreat; for if a man engage himself by a manifest declaration, he must go through, or take a fall. The third is, the better to discover the mind of another; for to him that opens himself men will hardly show themselves adverse, but will (fair) let him go on, and turn their freedom of speech to freedom of thought. And therefore it is a good shrewd proverb of the Spaniard, *tell a lie and find a troth*: as if there were no way of discovery but by Simulation. There be also three disadvantages to set it even. The first, that Simulation and Dissimulation commonly carry with them a show of fearfulness, which, in any business, doth spoil the feathers of round flying up to the mark. The second, that it puzzleth and perplexeth the conceits of many, that perhaps would otherwise co-operate with him, and makes a man walk almost alone to his own ends. The third, and greatest, is, that it depriveth a man of one of the most principal instruments for action; which is trust and belief. The best composition and temperature is to have openness in fame and opinion; secrecy in habit; dissimulation in seasonable use; and a power to feign, if there be no remedy.

VII

Of Parents and Children

THE joys of parents are secret, and so are their griefs and fears. They cannot utter the one, nor they will not utter the other. Children sweeten labours, but they make misfortunes more bitter; they increase the cares of life, but they mitigate the remembrance of death. The perpetuity by generation is common to beasts; but memory, merit, and noble works, are proper to men. And surely a man shall see the noblest works and foundations have proceeded from childless men, which have sought to express the images of their minds, where those of their bodies have failed. So the care of posterity is most in them that have no posterity. They that are the first raisers of their houses are most indulgent towards their children, beholding them as the continuance, not only of their kind, but of their work; and so both children and creatures.

The difference in affection of parents towards their several children is many times unequal, and sometimes unworthy, especially in the mother; as Salomon saith, *A wise son rejoiceth the father, but an ungracious son shames the mother.* A man shall see, where there is a house full of children, one or two of the eldest respected, and the youngest made wantons; but in the midst some that are as it were forgotten, who, many times, nevertheless, prove the best.

The illiberality of parents, in allowance towards their children, is a harmful error, makes them base, acquaints them with shifts, makes them sort with mean company, and makes them surfeit more when they come to plenty. And therefore the proof is best when men keep their authority towards their children, but not their purse. Men have a foolish manner (both parents, and schoolmasters, and servants), in creating and breeding an emulation between brothers during childhood; which many times sorteth to discord when they are men, and disturbeth families.

The Italians make little difference between children and nephews, or near kinsfolk; but, so they be of the lump, they care not, though they pass not through their own body. And, to say truth, in nature it is much a like matter: insomuch that we see a nephew sometimes resembleth an uncle, or a kinsman, more than his own parent, as the blood happens.

Let parents choose betimes the vocations and courses they mean their children should take; for then they are most flexible. And let them not too much apply themselves to the disposition of their children, as thinking they will take best to that which they have most mind to. It is true that, if the affection or aptness of the children be extraordinary, then it is good not to cross it; but generally the precept is good, *Optimum elige, suave et facile illud faciet consuetudo.* Younger brothers are commonly fortunate, but seldom or never where the elder are disinherited.

VIII

Of Marriage and Single Life

HE that hath wife and children hath given hostages to fortune; for they are impediments to great enterprises, either of virtue or mischief. Certainly the best works, and of greatest merit for the public, have proceeded from the unmarried or childless men; which, both in affection and means, have married and endowed the public. Yet it were great reason that those that have children should have greatest care of future times; unto which they know they must transmit their dearest pledges.

Some there are, who, though they lead a single life, yet their thoughts do end with themselves, and account future times impertinencies. Nay, there are some other that account wife and children but as bills of charges. Nay, more, there are some foolish rich covetous men that take a pride in having no children, because they may be thought so much the richer. For, perhaps, they have heard some talk, *Such a one is a great rich man,* and another except to it, *Yea, but he hath a great charge of children,* as if it were an abatement to his riches.

But the most ordinary cause of a single life is liberty, especially in certain self-pleasing and humorous minds, which are so sensible of every restraint, as they will go near to think their girdles and garters to be bonds and shackles.

Unmarried men are best friends, best masters, best servants; but not always best subjects. For they are light to run away; and almost all fugitives are of that condition. A single life doth well with churchmen; for charity will hardly water the ground where it must first fill a pool. It is indifferent for judges and magistrates; for if they be facile and corrupt, you shall have a servant five times worse than a wife. For soldiers, I find the generals commonly, in their hortatives, put men in mind of their wives and children; and I think the despising of marriage among the Turks maketh the vulgar soldier more base.

Certainly wife and children are a kind of discipline of humanity; and single men, though they be many times more charitable, because their means are less exhaust, yet, on the other side, they are more cruel and hard-hearted (good to make severe inquisitors), because their tenderness is not so oft called upon. Grave natures, led by custom, and therefore constant, are commonly loving husbands, as was said of Ulysses, *Vetulam suam prætulit immortalitati*. Chaste women are often proud and froward, as presuming upon the merit of their chastity. It is one of the best bonds, both of chastity and obedience, in the wife, if she thinks her husband wise; which she will never do if she find him jealous.

Wives are young men's mistresses, companions for middle age, and old men's nurses; so as a man may have a quarrel to marry, when he will. But yet he was reputed one of the wise men that made answer to the question when a man should marry—*A young man not yet, an elder man not at all.* It is often seen that bad husbands have very good wives; whether it be that it raiseth the price of their husbands' kindness when it comes, or that the wives take a pride in their patience. But this never fails, if the bad husbands were of their own choosing, against their friends' consent; for then they will be sure to make good their own folly.

IX
Of Envy

THERE be none of the affections which have been noted to fascinate or bewitch, but Love and Envy. They both have vehement wishes; they frame themselves readily into imaginations and suggestions, and they come easily into the eye, especially upon the presence of the objects: which are the points that conduce to fascination, if any such thing there be. We see, likewise, the Scripture calleth envy *an evil eye*; and the astrologers call the evil influences of the stars *evil aspects*: so that still there seemeth to be acknowledged, in the act of envy, an ejaculation or irradiation of the eye. Nay, some have been so curious as to note that the times when the stroke or percussion of an envious eye doth most hurt, are when the party envied is beheld in glory or triumph. For that sets an edge upon envy; and, besides, at such time, the spirits of the person envied do come forth most into the outward parts, and so meet the blow.

But leaving these curiosities (though not unworthy to be thought on in fit place), we will handle *what persons are apt to envy others*; *what persons are most subject to* be envied themselves; and *what is the difference between public and private envy.*

A man that hath no virtue in himself ever envieth virtue in others. For men's minds will either feed upon their own good, or upon other's evil; and who wanteth the one will prey upon the other; and whoso is out of hope to attain another's virtue, will seek to come at even hand, by depressing another's fortune.

A man that is busy and inquisitive is commonly envious. For to know much of other men's matters cannot be because all that ado may concern his own estate. Therefore it must needs be that he taketh a kind of play-pleasure in looking upon the fortunes of others. Neither can he that mindeth but his own business find much matter for envy. For envy is a gadding passion, and walketh the streets, and doth not keep home; *Non est curiosus, quin idem sit malevolus.*

Men of noble birth are noted to be envious towards new men when they rise. For the distance is altered: and it is like a deceit of the eye that, when others come on, they think themselves go back.

Deformed persons, and eunuchs, and old men, and bastards, are envious. For he that cannot possibly mend his own case, will do what he can to impair another's: except these defects light upon a very brave and heroical nature, which thinketh to make his natural wants part of his honour; in that it should be said that an eunuch, or a lame man, did such great matters; affecting the honour of a miracle; as it was in Narses the eunuch, and Agesilaus and Tamerlane, that were lame men.

The same is the case of men that rise after calamities and misfortunes. For they are as men fallen out with the times, and think other men's harms a redemption of their own sufferings.

They that desire to excel in too many matters, out of

levity and vain-glory, are ever envious. For they cannot want work; it being impossible but many, in some one of those things, should surpass them. Which was the character of Adrian the emperor, that mortally envied poets and painters, and artificers in works wherein he had a vein to excel.

Lastly, near kinsfolk and fellows in office, and those that are bred together, are more apt to envy their equals when they are raised. For it doth upbraid unto them their own fortunes, and pointeth at them, and cometh oftener into their remembrance, and incurreth likewise more into the note of others; and envy ever redoubleth from speech and fame. Cain's envy was the more vile and malignant towards his brother Abel, because, when his sacrifice was better accepted, there was nobody to look on. Thus much for those that are apt to envy.

Concerning those that are more or less subject to envy. First, persons of eminent virtue, when they are advanced, are less envied. For their fortune seemeth but due unto them; and no man envieth the payment of a debt, but rewards and liberality rather. Again, envy is ever joined with the comparing of a man's self; and where there is no comparison, no envy: and therefore kings are not envied but by kings. Nevertheless, it is to be noted that unworthy persons are most envied at their first coming in, and afterwards overcome it better; whereas, contrariwise, persons of worth and merit are most envied when their fortune continueth long. For by that time, though their virtue be the same, yet it hath not the same lustre: for fresh men grow up that darken it.

Persons of noble blood are less envied in their rising. For it seemeth but right done to their birth. Besides, there seemeth not much added to their fortune; and envy is as the sunbeams, that beat hotter upon a bank, or steep rising ground, than upon a flat. And, for the same reason, those that are advanced by degrees are less envied than those that are advanced suddenly, and *per saltum.*

Those that have joined with their honour great travels, cares, or perils, are less subject to envy. For men think that they earn their honours hardly, and pity them sometimes; and pity ever healeth envy. Wherefore you shall observe, that the more deep and sober sort of politic persons, in their greatness, are ever bemoaning themselves what a life they lead, chanting a *quanta patimur.* Not that they feel it so, but only to abate the edge of envy. But this is to be understood of business that is laid upon men, and not such as they call unto themselves. For nothing increaseth envy more than an unnecessary and ambitious engrossing of business. And nothing doth extinguish envy more than for a great person to preserve all other inferior officers in their full rights and pre-eminences of their places. For, by that means, there be so many screens between him and envy.

Above all, those are most subject to envy which carry the greatness of their fortunes in an insolent and proud manner; being never well but while they are showing how great they are, either by outward pomp, or by triumphing over all opposition or competition. Whereas wise men will rather do sacrifice to envy, in suffering themselves, sometimes of purpose, to be crossed and overborne in things that do not much concern them. Notwithstanding, so much is true, that the carriage of greatness in a plain and open manner (so it be without arrogancy and vain-glory), doth draw less envy than if it be in a more crafty and cunning fashion. For in that course a man doth but disavow fortune, and seemeth to be conscious of his own want in worth, and doth but teach others to envy him.

Lastly, to conclude this part : as we said in the beginning that the act of envy had somewhat in it of witchcraft, so there is no other cure of envy but the cure of witchcraft ; and that is to remove the lot (as they call it), and to lay it upon another. For which purpose, the wiser sort of great persons bring in ever upon the stage somebody upon whom to derive the envy that would come upon themselves ; sometimes upon ministers and servants, sometimes upon colleagues and associates, and the like. And, for that turn, there are never wanting some persons of violent and undertaking natures, who, so they may have power and business, will take it at any cost.

Now, to speak of public envy. There is yet some good in public envy, whereas in private there is none. For public envy is as an ostracism, that eclipseth men when they grow too great. And therefore it is a bridle also to great ones to keep within bounds.

This envy, being in the Latin word *invidia*, goeth in the modern languages by the name of *discontentment*; of which we shall speak in handling Sedition. It is a disease in a State like to infection. For, as infection spreadeth upon that which is sound, and tainteth it ; so, when envy is gotten once into a State, it traduceth even the best actions thereof, and turneth them into an ill odour. And therefore there is little won by intermingling of plausible actions. For that doth argue but a weakness and fear of envy, which hurteth so much the more ; as it is likewise usual in infections, which, if you fear them, you call them upon you.

This public envy seemeth to bear chiefly upon principal officers or ministers, rather than upon Kings and Estates themselves. But this is a sure rule, that if the envy upon the minister be great, when the cause of it in him is small, or if the envy be general in a manner upon all the ministers of an estate, then the envy (though hidden) is truly upon the State itself. And so much of public envy or discontentment, and the difference thereof from private envy, which was handled in the first place.

We will add this in general, touching the affection of envy, that of all other affections it is the most importune and continual. For of other affections there is occasion given but now and then; and therefore it was well said, *Invidia festos dies non agit.* For it is ever working upon some or other. And it is also noted, that love and envy do make a man pine, which other affections do not, because they are not so continual. It is also the vilest affection, and the most depraved; for which cause it is the proper attribute of the Devil, who is called *The envious man that soweth tares among the wheat by night;* as it always cometh to pass, that envy worketh subtilly, and in the dark, and to the prejudice of good things, such as is the wheat.

X
Of Love

THE stage is more beholding to Love than the life of man. For, as to the stage, love is ever matter of comedies, and now and then of tragedies; but in life it doth much mischief, sometimes like a Siren, sometimes like a Fury. You may observe that amongst all the great and worthy persons (whereof the memory remaineth, either ancient or recent), there is not one that hath been transported to the mad degree of love : which shews that great spirits and great business do keep out this weak passion. You must except, nevertheless, Marcus Antonius, the half-partner of the empire of Rome, and Appius Claudius, the decemvir and law-giver; whereof the former was indeed a voluptuous man, and inordinate, but the latter was an austere and wise man : and therefore it seems (though rarely) that love can find entrance, not only in an open heart, but also into a heart well fortified, if watch be not well kept.

It is a poor saying of Epicurus, *Satis magnum alter alteri theatrum sumus:* as if Man, made for the contemplation of heaven, and all noble objects, should do nothing but kneel before a little idol, and make himself a subject, though not of the mouth (as beasts are), yet of the eye; which was given him for higher purposes.

It is a strange thing to note the excess of this passion, and how it braves the nature and value of things, by this: that the speaking in a perpetual hyperbole is comely in nothing but in love. Neither is it merely in the phrase. For, whereas it hath been well said, that the archflatterer, with whom all the petty flatterers have intelligence, is a man's self: certainly the lover is more. For there was never a proud man thought so absurdly well of himself as the lover doth of the person loved. And therefore it was well said, that *it is impossible to love and be wise.* Neither doth this weakness appear to others only, and not to the party loved; but to the loved most of all, except the love be reciproque. For it is a true rule, that love is ever rewarded either with the reciproque, or with an inward or secret contempt. By how much the more, men ought to beware of this passion, which loseth not only other things, but itself. As for the other losses, the poet's relation doth well figure them: that he that preferred Helena, quitted the gifts of Juno and Pallas; for whosoever esteemeth too much of amorous affection quitteth both riches and wisdom.

This passion hath his floods in the very times of weakness, which are great prosperity and great adversity (though this latter hath been less observed); both which times kindle love, and make it more fervent, and therefore shew it to be the child of folly. They do best who, if they cannot but admit love, yet make it keep quarter, and sever it wholly from their serious affairs and actions of life. For if it check once with business, it troubleth men's fortunes, and maketh men that they can no ways be true to their own ends. I know not how, but martial men are given to love: I think it is but as they are given to wine; for perils commonly ask to be paid in pleasures.

There is in man's nature a secret inclination and motion towards love of others, which, if it be not spent upon some one or a few, doth naturally spread itself towards many, and maketh men become humane and charitable, as it is seen sometime in friars. Nuptial love maketh mankind; friendly love perfecteth it; but wanton love corrupteth and embaseth it.

XI

Of Great Place

MEN in Great Place are thrice servants; servants of the Sovereign or State, servants of fame, and servants of business. So as they have no freedom, neither in their persons, nor in their actions, nor in their times. It is a strange desire to seek power and to lose liberty: or to seek power over others and to lose power over a man's self. The rising unto place is laborious; and by pains men come to greater pains: and it is sometimes base; and by indignities men come to dignities. The standing is slippery, and the regress is either a downfall or at least an eclipse, which is a melancholy thing. *Cum non sis qui fueris, non esse cur velis vivere.* Nay, retire men cannot when they would, neither will they when it were reason, but are impatient of privateness, even in age and sickness, which require the shadow; like old townsmen, that will be still sitting at their street door, though thereby they offer age to scorn. Certainly great persons had need to borrow other men's opinions to think themselves happy. For if they judge by their own feeling, they cannot find it; but if they think with themselves what other men think of them, and that other men would fain be as they are, then they are happy as it were by report, when, perhaps, they find the contrary within. For they are the first that find their own griefs, though they be the last that find their own faults. Certainly, men in great fortunes are strangers to themselves, and while they are in the puzzle of business, they have no time to tend their health, either of body or mind. *Illi mors gravis incubat, qui notus nimis omnibus, ignotus moritur sibi.*

In place there is license to do good and evil, whereof the latter is a curse; for in evil, the best condition is not to will, the second not to can. But power to do good is the true and lawful end of aspiring. For good thoughts, though God accept them, yet towards men are little better than good dreams, except they be put in act; and that cannot be without power and place, as the vantage and commanding ground. Merit and good works is the end of man's motion, and conscience of the same is the accomplishment of man's rest. For if a man can be a partaker of God's theatre, he shall likewise be partaker of God's rest. *Et conversus Deus, ut aspiceret opera, quæ fecerunt manus suæ, vidit quod omnia essent bona nimis*; and then the Sabbath.

In the discharge of thy place set before thee the best examples; for imitation is a globe of precepts. And after a time set before thee thine own example, and examine thyself strictly whether thou didst not best at first. Neglect not also the examples of those that have carried themselves ill in the same place; not to set off thyself by taxing their memory, but to direct thyself what to avoid. Reform, therefore, without bravery, or scandal of former times and persons: but yet set it down to thyself, as well to create good precedents as to follow them. Reduce things to the first institution, and observe wherein and how they have degenerated: but yet ask counsel of both times;

of the ancient time, what is best; and of the latter time, what is fittest. Seek to make thy course regular, that men may know beforehand what they may expect; but be not too positive and peremptory, and express thyself well when thou digressest from thy rule. Preserve the right of thy place, but stir not questions of jurisdiction; and rather assume thy right in silence, and *de facto*, than voice it with claims and challenges. Preserve likewise the rights of inferior places, and think it more honour to direct in chief than to be busy in all. Embrace and invite helps and advices touching the execution of thy place; and do not drive away such as bring thee information, as meddlers, but accept of them in good part.

The vices of authority are chiefly four: delays, corruption, roughness, and facility. For delays; give easy access; keep times appointed; go through with that which is in hand, and interlace not business but of necessity. For corruption; do not only bind thine own hands or thy servants' hands from taking, but bind the hands of suitors also from offering. For integrity used doth the one; but integrity professed, and with a manifest detestation of bribery, doth the other. And avoid not only the fault, but the suspicion. Whosoever is found variable and changeth manifestly without manifest cause, giveth suspicion of corruption. Therefore always when thou changest thine opinion or course, profess it plainly, and declare it, together with the reasons that move thee to change; and do not think to steal it. A servant or a favourite, if he be inward, and no other apparent cause of esteem, is commonly thought but a by-way to close corruption. For roughness; it is a needless cause of discontent: severity breedeth fear, but roughness breedeth hate. Even reproofs from authority ought to be grave, and not taunting. As for facility, it is

worse than bribery. For bribes come but now and
then; but if importunity or idle respects lead a man,
he shall never be without. As Salomon saith, *To respect
persons it is not good, for such a man will transgress
for a piece of bread.*

It is most true that was anciently spoken, *A place
showeth the man.* And it showeth some to the better,
and some to the worse. *Omnium consensu, capax
imperii, nisi imperasset,* saith Tacitus of Galba: but
of Vespasian he saith, *Solus imperantium, Vespasianus
mutatus in melius.* Though the one was meant of
sufficiency, the other of manners and affection. It is
an assured sign of a worthy and generous spirit, whom
honour amends. For honour is, or should be, the place
of virtue: and as in nature things move violently to
their place, and calmly in their place, so virtue in
ambition is violent, in authority settled and calm.

All rising to great place is by a winding stair; and
if there be factions, it is good to side a man's self whilst
he is in the rising, and to balance himself when he is
placed. Use the memory of thy predecessor fairly and
tenderly; for if thou dost not, it is a debt will surely
be paid when thou art gone. If thou have colleagues,
respect them; and rather call them when they look
not for it, than exclude them when they have reason
to look to be called. Be not too sensible or too remembering of thy place in conversation and private
answers to suitors; but let it rather be said, *When he
sits in place, he is another man.*

XII

Of Boldness

IT is a trivial grammar-school text, but yet worthy a wise man's consideration: question was asked of Demosthenes, *What was the chief part of an orator?* he answered, *Action: What next? Action: What next again?*
⁵ *Action.* He said it that knew it best, and had by nature himself no advantage in that he commended. A strange thing, that that part of an orator which is but superficial, and rather the virtue of a player, should be placed so high above those other noble parts, of invention, elocution, and
¹⁰ the rest; nay, almost alone, as if it were all in all. But the reason is plain. There is in human nature generally more of the fool than of the wise; and therefore those faculties by which the foolish part of men's minds is taken are most potent. Wonderful like is the case of
¹⁵ boldness in civil business; What first? boldness: What second and third? boldness. And yet boldness is a child of ignorance and baseness, far inferior to other parts. But nevertheless it doth fascinate and bind hand and foot those that are either shallow in judgment or weak in
²⁰ courage, which are the greatest part; yea, and prevaileth

with wise men at weak times. Therefore we see it hath done wonders in popular States; but with senates and princes less: and more ever upon the first entrance of bold persons into action, than soon after; for boldness is an ill keeper of promise.

Surely, as there are mountebanks for the natural body, so there are mountebanks for the politic body; men that undertake great cures, and perhaps have been lucky in two or three experiments, but want the grounds of science, and therefore cannot hold out. Nay, you shall see a bold fellow many times do Mahomet's miracle. Mahomet made the people believe that he would call a hill to him, and from the top of it offer up his prayers for the observers of his law. The people assembled; Mahomet called the hill to come to him again and again; and when the hill stood still, he was never a whit abashed, but said, *If the hill will not come to Mahomet, Mahomet will go to the hill.* So these men, when they have promised great matters, and failed most shamefully, yet, if they have the perfection of boldness, they will but slight it over, and make a turn, and no more ado.

Certainly to men of great judgment bold persons are sport to behold; nay, and to the vulgar also boldness hath somewhat of the ridiculous. For, if absurdity be the subject of laughter, doubt you not but great boldness is seldom without some absurdity. Especially it is a sport to see when a bold fellow is out of countenance, for that puts his face into a most shrunken and wooden posture: as needs it must; for in bashfulness the spirits do a little go and come, but with bold men, upon like occasion, they stand at a stay; like a stale at chess, where it is no mate, but yet the game cannot stir. But this last were fitter for a satire than for a serious observation.

This is well to be weighed, that boldness is ever blind, for it seeth not dangers and inconveniences. Therefore it is ill in counsel, good in execution. So that the right use of bold persons is, that they never command in chief, but be seconds, and under the direction of others. For in counsel it is good to see dangers, and in execution not to see them, except they be very great.

XIII

Of Goodness, and Goodness of Nature

I TAKE Goodness in this sense,—the affecting of the weal of men, which is that the Grecians call Philanthropia ; and the word *humanity* (as it is used) is a little too light to express it. Goodness I call the habit, and Goodness of Nature the inclination. This, of all virtues and dignities of the mind, is the greatest, being the character of the Deity ; and without it, man is a busy, mischievous, wretched thing, no better than a kind of vermin. Goodness answers to the theological virtue, Charity, and admits no excess, but error. The desire of power, in excess, caused the angels to fall ; the desire of knowledge, in excess, caused man to fall : but in charity there is no excess ; neither can angel or man come in danger by it. The inclination to goodness is imprinted deeply in the nature of man ; insomuch that, if it issue not towards men, it will take unto other living creatures : as it is seen in the Turks, a cruel people, who, nevertheless, are kind to beasts, and give alms to dogs and birds ; insomuch as Busbechius reporteth, a Christian boy in Constantinople had like to have been stoned for gagging, in a waggishness, a long-billed fowl.

Errors, indeed, in this virtue of goodness or charity, may be committed. The Italians have an ungracious proverb, *Tanto buon che val niente: So good that he is good for nothing.* And one of the doctors of Italy, Nicholas Machiavel, had the confidence to put in writing, almost in plain terms, that *the Christian faith had given up good men in prey to those who are tyrannical and unjust.* Which he spake because, indeed, there was never law, or sect, or opinion, did so much magnify goodness as the Christian religion doth. Therefore, to avoid the scandal, and the danger both, it is good to take knowledge of the errors of an habit so excellent. Seek the good of other men, but be not in bondage to their faces or fancies: for that is but facility or softness; which taketh an honest mind prisoner. Neither give thou Æsop's cock a gem, who would be better pleased and happier if he had had a barley-corn. The example of God teacheth the lesson truly: *He sendeth his rain, and maketh his sun to shine upon the just and the unjust;* but he doth not rain wealth nor shine honour and virtues upon men equally. Common benefits are to be communicate with all; but peculiar benefits with choice. And beware how, in making the portraiture, thou breakest the pattern. For divinity maketh the love of ourselves the pattern, the love of our neighbours but the portraiture. *Sell all thou hast, and give it to the poor, and follow me;* but sell not all thou hast, except thou come and follow me: that is, except thou have a vocation wherein thou mayest do as much good with little means as with great; for otherwise, in feeding the streams, thou driest the fountain.

Neither is there only a habit of goodness directed by right reason; but there is in some men, even in nature, a disposition towards it; as, on the other side, there is a natural malignity; for there be that in their nature do not affect the good of others. The lighter sort of malignity turneth but to a crossness, or frowardness, or aptness to oppose, or difficilness, or the like; but the deeper sort to envy, and mere mischief. Such men, in other men's calamities, are, as it were, in season, and are ever on the loading part: not so good as the dogs that licked Lazarus' sores, but like flies that are still buzzing upon anything that is raw: *Misanthropi*, that make it their practice to bring men to the bough, and yet never have a tree for the purpose in their gardens, as Timon had: Such dispositions are the very errors of human nature; and yet they are the fittest timber to make great politiques of: like to knee-timber, that is good for ships that are ordained to be tossed, but not for building houses that shall stand firm.

The parts and signs of goodness are many. If a man be gracious and courteous to strangers, it shows he is a citizen of the world, and that his heart is no island cut off from other lands, but a continent that joins to them. If he be compassionate towards the affliction of others, it shows that his heart is like the noble tree that is wounded itself when it gives the balm. If he easily pardons and remits offences, it shows that his mind is planted above injuries, so that he cannot be shot. If he be thankful for small benefits, it shows that he weighs men's minds, and not their trash. But, above all, if he have St. Paul's perfection, that he would wish to be an *anathema* from Christ, for the salvation of his brethren, it shows much of a divine nature, and a kind of conformity with Christ Himself.

XIV

Of Nobility

WE will speak of Nobility first as a portion of an estate, then as a condition of particular persons. A monarchy where there is no nobility at all is ever a pure and absolute tyranny, as that of the Turks. For nobility attempers sovereignty, and draws the eyes of the people somewhat aside from the line royal. But for democracies, they need it not; and they are commonly more quiet, and less subject to sedition than where there are stirps of nobles. For men's eyes are upon the business, and not upon the persons; or, if upon the persons, it is for the business' sake, as fittest, and not for flags and pedigree. We see the Switzers last well, notwithstanding their diversity of religion and of Cantons; for utility is their bond, and not respects. The United Provinces of the Low Countries in their government excel. For where there is an equality, the consultations are more indifferent, and the payments and tributes more cheerful. A great and potent nobility addeth majesty to a monarch, but diminisheth power and putteth life and spirit into the people, but presseth their fortune. It is well when nobles are not too great for sovereignty, nor for justice; and yet maintained in that height, as the insolency of inferiors may be broken upon them before it come on too fast upon the majesty of kings. A numerous nobility causeth poverty and inconvenience in a State; for it is a surcharge of expense; and besides, it being of necessity that many of the nobility fall in time to be weak in fortune, it maketh a kind of disproportion between honour and means.

As for nobility in particular persons: it is a reverend thing to see an ancient castle or building not in decay, or to see a fair timber tree sound and perfect; how much more to behold an ancient noble family, which hath stood against the waves and weathers of time. For new nobility is but the act of power, but ancient nobility is the act of time. Those that are first raised to nobility are commonly more virtuous, but less innocent, than their descendants; for there is rarely any rising but by a commixture of good and evil arts. But it is reason the memory of their virtues remain to their posterity, and their faults die with themselves. Nobility of birth commonly abateth industry; and he that is not industrious, envieth him that is. Besides, noble persons cannot go much higher; and he that standeth at a stay when others rise, can hardly avoid motions of envy. On the other side, nobility extinguisheth the passive envy from others towards them, because they are in possession of honour. Certainly, kings that have able men of their nobility shall find ease in employing them, and a better slide into their business; for people naturally bend to them as born in some sort to command.

XV
Of Seditions and Troubles

SHEPHERDS of people had need know the calendars of tempests in State; which are commonly greatest when things grow to equality, as natural tempests are greatest about the equinoctia. And as there are certain hollow blasts of wind and secret swellings of seas before a tempest, so are there in States:

> *Ille etiam cæcos instare tumultus*
> *Sæpe monet, fraudesque et operta tumescere bella.*

Libels and licentious discourses against the State, when they are frequent and open; and in like sort, false news often running up and down to the disadvantage of the State, and hastily embraced, are amongst the signs of troubles. Virgil, giving the pedigree of Fame, saith, she was sister to the giants:

> *Illam terra parens, ira irritata deorum,*
> *Extremam (ut perhibent) Cæo Enceladoque sororem*
> *Progenuit.*

As if fames were the relics of seditions past. But they are no less indeed the preludes of seditions to come.

Howsoever, he noteth it right, that seditious tumults and seditious fames differ no more but as brother and sister, masculine and feminine: especially if it come to that, that the best actions of a State, and the most plausible, and which ought to give greatest contentment, are taken in ill sense and traduced. For that shows the envy great, as Tacitus saith, *Conflata magna invidia, seu bene, seu male, gesta premunt*. Neither doth it follow that because these fames are a sign of troubles, that the suppressing of them with too much severity should be a remedy of troubles. For the despising of them many times checks them best; and the going about to stop them doth but make a wonder long-lived. Also that kind of obedience, which Tacitus speaketh of, is to be held suspected: *Erant in officio, sed tamen qui mallent mandata imperantium interpretari, quam exequi*. Disputing, excusing, cavilling upon mandates and directions, is a kind of shaking off the yoke, and assay of disobedience: especially if in those disputings they which are for the direction speak fearfully and tenderly, and those that are against it, audaciously.

Also, as Machiavel noteth well, when princes, that ought to be common parents, make themselves as a party, and lean to a side, that is, as a boat that is overthrown by uneven weight on the one side: as was well seen in the time of Henry III. of France; for, first himself entered League for the extirpation of the Protestants, and, presently after, the same League was turned upon himself. For when the authority of princes is made but an accessary to a cause, and that there be other bands that tie faster than the band of sovereignty, kings begin to be put almost out of possession.

Also, when discords, and quarrels, and factions are carried openly and audaciously, it is a sign the reverence of government is lost. For the motions of the greatest persons in a government ought to be as the motions of the planets under *primum mobile* (according to the old opinion), which is, that every of them is carried swiftly by the highest motion, and softly in their own motion. And, therefore, when great ones in their own particular motion move violently, and, as Tacitus expresseth it well, *liberius quam ut imperantium meminissent*, it is a sign the orbs are out of frame. For reverence is that wherewith princes are girt from God, who threateneth the dissolving thereof: *Solvam cingula regum.*

So when any of the four pillars of government are mainly shaken, or weakened (which are Religion, Justice, Counsel, and Treasure), men had need to pray for fair weather. But let us pass from this part of predictions (concerning which, nevertheless, more light might be taken from that which followeth), and let us speak first of the materials of seditions, then of the motives of them, and thirdly of the remedies.

Concerning the Materials of seditions. It is a thing well to be considered: for the surest way to prevent seditions (if the times do bear it), is to take away the matter of them. For if there be fuel prepared, it is hard to tell whence the spark shall come that shall set it on fire. The matter of seditions is of two kinds, much poverty, and much discontentment. It is certain, so many overthrown estates, so many votes for troubles. Lucan noteth well the state of Rome before the civil war:

> *Hinc usura vorax rapidumque in tempore fœnus,*
> *Hinc concussa fides, et multis utile bellum.*

This same *multis utile bellum* is an assured and infallible sign of a State disposed to seditions and troubles. And if this poverty and broken estate in the

better sort be joined with a want and necessity in the
mean people, the danger is imminent and great. For
the rebellions of the belly are the worst. As for discontentments, they are in the politic body like to humours
in the natural, which are apt to gather a preternatural
heat, and to inflame. And let no prince measure the
danger of them by this, whether they be just or unjust
(for that were to imagine people to be too reasonable;
who do often spurn at their own good,) nor yet by this,
whether the griefs whereupon they rise be in fact great
or small; for they are the most dangerous discontentments, where the fear is greater than the feeling.
Dolendi modus, timendi non item. Besides, in great
oppressions, the same things that provoke the patience
do withal mate the courage; but in fears it is not so.
Neither let any prince, or state, be secure concerning
discontentments, because they have been often, or have
been long, and yet no peril hath ensued. For as it is
true that every vapour or fume doth not turn into a
storm, so it is nevertheless true, that storms, though they
blow over divers times, yet may fall at last. And, as
the Spanish proverb noteth well, *The cord breaketh at
the last by the weakest pull.*

The Causes and Motives of seditions are innovation
in religion, taxes, alteration of laws and customs, breaking of privileges, general oppression, advancement of unworthy persons, strangers, dearths, disbanded soldiers,
factions grown desperate, and whatsoever in offending
people joineth and knitteth them in a common cause.

For the Remedies; there may be some general preservatives, whereof we will speak: as for the just cure, it
must answer to the particular disease, and so be left to
counsel rather than rule.

The first remedy or prevention, is to remove, by all
means possible, that material cause of sedition whereof

we speak, which is want and poverty in the estate. To which purpose serveth the opening and well-balancing of trade; the cherishing of manufactures; the banishing of idleness; the repressing of waste and excess by sumptuary laws; the improvement and husbanding of the soil; the regulating of prices of things vendible; the moderating of taxes and tributes; and the like. Generally, it is to be foreseen that the population of a kingdom (especially if it be not mown down by wars), do not exceed the stock of the kingdom which should maintain them. Neither is the population to be reckoned only by number. For a smaller number, that spend more and earn less, do wear out an estate sooner than a greater number that live low and gather more. Therefore the multiplying of nobility, and other degrees of quality, in an over-proportion to the common people, doth speedily bring a State to necessity; and so doth likewise an overgrown clergy; for they bring nothing to the stock; and in like manner, when more are bred scholars than preferments can take off.

It is likewise to be remembered, that, forasmuch as the increase of any estate must be upon the foreigner (for whatsoever is somewhere gotten is somewhere lost), there be but three things which one nation selleth unto another; the commodity as nature yieldeth it, the manufacture, and the vecture, or carriage. So that, if these three wheels go, wealth will flow as in a spring tide. And it cometh many times to pass, that *materiam superabit opus*, that the work and carriage is worth more than the material, and enricheth a State more; as is notably seen in the Low Countrymen, who have the best mines above ground in the world.

Above all things, good policy is to be used, that the treasures and monies in a State be not gathered into few hands. For otherwise, a State may have a great stock,

Essay 15] **Of Seditions and Troubles** 51

and yet starve ; and money is like muck, not good except it be spread. This is done chiefly by suppressing, or at the least keeping a strait hand upon, the devouring trades of usury, engrossing, great pasturages, and the like.

For removing discontentments, or, at least, the danger of them : there is in every state (as we know), two portions of subjects, the nobles and the commonalty. When one of these is discontent, the danger is not great : for common people are of slow motion, if they be not excited by the greater sort ; and the greater sort are of small strength, except the multitude be apt and ready to move of themselves. Then is the danger, when the greater sort do but wait for the troubling of the waters amongst the meaner, that then they may declare themselves. The poets feign that the rest of the gods would have bound Jupiter ; which he hearing of, by the counsel of Pallas sent for Briareus, with his hundred hands, to come in to his aid. An emblem, no doubt, to show how safe it is for monarchs to make sure of the good-will of common people.

To give moderate liberty for griefs and discontentments to evaporate (so it be without too great insolency or bravery), is a safe way. For he that turneth the humours back, and maketh the wound bleed inwards, endangereth malign ulcers and pernicious imposthumations.

The part of Epimetheus mought well become Prometheus, in the case of discontentments ; for there is not a better provision against them. Epimetheus, when griefs and evils flew abroad, at last shut the lid, and kept hope in the bottom of the vessel. Certainly, the politic and artificial nourishing and entertaining of hopes, and carrying men from hopes to hopes, is one of the best antidotes against the poison of discontentments. And it is a certain sign of a wise government and proceeding, when it can hold men's hearts by hopes, when it cannot by satisfaction; and when it can handle things in such manner as no evil shall appear so peremptory but that it hath some outlet of hope: which is the less hard to do, because both particular persons and factions are apt enough to flatter themselves, or, at least, to brave that which they believe not.

Also the foresight and prevention, that there be no likely or fit head whereupon discontented persons may resort, and under whom they may join, is a known, but an excellent point of caution. I understand a fit head to be one that hath greatness and reputation, that hath confidence with the discontented party, and upon whom they turn their eyes, and that is thought discontented in his own particular; which kind of persons are either to be won and reconciled to the State, and that in a fast and true manner, or to be fronted with some other of the same party that may oppose them, and so divide the reputation. Generally, the dividing and breaking of all factions and combinations that are adverse to the State, and setting them at distance, or, at least, distrust among themselves, is not one of the worst remedies. For it is a desperate case, if those that hold with the proceeding of the State be full of discord and faction, and those that are against it be entire and united.

I have noted, that some witty and sharp speeches, which have fallen from princes, have given fire to seditions. Cæsar did himself infinite hurt in that speech, *Sylla nescivit literas, non potuit dictare:* for it did utterly cut off that hope which men had entertained, that he would at one time or other give over his dictatorship. Galba undid himself by that speech, *legi a se militem, non emi:* for it put the soldiers out of hope of the donative. Probus, likewise, by that speech, *Si vixero, non opus erit amplius Romano imperio militibus*; a speech of great despair for the soldiers. And many the like. Surely princes had need, in tender matters and ticklish times, to beware what they say, especially in these short speeches, which fly abroad like darts, and are thought to be shot out of their secret intentions. For, as for large discourses, they are flat things, and not so much noted.

Lastly, let princes, against all events, not be without some great person, one or rather more, of military valour, near unto them, for the repressing of seditions in their beginnings. For, without that, there useth to be more trepidation in court upon the first breaking out of trouble than were fit. And the State runneth the danger of that which Tacitus saith—*Atque is habitus animorum fuit, ut pessimum facinus auderent pauci, plures vellent, omnes paterentur.* But let such military persons be assured and well reputed of, rather than factious and popular; holding also good correspondence with the other great men in the State : or else the remedy is worse than the disease.

XVI
Of Atheism

I HAD rather believe all the fables in the Legend, and the Talmud, and the Alcoran, than that this universal frame is without a mind. And therefore God never wrought miracles to convince atheism, because his ordinary works convince it. It is true that a little philosophy inclineth Man's mind to atheism; but depth in philosophy bringeth men's minds about to religion. For while the mind of Man looketh upon second causes scattered, it may sometimes rest in them, and go no farther; but when it beholdeth the chain of them confederate and linked together, it must needs fly to Providence and Deity. Nay, even that school which is most accused of atheism, doth most demonstrate religion; that is, the school of Leucippus, and Democritus, and Epicurus. For it is a thousand times more credible, that four mutable elements and one immutable fifth essence, duly and eternally placed, need no God, than that an army of infinite small portions or seeds, unplaced, should have produced this order and beauty without a divine marshal.

Of Atheism

The Scripture saith, *The fool hath said in his heart, there is no God*; it is not said, *The fool hath thought in his heart*: so as he rather saith it by rote to himself, as that he would have, than that he can thoroughly believe it, or be persuaded of it; for none deny there is a God, but those for whom it maketh that there were no God. It appeareth in nothing more, that atheism is rather in the lip than in the heart of man, than by this, that atheists will ever be talking of that their opinion, as if they fainted in it themselves, and would be glad to be strengthened by the consent of others. Nay, more, you shall have atheists strive to get disciples, as it fareth with other sects. And, which is most of all, you shall have of them that will suffer for atheism, and not recant: whereas, if they did truly think that there were no such thing as God, why should they trouble themselves? Epicurus is charged, that he did but dissemble for his credit's sake, when he affirmed there were Blessed Natures, but such as enjoy themselves without having respect to the government of the world. Wherein they say he did temporize, though in secret he thought there was no God. But certainly he is traduced; for his words are noble and divine: *Non deos vulgi negare profanum; sed vulgi opiniones diis applicare profanum.* Plato could have said no more. And although he had the confidence to deny the administration, he had not the power to deny the nature. The Indians of the West have names for their particular gods, though they have no name for God (as if the heathens should have had the names Jupiter, Apollo, Mars, &c., but not the word Deus) which shews that even those barbarous people have the notion, though they have not the latitude and extent of it. So that against atheists the very savages take part with the very subtlest philosophers. The contemplative atheist is rare: a Diagoras, a Bion, a Lucian perhaps, and some others. And yet they seem to be more than they are, for that all that impugn a received religion, or superstition, are, by the adverse part, branded with the name of atheists. But the great atheists indeed are hypocrites, which are ever handling holy things, but without feeling, so as they must needs be cauterized in the end.

The causes of atheism are, divisions in religion, if there be many (for any one main division addeth zeal to both sides, but many divisions introduce atheism); another is, scandal of priests, when it is come to that which St. Bernard saith, *Non est jam dicere, ut populus, sic sacerdos; quia nec sic populus, ut sacerdos*; a third is, a custom of profane scoffing in holy matters, which doth by little and little deface the reverence of religion; and lastly, learned times, especially with peace and prosperity; for troubles and adversities do more bow men's minds to religion.

They that deny a God destroy man's nobility, for certainly Man is of kin to the beasts by his body; and if he be not of kin to God by his spirit, he is a base and ignoble creature. It destroys likewise magnanimity, and the raising of human nature. For take an example of a dog, and mark what a generosity and courage he will put on when he finds himself maintained by a man, who to him is instead of a God, or *melior natura*: which courage is manifestly such as that creature, without that confidence of a better nature than his own, could never attain. So Man, when he resteth and assureth himself upon divine protection and favour, gathereth a force and faith which human nature in itself could not obtain; therefore, as atheism is in all respects hateful, so in this, that it depriveth human nature of the means to exalt itself above human frailty. As it is in particular persons, so it is in nations. Never was there such a

State for magnanimity as Rome. Of this State hear what Cicero saith : *Quam volumus, licet, patres conscripti, nos amemus, tamen nec numero Hispanos, nec robore Gallos, nec calliditate Pœnos, nec artibus Græcos, nec denique hoc ipso hujus gentis et terræ domestico nativoque sensu Italos ipsos et Latinos; sed pietate, ac religione, atque hac una sapientia, quod deorum immortalium numine omnia regi, gubernarique perspeximus, omnes gentes nationesque superavimus.*

XVII

Of Superstition

IT were better to have no opinion of God at all, than such an opinion as is unworthy of him. For the one is unbelief, the other is contumely: and certainly superstition is the reproach of the Deity. Plutarch saith
5 well to that purpose: *Surely,* saith he, *I had rather a great deal men should say there was no such a man at all as Plutarch, than that they should say there was one Plutarch that would eat his children as soon as they were born;* as the poets speak of Saturn. And as the con-
10 tumely is greater towards God, so the danger is greater towards men. Atheism leaves a man to sense, to philosophy, to natural piety, to laws, to reputation: all which may be guides to an outward moral virtue, though religion were not. But superstition dismounts all these,
15 and erecteth an absolute monarchy in the minds of men. Therefore atheism did never perturb States; for it makes men weary of themselves, as looking no further: and we see the times inclined to atheism, as the time of Augustus Cæsar, were civil times. But superstition
20 hath been the confusion of many States, and bringeth in a new *primum mobile,* that ravisheth all the spheres of government.

The master of superstition is the people, and in all superstition wise men follow fools; and arguments are fitted to practice, in a reversed order. It was gravely said by some of the prelates in the Council of Trent, where the doctrine of the schoolmen bare great sway, that *the schoolmen were like astronomers, which did feign eccentrics and epicycles, and such engines of orbs, to save the phenomena, though they knew there were no such things;* and, in like manner, that the schoolmen had framed a number of subtle and intricate axioms and theorems to save the practice of the Church.

The causes of superstition are pleasing and sensual rites and ceremonies; excess of outward and pharisaical holiness; over-great reverence of traditions, which cannot but load the Church; the stratagems of prelates for their own ambition and lucre; the favouring too much of good intentions, which openeth the gate to conceits and novelties; the taking an aim at divine matters by human, which cannot but breed mixture of imaginations; and, lastly, barbarous times, especially joined with calamities and disasters.

Superstition, without a veil, is a deformed thing; for, as it addeth deformity to an ape to be so like a man, so the similitude of superstition to religion makes it the more deformed. And as wholesome meat corrupteth to little worms, so good forms and orders corrupt into a number of petty observances.

There is a superstition in avoiding superstition, when men think to do best if they go farthest from the superstition formerly received; therefore care would be had that (as it fareth in ill purgings) the good be not taken away with the bad, which commonly is done when the people is the reformer.

XVIII
Of Travel

TRAVEL, in the younger sort, is a part of education; in the elder, a part of experience. He that travelleth into a country, before he hath some entrance into the language, goeth to school, and not to travel. That young men travel under some tutor, or grave servant, I allow well; so that he be such a one that hath the language, and hath been in the country before; whereby he may be able to tell them what things are worthy to be seen in the country where they go, what acquaintances they are to seek, what exercises or discipline the place yieldeth; for else young men shall go hooded, and look abroad little.

It is a strange thing that, in sea-voyages, where there is nothing to be seen but sky and sea, men should make diaries; but in land-travel, wherein so much is to be observed, for the most part they omit it : as if chance were fitter to be registered than observation. Let diaries, therefore, be brought in use.

The things to be seen and observed are the courts of princes, especially when they give audience to ambassadors; the courts of justice, while they sit and hear causes,

Essay 18]   Of Travel   61

and so of consistories ecclesiastic; the churches and monasteries with the monuments which are therein extant; the walls and fortifications of cities and towns, and so the havens and harbours; antiquities and ruins; libraries, colleges, disputations and lectures, where any are; shipping and navies; houses and gardens of state and pleasure near great cities; armories, arsenals, magazines; exchanges, burses, warehouses; exercises of horsemanship, fencing, training of soldiers, and the like; comedies, such whereunto the better sort of persons do resort; treasuries of jewels and robes; cabinets and rarities; and, to conclude, whatsoever is memorable in the places where they go. After all which, the tutor or servants ought to make diligent inquiry. As for triumphs, masks, feasts, weddings, funerals, capital executions, and such shows, men need not be put in mind of them; yet they are not to be neglected. If you will have a young man to put his travel into a little room, and in short time to gather much, this you must do. First, as was said, he must have some entrance into the language before he goeth. Then he must have such a servant, or tutor, as knoweth the country, as was likewise said. Let him carry with him also some card, or book, describing the country where he travelleth, which will be a good key to his inquiry. Let him keep also a diary. Let him not stay long in one city or town: more or less, as the place deserveth, but not long. Nay, when he stayeth in one city or town, let him change his lodging from one end and part of the town to another; which is a great adamant of acquaintance. Let him sequester himself from the company of his countrymen, and diet in such places where there is good company of the nation where he travelleth. Let him, upon his removes from one place to another, procure recommendation to some person of quality residing in the place whither he removeth, that he may use his favour in those things he desireth to see or know. Thus he may abridge his travel with much profit.

As for the acquaintance which is to be sought in travel, that which is most of all profitable, is acquaintance with the secretaries, and employed men of ambassadors. For so, in travelling in one country, he shall suck the experience of many. Let him also see and visit eminent persons in all kinds, which are of great name abroad, that he may be able to tell how the life agreeth with the fame. For quarrels, they are with care and discretion to be avoided. They are commonly for mistresses, healths, place, and words. And let a man beware how he keepeth company with choleric and quarrelsome persons. For they will engage him into their own quarrels. When a traveller returneth home, let him not leave the countries where he hath travelled altogether behind him, but maintain a correspondence by letters with those of his acquaintance which are of most worth. And let his travel appear rather in his discourse, than in his apparel or gesture ; and in his discourse let him be rather advised in his answers, than forward to tell stories : and let it appear that he doth not change his country manners for those of foreign parts, but only prick in some flowers of that he hath learned abroad into the customs of his own country.

XIX

Of Empire

It is a miserable state of mind to have few things to desire and many things to fear. And yet that commonly is the case with kings; who, being at the highest, want matter of desire, which makes their minds more languishing; and have many representations of perils and shadows, which make their minds the less clear. And this is one reason also of that effect which the Scripture speaketh of, that *the king's heart is inscrutable.* For multitude of jealousies, and lack of some predominant desire, that should marshal and put in order all the rest, maketh any man's heart hard to find or sound. Hence it comes likewise, that princes many times make themselves desires, and set their hearts upon toys; sometimes upon a building; sometimes upon erecting of an Order; sometimes upon the advancing of a person; sometimes upon obtaining excellency in some art, or feat of the hand: as Nero for playing on the harp; Domitian for certainty of the hand with the arrow; Commodus for playing at fence; Caracalla for driving chariots; and the like. This seemeth incredible unto those that know not the principle, that *the mind of man is more cheered and refreshed by profiting in small things, than by standing at a stay in great.* We see also that kings that have been fortunate conquerors in their first years, it being not possible for them to go forward infinitely, but that they must have some check or arrest in their fortunes, turn in their latter years to be superstitious and melancholy; as did Alexander the Great, Dioclesian, and in our memory Charles V.; and others: for he that is used to go forward, and findeth a stop, falleth out of his own favour, and is not the thing he was.

To speak now of the true temper of empire: it is a thing rare and hard to keep; for both temper and distemper consist of contraries. But it is one thing to mingle contraries, another to interchange them. The answer of Apollonius to Vespasian is full of excellent instruction. Vespasian asked him, *What was Nero's overthrow?* He answered, *Nero could touch and tune the harp well; but in government sometimes he used to wind the pins too high, sometimes to let them down too low.* And certain it is, that nothing destroyeth authority so much as the unequal and untimely interchange of power pressed too far, and relaxed too much.

This is true, that the wisdom of all these latter times in princes' affairs, is rather fine deliveries, and shiftings of dangers and mischiefs, when they are near, than solid and grounded courses to keep them aloof. But this is but to try masteries with fortune. And let men beware how they neglect and suffer matter of trouble to be prepared. For no man can forbid the spark, nor tell whence it may come. The difficulties in princes' business are many and great, but the greatest difficulty is often in their own mind. For it is common with princes (saith Tacitus) to will contradictories: *Sunt plerumque regum voluntates vehementes, et inter se contrariæ.* For it is the solecism of power to think to command the end, and yet not to endure the mean.

Kings have to deal with their neighbours, their wives, their children, their prelates or clergy, their nobles, their second nobles or gentlemen, their merchants, their commons, and their men of war; and from all these arise dangers, if care and circumspection be not used.

First, for their neighbours; there can no general rule be given (the occasions are so variable), save one which ever holdeth. Which is, that princes do keep due sentinel, that none of their neighbours do overgrow so (by increase of territory, by embracing of trade, by approaches, or the like), as they become more able to annoy them than they were. And this is generally the work of standing councils to foresee and to hinder it. During that triumvirate of kings, King Henry VIII. of England, Francis I., king of France, and Charles V., emperor, there was such a watch kept that none of the three could win a palm of ground, but the other two would straightways balance it, either by confederation, or, if need were, by a war, and would not in anywise take up peace at interest. And the like was done by that league (which Guicciardini saith was the security of Italy), made between Ferdinando, king of Naples, Lorenzius Medices, and Ludovicus Sforsa, potentates, the one of Florence, the other of Milan. Neither is the opinion of some of the schoolmen to be received, that a war cannot justly be made, but upon a precedent injury or provocation. For there is no question but a just fear of an imminent danger, though there be no blow given, is a lawful cause of war.

For their wives; there are cruel examples of them. Livia is infamed for the poisoning of her husband; Roxolana, Solyman's wife, was the destruction of that renowned prince, Sultan Mustapha, and otherwise troubled his house and succession; Edward II. of England his queen had the principal hand in the deposing and murder of her husband. This kind of danger is then to be feared chiefly when the wives have plots for the raising of their own children, or else that they be advoutresses.

For their children; the tragedies likewise of dangers from them have been many. And generally the entering of the fathers into suspicion of their children hath been ever unfortunate. The destruction of Mustapha (that we named before) was fatal to Solyman's line, as the succession of the Turks from Solyman until this day is suspected to be untrue, and of strange blood; for that Selymus II. was thought to be supposititious. The destruction of Crispus, a young prince of rare towardness, by Constantinus the Great, his father, was in like manner fatal to his house, for both Constantinus and Constance, his sons, died violent deaths; and Constantius, his other son, did little better; who died, indeed of sickness, but after that Julianus had taken arms against him. The destruction of Demetrius, son to Philip II. of Macedon, turned upon the father, who died of repentance. And many like examples there are; but few or none where the fathers had good by such distrust: except it were where the sons were in open arms against them, as was Selymus I. against Bajazet, and the three sons of Henry II. king of England.

For their prelates; when they are proud and great, there is also danger from them; as it was in the times of Anselmus and Thomas Beckett, archbishops of Canterbury, who, with their crosiers, did almost try it with the king's sword: and yet they had to deal with stout and haughty kings, William Rufus, Henry I., and Henry II. The danger is not from that state, but where it hath a dependence of foreign authority, or where the churchmen come in and are elected, not by the collation of the king, or particular patrons, but by the people.

For the nobles; to keep them at a distance, it is not amiss; but to depress them may make a king more absolute, but less safe, and less able to perform anything that he desires. I have noted it in my history of King Henry VII. of England, who depressed his nobility; whereupon it came to pass, that his times were full of difficulties and troubles. For the nobility, though they continued loyal unto him, yet did they not co-operate with him in his business. So that in effect he was fain to do all things himself.

For their second nobles; there is not much danger from them, being a body dispersed. They may sometimes discourse high; but that doth little hurt. Besides, they are a counterpoise to the high nobility, that they grow not too potent. And, lastly, being the most immediate in authority with the common people, they do best temper popular commotions.

For their merchants; they are *vena porta*, and if they flourish not, a kingdom may have good limbs, but will have empty veins, and nourish little. Taxes and imposts upon them do seldom good to the king's revenue. For that that he wins in the hundred he loseth in the shire: the particular rates being increased, but the total bulk of trading rather decreased.

For their commons; there is little danger from them, except it be where they have great and potent heads; or where you meddle with the point of religion, or their customs, or means of life.

For their men of war; it is a dangerous state where they live and remain in a Body, and are used to donatives; whereof we see examples in the janizaries, and pretorian bands of Rome. But trainings of men, and arming them, in several places, and under several commanders, and without donatives, are things of defence, and no danger.

Princes are like to heavenly bodies, which cause good or evil times, and which have much veneration, but no rest. All precepts concerning kings are in effect comprehended in those two remembrances: *Memento quod. es homo*, and *Memento quod es Deus*, or *vice Dei*. The one bridleth their power, and the other their will.

XX
Of Counsel

THE greatest trust between man and man, is the trust of giving counsel. For in other confidences men commit the parts of life, their lands, their goods, their children, their credit, some particular affair; but to such as they make their counsellors they commit the whole: by how much the more they are obliged to all faith and integrity. The wisest princes need not think it any diminution to their greatness, or derogation to their sufficiency, to rely upon counsel. God himself is not without, but hath made it one of the names of the blessed Son: *The Counsellor.* Salomon hath pronounced that *in counsel is stability*. Things will have their first or second agitation. If they be not tossed upon the arguments of counsel, they will be tossed upon the waves of fortune, and be full of inconstancy, doing and undoing, like the reeling of a drunken man. Salomon's son found the force of counsel, as his father saw the necessity of it. For the beloved kingdom of God was first rent and broken by ill counsel. Upon which counsel there are set for our instruction the two marks whereby bad counsel is for ever best discerned: that it was young counsel, for the persons; and violent counsel, for the matter.

The ancient times do set forth in figure both the incorporation and inseparable conjunction of counsel with Kings, and the wise and politic use of counsel by Kings: the one, in that they say Jupiter did marry Metis, which signifieth counsel, whereby they intend that Sovereignty is married to Counsel; the other in that which followeth, which was thus: They say, after Jupiter was married to Metis, she conceived by him, and was with child: but Jupiter suffered her not to stay till she brought forth, but ate her up; whereby he became himself with child, and was delivered of Pallas armed out of his head. Which monstrous fable containeth a secret of empire how kings are to make use of their counsel of state: that first, they ought to refer matters unto them, which is the first begetting or impregnation; but when they are elaborate, moulded, and shaped in the womb of their counsel, and grow ripe and ready to be brought forth, that then they suffer not their counsel to go through with the resolution and direction, as if it depended on them, but take the matter back into their own hands, and make it appear to the world, that the decrees and final directions (which, because they come forth with prudence and power, are resembled to Pallas armed) proceeded from themselves, and not only from their authority, but (the more to add reputation to themselves) from their head and device.

Let us now speak of the inconveniences of counsel, and of the remedies. The inconveniences that have been noted in calling and using counsel, are three. First, the revealing of affairs, whereby they become less secret. Secondly, the weakening of the authority of princes, as if they were less of themselves. Thirdly, the danger of being unfaithfully counselled, and more for the good of them that counsel, than of him that is counselled. For which inconveniences, the doctrine of Italy, and practice of France, in some kings' times, hath introduced cabinet councils, a remedy worse than the disease.

As to secrecy; princes are not bound to communicate all matters with all counsellors, but may extract and select. Neither is it necessary, that he that consulteth what he should do, should declare what he will do. But let princes beware that the unsecreting of their affairs comes not from themselves. And as for cabinet councils, it may be their motto, *Plenus rimarum sum.* One futile person, that maketh it his glory to tell, will do more hurt than many that know it their duty to conceal. It is true there be some affairs which require extreme secrecy, which will hardly go beyond one or two persons besides the king. Neither are those counsels unprosperous. For, besides the secrecy, they commonly go on constantly in one spirit of direction without distraction. But then it must be a prudent king, such as is able to grind with a hand-mill. And those inward counsellors had need also be wise men, and especially true and trusty to the king's ends: as it was with King Henry VII. of England, who in his greatest business imparted himself to none, except it were to Morton and Fox.

For weakness of authority; the fable showeth the remedy. Nay, the majesty of kings is rather exalted than diminished when they are in the chair of counsel: neither was there ever prince bereaved of his dependencies by his counsel; except where there hath been either an over-greatness in one counsellor, or an over-strict combination in divers: which are things soon found and holpen.

For the last inconvenience, that men will counsel with an eye to themselves: certainly, *non inveniet fidem super terram* is meant of the nature of times, and not of all particular persons. There be that are in nature faithful and sincere, and plain and direct, not crafty and involved. Let princes, above all, draw to themselves such natures. Besides, counsellors are not commonly so united but that one counsellor keepeth sentinel over another. So that if any counsel out of faction or private ends, it commonly comes to the king's ear. But the best remedy is, if princes know their counsellors, as well as their counsellors know them:

Principis est virtus maxima nosse suos.

And on the other side, counsellors should not be too speculative into their sovereign's person. The true composition of a counsellor is, rather to be skilful in his master's business, than in his nature. For then he is like to advise him, and not to feed his humour. It is of singular use to princes if they take the opinions of their council both separately and together. For private opinion is more free, but opinion before others is more reverend. In private, men are more bold in their own humours, and, in consort, men are more obnoxious to others' humours. Therefore it is good to take both; and of the inferior sort, rather in private, to preserve freedom; of the greater, rather in consort, to preserve respect. It is in vain for princes to take counsel concerning matters, if they take no counsel likewise concerning persons. For all matters are as dead images; and the life of the execution of affairs resteth in the good choice of persons. Neither is it enough to consult concerning persons, *secundum genera* (as in an idea, or mathematical description), what the kind and character of the person should be. For the greatest errors are committed, and the most judgment is shown, in the choice of individuals. It was truly said, *Optimi consiliarii mortui*: Books will speak plain when counsellors blanch. Therefore it is good to be conversant in them, specially the books of such as themselves have been actors upon the stage.

The councils at this day in most places are but familiar meetings, where matters are rather talked on than debated. And they run too swift to the order or act of council. It were better that, in causes of weight, the matter were propounded one day, and not spoken to till next day; *in nocte consilium*. So was it done in the commission of union between England and Scotland, which was a grave and orderly assembly. I commend set days for petitions. For both it gives the suitors more certainty for their attendance, and it frees the meetings for matters of estate, that they may *hoc agere*. In choice of committees for ripening business for the council, it is better to choose indifferent persons, than to make an indifferency by putting in those that are strong on both sides. I commend also standing commissions; as, for trade, for treasure, for war, for suits, for some provinces. For where there be divers particular councils, and but one council of estate (as it is in Spain), they are, in effect, no more than standing commissions, save that they have greater authority. Let such as are to inform councils out of their particular professions (as lawyers, seamen, mintmen, and the like), be first heard before committees, and then, as occasion serves, before the council. And let them not come in multitudes, or in a tribunitious manner; for that is to clamour councils, not to inform them. A long table and a square table, or seats about the walls, seem things of form, but are things of substance. For at a long table, a few at the upper end, in effect, sway all the business; but in the other form there is more use of the counsellors' opinions that sit lower. A king, when he presides in council, let him beware how he opens his own inclination too much in that which he propoundeth. For else counsellors will but take the wind of him, and instead of giving free counsel, will sing him a song of *placebo*.

XXI

Of Delays

FORTUNE is like the market; where, many times, if you can stay a little, the price will fall. And again, it is sometimes like Sibylla's offer; which at first offereth the commodity at full, then consumeth part and part, and still holdeth up the price. For *Occasion* (as it is in the common verse) *turneth a bald noddle after she hath presented her locks in front, and no hold taken;* or, at least, turneth the handle of the bottle first to be received, and after the belly, which is hard to clasp. There is surely no greater wisdom than well to time the beginnings and onsets of things. Dangers are no more light, if they once seem light; and more dangers have deceived men than forced them. Nay, it were better to meet some dangers half way, though they come nothing near, than to keep too long a watch upon their approaches. For if a man watch too long, it is odds he will fall asleep. On the other side, to be deceived with too long shadows (as some have been when the moon was low, and shone on their enemies' back), and so to shoot off before the time, or to teach dangers to come on by over-early buckling towards them, is another extreme. The ripeness or unripeness of the occasion (as we said) must ever be well weighed. And generally it is good to commit the beginnings of all great actions to Argus with his hundred eyes, and the ends to Briareus with his hundred hands: first to watch, and then to speed. For the helmet of Pluto, which maketh the politic man go invisible, is secrecy in the council, and celerity in the execution. For when things are once come to the execution, there is no secrecy comparable to celerity—like the motion of a bullet in the air, which flieth so swift as it outruns the eye.

XXII

Of Cunning

WE take Cunning for a sinister or crooked wisdom. And certainly there is a great difference between a cunning man and a wise man, not only in point of honesty, but in point of ability. There be that can pack the cards, and yet cannot play well; so there are some that are good in canvasses and factions, that are otherwise weak men. Again, it is one thing to understand persons, and another thing to understand matters. For many are perfect in men's humours, that are not greatly capable of the real part of business; which is the constitution of one that hath studied men more than books. Such men are fitter for practice than for counsel, and they are good but in their own alley: turn them to new men, and they have lost their aim; so as the old rule, to know a fool from a wise man, *Mitte ambos nudos ad ignotos, et videbis,* doth scarce hold for them. And because these cunning men are like haberdashers of small wares, it is not amiss to set forth their shop.

It is a point of cunning to wait upon him with whom you speak, with your eye; as the Jesuits give it in precept.

For there be many wise men that have secret hearts and transparent countenances. Yet this would be done with a demure abasing of your eye sometimes, as the Jesuits also do use.

Another is, that when you have anything to obtain of present dispatch, you entertain and amuse the party with whom you deal with some other discourse, that he be not too much awake to make objections. I know a counsellor and secretary, that never came to Queen Elizabeth of England with bills to sign, but he would always first put her into some discourse of state, that she mought the less mind the bills.

The like surprise may be made by moving things when the party is in haste, and cannot stay to consider advisedly of that is moved.

If a man would cross a business that he doubts some other would handsomely and effectually move, let him pretend to wish it well, and move it himself, in such sort as may foil it.

The breaking off in the midst of that one was about to say, as if he took himself up, breeds a greater appetite in him with whom you confer to know more.

And because it works better when anything seemeth to be gotten from you by question, than if you offer it of yourself, you may lay a bait for a question, by shewing another visage and countenance than you are wont; to the end, to give occasion for the party to ask what the matter is of the change; as Nehemiah did, *And I had not before that time been sad before the king.*

In things that are tender and unpleasing, it is good to break the ice by some whose words are of less weight, and to reserve the more weighty voice to come in as by chance, so that he may be asked the question upon the other's speech; as Narcissus did, in relating to Claudius the marriage of Messalina and Silius.

In things that a man would not be seen in himself, it is a point of cunning to borrow the name of the world; as to say, *The world says*, or, *There is a speech abroad.*

I knew one that, when he wrote a letter, he would put that which was most material in the postscript, as if it had been a bye matter.

I knew another that, when he came to have speech, he would pass over that he intended most, and go forth, and come back again, and speak of it as a thing he had almost forgot.

Some procure themselves to be surprised at such times as it is like the party, that they work upon, will suddenly come upon them, and be found with a letter in their hand, or doing somewhat which they are not accustomed, to the end they may be apposed of those things which of themselves they are desirous to utter.

It is a point of cunning to let fall those words in a man's own name which he would have another man learn and use, and thereupon take advantage. I knew two that were competitors for the secretary's place, in Queen Elizabeth's time, and yet kept good quarter between themselves, and would confer one with another upon the business; and the one of them said, that to be a secretary *in the declination of a monarchy* was a ticklish thing, and that he did not affect it. The other straight caught up those words, and discoursed with divers of his friends, that he had no reason to desire to be secretary *in the declination of a monarchy*. The first man took hold of it, and found means it was told the Queen; who, hearing of a *declination of a monarchy*, took it so ill, as she would never after hear of the other's suit.

There is a cunning, which we in England call *the turning of the cat in the pan;* which is, when that which a man says to another, he lays it as if another had said it to him. And, to say truth, it is not easy when such a matter passed between two, to make it appear from which of them it first moved and began.

It is a way that some men have, to glance and dart at others by justifying themselves by negatives; as to say, *This I do not;* as Tigellinus did towards Burrhus, saying, *Se non diversas spes, sed incolumitatem imperatoris simpliciter spectare.*

Some have in readiness so many tales and stories, as there is nothing they would insinuate but they can wrap it into a tale; which serveth both to keep themselves more in guard, and to make others carry it with more pleasure.

It is a good point of cunning for a man to shape the answer he would have, in his own words and propositions; for it makes the other party stick the less.

It is strange how long some men will lie in wait to speak somewhat they desire to say, and how far about they will fetch, and how many other matters they will beat over to come near it. It is a thing of great patience, but yet of much use.

A sudden, bold, and unexpected question doth many times surprise a man, and lay him open. Like to him that, having changed his name, and walking in Paul's, another suddenly came behind him, and called him by his true name; whereat straightways he looked back.

But these small wares and petty points of cunning are infinite, and it were a good deed to make a list of them; for that nothing doth more hurt in a State than that cunning men pass for wise.

But certainly some there are that know the resorts and falls of business, that cannot sink into the main of it; like a house that hath convenient stairs and entries, but never a fair room. Therefore you shall see them find out pretty looses in the conclusion, but are no ways able to examine or debate matters. And yet commonly they take advantage of their inability, and would be thought wits of direction. Some build rather upon the abusing of others, and (as we now say) putting tricks upon them, than upon the soundness of their own proceedings. But Solomon saith, *Prudens advertit ad gressus suos; stultus divertit ad dolos.*

XXIII

Of Wisdom for a Man's Self

An ant is a wise creature for itself, but it is a shrewd thing in an orchard or garden. And certainly men that are great lovers of themselves waste the public. Divide with reason between self-love and society; and be so true to thyself as thou be not false to others, especially to thy king and country. It is a poor centre of a man's actions, *himself.* It is right earth. For that only stands fast upon its own centre; whereas all things that have affinity with the heavens move upon the centre of another, which they benefit.

The referring of all to a man's self is more tolerable in a sovereign prince, because themselves are not only themselves, but their good and evil is at the peril of the public fortune. But it is a desperate evil in a servant to a prince, or a citizen in a republic. For whatsoever affairs pass such a man's hands, he crooketh them to his own ends; which must needs be often eccentric to the ends of his master or State. Therefore, let princes or States choose such servants as have not this mark; except they mean their service should be made but the accessary.

That which maketh the effect more pernicious is, that all proportion is lost. It were disproportion enough for the servant's good to be preferred before the master's; but yet it is a greater extreme, when a little good of the servant shall carry things against a great good of the master's. And yet that is the case of bad officers, treasurers, ambassadors, generals, and other false and corrupt servants; which set a bias upon their bowl, of their own petty ends and envies, to the overthrow of their master's great and important affairs. And for the most part the good such servants receive is after the model of their own fortune; but the hurt they sell for that good is after the model of their master's fortune. And certainly it is the nature of extreme self-lovers as they will set a house on fire and it were but to roast their eggs. And yet these men many times hold credit with their masters, because their study is but to please them, and profit themselves; and for either respect they will abandon the good of their affairs.

Wisdom for a man's self is, in many branches thereof, a depraved thing. It is the wisdom of rats, that will be sure to leave a house somewhat before it fall. It is the wisdom of the fox, that thrusts out the badger, who digged and made room for him. It is the wisdom of crocodiles, that shed tears when they would devour. But that which is specially to be noted is, that those which (as Cicero says of Pompey) are *sui amantes sine rivali*, are many times unfortunate. And whereas they have all their time sacrificed to themselves, they become in the end themselves sacrifices to the inconstancy of fortune; whose wings they thought by their self-wisdom to have pinioned.

XXIV

Of Innovations

As the births of living creatures at first are ill-shapen, so are all Innovations, which are the births of time. Yet, notwithstanding, as those that first bring honour into their family are commonly more worthy than most
5 that succeed, so the first precedent (if it be good) is seldom attained by imitation. For Ill, to man's nature as it stands perverted, hath a natural motion, strongest in continuance; but Good, as a forced motion, strongest at first. Surely every medicine is an innovation, and
10 he that will not apply new remedies must expect new evils. For time is the greatest innovator; and if time of course alters things to the worse, and wisdom and counsel shall not alter them to the better, what shall be the end?
15 It is true that what is settled by custom, though it be not good, yet at least it is fit;. and those things which have long gone together, are, as it were, confederate with themselves; whereas new things piece not so well; but, though they help by their utility, yet
20 they trouble by their inconformity. Besides, they are

like strangers, more admired, and less favoured. All this is true, if time stood still: which contrariwise moveth so round that a froward retention of custom is as turbulent a thing as an innovation; and they that reverence too much old times, are but a scorn to the new.

It were good, therefore, that men in their innovations, would follow the example of time itself; which indeed innovateth greatly, but quietly, and by degrees scarce to be perceived. For otherwise, whatsoever is new is unlooked for: and ever it mends some, and pairs others; and he that is holpen takes it for a fortune, and thanks the time; and he that is hurt, for a wrong, and imputeth it to the author.

It is good also not to try experiments in States, except the necessity be urgent, or the utility evident; and well to beware, that it be the reformation that draweth on the change, and not the desire of change that pretendeth the reformation: and lastly, that the novelty, though it be not rejected, yet be held for a suspect; and, as the Scripture saith, that *we make a stand upon the ancient way, and then look about us, and discover what is the straight and right way, and so to walk in it.*

XXV

Of Dispatch

AFFECTED Dispatch is one of the most dangerous things to business that can be; it is like that which the physicians call predigestion, or hasty digestion, which is sure to fill the body full of crudities, and secret seeds of diseases. Therefore measure not dispatch by the time of sitting, but by the advancement of the business. And as in races it is not the large stride or high lift that makes the speed, so in business the keeping close to the matter and not taking of it too much at once, procureth dispatch. It is the care of some, only to come off speedily for the time, or to contrive some false periods of business, because they may seem men of dispatch. But it is one thing to abbreviate by contracting, another by cutting off; and business so handled at several sittings or meetings goeth commonly backward and forward in an unsteady manner. I knew a wise man that had it for a by-word, when he saw men hasten to a conclusion, *Stay a little, that we may make an end the sooner.*

On the other side, true dispatch is a rich thing. For

time is the measure of business, as money is of wares; and business is bought at a dear hand where there is small dispatch. The Spartans and Spaniards have been noted to be of small dispatch: *Mi venga la muerte de Spagna*; Let my death come from Spain; for then it will be sure to be long in coming.

Give good hearing to those that give the first information in business; and rather direct them in the beginning than interrupt them in the continuance of their speeches. For he that is put out of his own order will go forward and backward, and be more tedious while he waits upon his memory, than he could have been if he had gone on in his own course. But sometimes it is seen that the moderator is more troublesome than the actor.

Iterations are commonly loss of time. But there is no such gain of time as to iterate often the state of the question; for it chaseth away many a frivolous speech as it is coming forth. Long and curious speeches are as fit for dispatch as a robe or mantle with a long train is for a race. Prefaces, and passages, and excusations, and other speeches of reference to the person, are great wastes of time; and though they seem to proceed of modesty, they are bravery. Yet beware of being too material when there is any impediment or obstruction in men's wills; for pre-occupation of mind ever requireth preface of speech, like a fomentation to make the unguent enter.

Above all things, order and distribution, and singling out of parts, is the life of dispatch; so as the distribution be not too subtle. For he that doth not divide will never enter well into business; and he that divideth too much will never come out of it clearly. To choose time is to save time; and an unseasonable motion is but beating the air. There be three parts of business;

the preparation, the debate or examination, and the perfection. Whereof, if you look for dispatch, let the middle only be the work of many, and the first and last the work of few. The proceeding upon somewhat conceived in writing doth for the most part facilitate dispatch. For, though it should be wholly rejected, yet that negative is more pregnant of direction than an indefinite; as ashes are more generative than dust.

XXVI

Of Seeming Wise

It hath been an opinion, that the French are wiser than they seem, and the Spaniards seem wiser than they are. But howsoever it be between nations, certainly it is so between man and man. For, as the Apostle saith of godliness, *Having a show of godliness, but denying the power thereof,* so, certainly there are, in point of wisdom and sufficiency, that do nothing or little very solemnly, *Magno conatu nugas.* It is a ridiculous thing, and fit for a satire to persons of judgment, to see what shifts these formalists have, and what prospectives, to make superficies to seem body that hath depth and bulk.

Some are so close and reserved, as they will not show their wares but by a dark light, and seem always to keep back somewhat: and when they know within themselves they speak of that they do not well know, would nevertheless seem to others to know of that which they may not well speak. Some help themselves with countenance and gesture, and are wise by signs; as Cicero saith of Piso, that when he answered him he fetched one of his brows up to his forehead, and bent the other down to his chin ; *Respondes, altero ad frontem sublato, altero ad mentum depresso supercilio, crudelitatem tibi non placere.* Some think to bear it by speaking a great word, and being peremptory ; and go on, and take by admittance that which they cannot make good. Some, whatsoever is beyond their reach, will seem to despise, or make light of it, as impertinent or curious ; and so would have their ignorance seem judgment. Some are never without a difference, and commonly by amusing men with a subtlety, blanch the matter ; of whom A. Gellius saith, *Hominem delirum, qui verborum minutiis rerum frangit pondera.* Of which kind also Plato, in his *Protagoras*, bringeth in Prodicus in scorn, and maketh him make a speech that consisteth of distinctions from the beginning to the end.

Generally, such men, in all deliberations, find ease to be of the negative side, and affect a credit to object and foretell difficulties. For when propositions are denied, there is an end of them ; but if they be allowed, it requireth a new work : which false point of wisdom is the bane of business.

To conclude, there is no decaying merchant, or inward beggar, hath so many tricks to uphold the credit of their wealth, as these empty persons have to maintain the credit of their sufficiency. Seeming wise-men may make shift to get opinion ; but let no man choose them for employment : for, certainly, you were better take for business a man somewhat absurd than over-formal.

XXVII

Of Friendship

It had been hard for him that spake it, to have put more truth and untruth together in few words, than in that speech, *Whosoever is delighted in solitude, is either a wild beast or a god.* For it is most true, that a natural and secret hatred and aversation towards society, in any man, hath somewhat of the savage beast; but it is most untrue, that it should have any character at all of the divine nature, except it proceed, not out of a pleasure in solitude, but out of a love and desire to sequester a man's self for a higher conversation: such as is found to have been falsely and feignedly in some of the heathens, as Epimenides the Candian, Numa the Roman, Empedocles the Sicilian, and Apollonius of Tyana, and truly and really in divers of the ancient hermits and holy fathers of the Church. But little do men perceive what solitude is, and how far it extendeth. For a crowd is not company, and faces are but a gallery of pictures, and talk but a tinkling cymbal, where there is no love. The Latin adage meeteth with it a little: *Magna civitas, magna solitudo:* because in a great town friends are scattered;

so that there is not that fellowship, for the most part, which is in less neighbourhoods. But we may go further, and affirm most truly, t at it is a mere and miserable solitude to want true friends, without which the world is but a wilderness. And, even in this sense also of solitude, whosoever in the frame of his nature and affections is unfit for friendship, he taketh it of the beast, and not from humanity.

A principal fruit of friendship is the ease and discharge of the fulness of the heart, which passions of all kinds do cause and induce. We know diseases of stoppings and suffocations are the most dangerous in the body; and it is not much otherwise in the mind. You may take sarza to open the liver, steel to open the spleen, flower of sulphur for the lungs, castoreum for the brain: but no receipt openeth the heart but a true friend; to whom you may impart griefs, joys, fears, hopes, suspicions, counsels, and whatsoever lieth upon the heart to oppress it, in a kind of civil shrift or confession.

It is a strange thing to observe how high a rate great kings and monarchs do set upon this fruit of friendship whereof we speak, so great as they purchase it many times at the hazard of their own safety and greatness. For princes, in regard of the distance of their fortune from that of their subjects and servants, cannot gather this fruit, except (to make themselves capable thereof) they raise some persons to be as it were companions, and almost equals to themselves, which many times sorteth to inconvenience. The modern languages give unto such persons the name of favourites, or privadoes; as if it were matter of grace or conversation. But the Roman name attaineth the true use and cause thereof, naming them *Participes curarum*; for it is that which tieth the knot. And we see plainly that this hath been done, not by weak and passionate princes only, but by the wisest and most politic that ever reigned : who have oftentimes joined to themselves some of their servants, whom both themselves have called friends, and allowed others likewise to call them in the same manner, using the word which is received between private men.

L. Sylla, when he commanded Rome, raised Pompey, after surnamed the Great, to that height that Pompey vaunted himself for Sylla's over-match. For when he had carried the consulship for a friend of his, against the pursuit of Sylla, and that Sylla did a little resent thereat, and began to speak great, Pompey turned upon him again, and in effect bade him be quiet ; *for that more men adored the sun rising than the sun setting.* With Julius Cæsar, Decimus Brutus had obtained that interest, as he set him down in his testament for heir in remainder after his nephew. And this was the man that had power with him to draw him forth to his death. For when Cæsar would have discharged the senate, in regard of some ill presages, and especially a dream of Calpurnia, this man lifted him gently by the arm out of his chair, telling him he hoped he would not dismiss the senate till his wife had dreamed a better dream. And it seemeth his favour was so great, as Antonius, in a letter, which is recited verbatim in one of Cicero's Philippics, called him *venefica, witch,* as if he had enchanted Cæsar. Augustus raised Agrippa, though of mean birth, to that height, as, when he consulted with Mæcenas about the marriage of his daughter Julia, Mæcenas took the liberty to tell him, that *he must either marry his daughter to Agrippa, or take away his life : there was no third way, he had made him so great.* With Tiberius Cæsar, Sejanus had ascended to that height as they two were termed and reckoned as a pair of friends. Tiberius, in a letter to him, saith, *Hæc pro amicitia nostra non occultavi;* and the whole senate dedicated an altar to Friendship, as to a goddess, in respect of the great dearness of friendship between them two. The like, or more, was between Septimus Severus and Plautianus. For he forced his eldest son to marry the daughter of Plautianus, and would often maintain Plautianus in doing affronts to his son; and did write also, in a letter to the senate, by these words: *I love the man so well, as I wish he may over-live me.* Now, if these princes had been as a Trajan, or a Marcus Aurelius, a man might have thought that this had proceeded of an abundant goodness of nature. But being men so wise, of such strength and severity of mind, and so extreme lovers of themselves, as all these were, it proveth, most plainly, that they found their own felicity, though as great as ever happened to mortal men, but as a half piece, except they might have a friend to make it entire. And yet, which is more, they were princes that had wives, sons, nephews; and yet all these could not supply the comfort of friendship.

It is not to be forgotten what Comineus observeth of his first master, Duke Charles the Hardy; namely, that he would communicate his secrets with none; and, least of all, those secrets which troubled him most. Whereupon he goeth on, and saith that towards his latter time *that closeness did impair and a little perish his understanding.* Surely Comineus mought have made the same judgment also, if it had pleased him, of his second master, Louis XI., whose closeness was indeed his tormentor. The parable of Pythagoras is dark, but true, *Cor ne edito*: Eat not the heart. Certainly, if a man would give it a hard phrase, those that want friends to open themselves unto are cannibals of their own hearts. But one thing is most admirable (wherewith I will conclude this first fruit of friendship), which is, that this communicating of a man's self to his friend, works two contrary effects: for it redoubleth joys, and cutteth griefs in halfs. For there is no man that imparteth his joys to his friend, but he joyeth the more; and no man that imparteth his griefs to his friend, but he grieveth the less. So that it is, in truth, of operation upon a man's mind of like virtue as the alchymists use to attribute to their stone for man's body, that it worketh all contrary effects, but still to the good and benefit of nature. But yet, without praying in aid of alchymists, there is a manifest image of this in the ordinary course of nature. For in bodies, union strengtheneth and cherisheth any natural action, and, on the other side, weakeneth and dulleth any violent impression: and even so is it of minds.

The second fruit of friendship is healthful and sovereign for the understanding, as the first is for the affections. For friendship maketh indeed a fair day in the affections from storm and tempests; but it maketh daylight in the understanding, out of darkness and confusion of thoughts. Neither is this to be understood only of faithful counsel, which a man receiveth from his friend; but before you come to that, certain it is, that whosoever hath his mind fraught with many thoughts, his wits and understanding do clarify and break up, in the communicating and discoursing with another: he tosseth his thoughts more easily; he marshalleth them more orderly; he seeth how they look when they are turned into words; finally, he waxeth wiser than himself: and that more by an hour's discourse than by a day's meditation. It was well said by Themistocles to the king of Persia, that *speech was like cloth of Arras, opened and put abroad, whereby the imagery doth appear in figure; whereas in thoughts they lie but as in packs.* Neither is this second fruit of friendship, in opening the understanding, restrained only to such friends as are able to give a man counsel. They indeed are best : but, even without that, a man learneth of himself, and bringeth his own thoughts to light, and whetteth his wits as against a stone, which itself cuts not. In a word, a man were better relate himself to a statua or picture, than to suffer his thoughts to pass in smother.

Add now, to make this second fruit of friendship complete, that other point which lieth more open, and falleth within vulgar observation; which is faithful counsel from a friend. Heraclitus saith well, in one of his enigmas, *Dry light is ever the best.* And certain it is, that the light that a man receiveth by counsel from another is drier and purer than that which cometh from his own understanding and judgment; which is ever infused and drenched in his affections and customs. So as there is as much difference between the counsel that a friend giveth, and that a man giveth himself, as there is between the counsel of a friend and of a flatterer. For there is no such flatterer as is a man's self, and there is no such remedy against flattery of a man's self as the liberty of a friend. Counsel is of two sorts; the one concerning manners, the other concerning business. For the first, the best preservative to keep the mind in health is the faithful admonition of a friend. The calling of a man's self to a strict account is a medicine sometimes too piercing and corrosive. Reading good books of morality is a little flat and dead. Observing our faults in others is sometimes unproper for our case; but the best receipt (best, I say, to work, and best to take) is the admonition of a friend. It is a strange thing to behold what gross errors and extreme absurdities many (especially of the greater sort) do commit, for want of a friend to tell them of them ; to the great damage both of their fame and fortune. For, as St. James saith, they are as men, *that look sometimes* into a glass, and presently forget their own shape and favour. As for business, a man may think, if he will, that two eyes see no more than one; or that a gamester seeth always more than a looker-on; or that a man in anger is as wise as he that hath said over the four-and-twenty letters; or that a musket may be shot off as well upon the arm as upon a rest; and such other fond and high imaginations, to think himself all in all. But when all is done, the help of good counsel is that which setteth business straight. And if any man think that he will take counsel, but it shall be by pieces; asking counsel in one business of one man, and in another business of another man; it is well (that is to say, better, perhaps, than if he asked none at all), but he runneth two dangers. One, that he shall not be faithfully counselled: for it is a rare thing, except it be from a perfect and entire friend, to have counsel given, but such as shall be bowed and crooked to some ends which he hath that giveth it. The other, that he shall have counsel given, hurtful and unsafe (though with good meaning), and mixed partly of mischief and partly of remedy. Even as if you would call a physician, that is thought good for the cure of the disease you complain of but is unacquainted with your body, and therefore, may put you in a way for present cure, but overthroweth your health in some other kind, and so cure the disease, and kill the patient. But a friend, that is wholly acquainted with a man's estate, will beware, by furthering any present business, how he dasheth upon other inconvenience. And, therefore, rest not upon scattered counsels, for they will rather distract and mislead than settle and direct.

After these two noble fruits of friendship (peace in the affections, and support of the judgment), followeth the last fruit, which is, like the pomegranate, full of many kernels: I mean, aid and bearing a part in all actions and occasions. Here, the best way to represent to life the manifold use of friendship, is to cast and see how many things there are which a man cannot do himself; and then it will appear that it was a sparing speech of the ancients, to say, that *a friend is another himself*; for that a friend is far more than himself. Men have their time, and die many times in desire of some things which they principally take to heart; the bestowing of a child, the finishing of a work, or the like. If a man have a true friend, he may rest almost secure that the care of those things will continue after him. So that a man hath, as it were, two lives in his desires. A man hath a body, and that body is confined to a place; but where friendship is, all offices of life are, as it were, granted to him and his deputy. For he may exercise them by his friend. How many things are there which a man cannot, with any face or comeliness, say or do himself! A man can scarce allege his own merits with modesty, much less extol them; a man cannot sometimes stoop to supplicate or beg, and a number of the like. But all these things are graceful in a friend's mouth, which are blushing in a man's own. So, again a man's person hath many proper relations which he cannot put off. A man cannot speak to his son but as a father; to his wife but as a husband; to his enemy but upon terms: whereas a friend may speak as the case requires, and not as it sorteth with the person. But to enumerate these things were endless: I have given the rule, where a man cannot fitly play his own part: if he have not a friend, he may quit the stage.

XXVIII

Of Expense

RICHES are for spending, and spending for honour and good actions. Therefore extraordinary expense must be limited by the worth of the occasion (for voluntary undoing may be as well for a man's country as for the kingdom of heaven); but ordinary expense ought to be limited by a man's estate, and governed with such regard as it be within his compass and not subject to deceit and abuse of servants; and ordered to the best show, that the bills may be less than the estimation abroad. Certainly, if a man will keep but of even hand, his ordinary expenses ought to be but to the half of his

Riches are for spending, and spending for honour, and good actions; therefore extraordinary expence must be limited by the worth of the occasion: for voluntary vndoing may be aswell for a mans countrey, as for the kingdome of heauen: but ordinary expence ought to be limited by a mans estate, and governed wth such regarde as it be wthin his compasse, and not subject to deceite, and abuse of servauntes, and ordered by the best showe, that the billes may be lesse then the estimation abroade: It is no basenes for the greatest to discende, and looke into their owne estate: some receipts; and if he think to wax rich, but to the third part. It is no baseness for the greatest to descend and look into their own estate. Some forbear it, not upon negligence alone, but doubting to bring themselves into melancholy, in respect they shall find it broken. But wounds cannot be cured without searching. He that cannot look into his own estate at all had need both choose well those whom he employeth, and change them often; for new are more timorous and less subtle. He that can look into his estate but seldom, it behoveth him to turn all to certainties. A man had need, if he be plentiful in some kind of expense, to be as saving again in some other; as, if he be plentiful in diet, to be saving in apparel; if he be plentiful in the hall, to be saving in the stable, and the like. For he that is plentiful in expenses of all kinds, will hardly be preserved from decay. In clearing of a man's estate, he may as well hurt himself in being too sudden as in letting it run on too long; for hasty selling is commonly as disadvantageable as interest. Besides, he that clears at once will relapse; for finding himself out of straits, he will revert to his customs: but he that cleareth by degrees induceth a habit of frugality, and gaineth as well upon his mind as upon his estate. Certainly, who hath a state to repair may not despise smal things: and commonly, it

forbeare it not of negligence alo e, but doubting to bring themselues into melancholy, in respect they shall finde it broken; but woundes cannot be cured wthout searching: he that cannot looke into his owne estate, had neede both choose well those whome he imployeth, and chaunge them often: for newe [men] are more timerous, and lesse subtile: in clearing of a mans estate he may aswell hurt himselfe in being too suddaine, as in letting it runne one to long; for hasty selling is commonly as disadvantageable as interest: he that hath a state to repaire may not despise small thinges: and commonly it is lesse dishonour to abridge petty is less dishonourable to abridge petty charges than to stoop to petty gettings. A man ought warily to begin charges which, once begun, will continue; but in matters that return not, he may be more magnificent.

charges, then to stoope to petty gettings: a man ought warily to begin charges wch begun must continue, but in matters that returne not, he may be more liberal.

XXIX

Of the True Greatness of Kingdoms and Estates

THE speech of Themistocles, the Athenian, which was haughty and arrogant, in taking so much to himself, had been a grave and wise observation and censure, applied at large to others. Desired at a feast to touch a lute, he said, *He could not fiddle, but yet he could make a small town a great city.* These words (holpen a little with a metaphor) may express two differing abilities in those that deal in business of estate. For, if a true survey be taken of counsellors and statesmen, there may be found (though rarely) those which can make a small State great and yet cannot fiddle: as, on the other side, there will be found a great many that can fiddle very cunningly, but yet are so far from being able to make a small State great, as their gift lieth the other way, to bring a great and flourishing estate to ruin and decay. And, certainly, th se degenerate arts and shifts, whereby many counsellors and governors gain both favour with their masters and estimation with the vulgar, deserve no better name than fiddling; being things rather pleasing for the time, and graceful to themselves only, than tending to the weal and advancement of the State which they serve. There are also (no doubt) counsellors and governors which may be held sufficient *negotiis pares*, able to manage affairs, and to keep them from precipices and manifest inconveniences; which, nevertheless, are far from the ability to raise and amplify an estate in power, means, and fortune. But be the workmen what they may be, let us speak of the work; that is, the true greatness of kingdoms and estates, and the means thereof. An argument fit for great and mighty princes to have in their hand: to the end that neither by over-measuring their forces, they lose themselves in vain enterprises; nor, on the other side, by undervaluing them, they descend to fearful and pusillanimous counsels.

The greatness of an estate, in bulk and territory, doth fall under measure; and the greatness of finances and revenue doth fall under computation. The population may appear by musters; and the number and greatness of cities and towns by cards and maps. But yet there is not anything, amongst civil affairs, more subject to error, than the right valuation and true judgment concerning the power and forces of an estate. The kingdom of heaven is compared, not to any great kernel, or nut, but to a grain of mustard seed; which is one of the least grains, but hath in it a property and spirit hastily to get up and spread. So are there states great in territory, and yet not apt to enlarge or command; and some that have but a small dimension of stem, and yet are apt to be the foundation of great monarchies.

Walled towns, stored arsenals and armouries, goodly races of horse, chariots of war, elephants, ordnance, artillery, and the like: all this is but a sheep in a lion's skin, except the breed and disposition of the people be stout and warlike. Nay, number itself in armies importeth not much, where the people are of weak courage;

for, as Virgil saith, *It never troubles the wolf how many the sheep be.* The army of the Persians, in the plains of Arbela, was such a vast sea of people as it did somewhat astonish the commanders in Alexander's army; who came to him, therefore, and wished him to set upon them by night; but he answered, *He would not pilfer the victory.* And the defeat was easy. When Tigranes, the Armenian, being encamped upon a hill with four hundred thousand men, discovered the army of the Romans, being not above fourteen thousand, marching towards him, he made himself merry with it, and said, *Yonder men are too many for an ambassage and too few for a fight.* But, before the sun set, he found them enow to give him the chase with infinite slaughter. Many are the examples of the great odds between number and courage; so that a man may truly make a judgment, that the principal point of greatness, in any State, is to have a race of military men. Neither is money the sinews of war (as it is trivially said), where the sinews of men's arms in base and effeminate people are failing. For Solon said well to Crœsus (when in ostentation he shewed him his gold), *Sir, if any other come that hath better iron than you, he will be master of all this gold.* Therefore, let any prince or State think soberly of his forces, except his militia of natives be of good and valiant soldiers. And let princes, on the other side, that have subjects of martial disposition, know their own strength, unless they be otherwise wanting unto themselves. As for mercenary forces (which is the help in this case), all examples show that, whatsoever estate or prince doth rest upon them, *he may spread his feathers for a time, but he will mew them soon after.*

The blessing of Judah and Issachar will never meet; that the same people, or nation, should be both the *lion's whelp*, and *the ass between burdens*: neither will it be, that a people overlaid with taxes should ever become valiant and martial. It is true that taxes, levied by consent of the estate, do abate men's courage less ; as it hath been seen notably in the excises of the Low Countries ; and in some degree, in the subsidies of England. For, you must note, that we speak now of the heart, and not of the purse. So that, although the same tribute and tax, laid by consent, or by imposing, be all one to the purse, yet it works diversely upon the courage. So that you may conclude, that no people overcharged with tribute is fit for empire.

Let states, that aim at greatness, take heed how their nobility and gentlemen do multiply too fast. For that maketh the common subject grow to be a peasant and base swain, driven out of heart, and in effect, but a gentleman's labourer. Even as you may see in coppice woods ; if you leave your staddles too thick, you shall never have clean underwood, but shrubs and bushes. So in countries, if the gentlemen be too many, the commons will be base ; and you will bring it to that, that not the hundredth poll will be fit for an helmet ; especially as to the infantry, which is the nerve of an army : and so there will be great population, and little strength. This which I speak of hath been no where better seen than by comparing of England and France ; whereof England, though far less in territory and population, hath been (nevertheless) an overmatch ; in regard the middle people of England make good soldiers, which the peasants of France do not. And herein the device of King Henry VII. (whereof I have spoken largely in the history of his life) was profound and admirable, in making farms and houses of husbandry of a standard ; that is, maintained with such a proportion of land unto them, as may breed a subject to live in convenient plenty and no servile condition ; and to keep the plough in the hands of the owners, and not mere hirelings. And thus indeed you shall attain to Virgil's character, which he gives to ancient Italy :

Terra potens armis atque ubere glebæ.

Neither is the state (which, for anything I know, is almost peculiar to England, and hardly to be found anywhere else, except it be, perhaps, in Poland) to be passed over ; I mean the state of free servants and attendants upon noblemen and gentlemen : which are no ways inferior unto the yeomanry for arms. And therefore, out of all question, the splendour and magnificence and great retinues, and hospitality of noblemen and gentlemen, received into custom, doth much conduce unto martial greatness. Whereas, contrariwise, the close and reserved living of noblemen and gentlemen causeth a penury of military forces.

By all means it is to be procured, that the trunk of Nebuchadnezzar's tree of monarchy be great enough to bear the branches and the boughs ; that is, that the natural subjects of the Crown, or State, bear a sufficient proportion to the strange subjects that they govern. Therefore all states that are liberal of naturalization towards strangers are fit for empire. For to think that an handful of people can, with the greatest courage and policy in the world, embrace too large extent of dominion —it may hold for a time, but it will fail suddenly. The Spartans were a nice people in point of naturalization : whereby, while they kept their compass, they stood firm ; but when they did spread, and their boughs were becomen too great for their stem, they became a windfall upon the sudden. Never any State was, in this point, so open to receive strangers into their Body as were the Romans. Therefore it sorted with them accordingly ; for they grew to the greatest monarchy. Their manner

Essay 29]   of 𝔎𝔦𝔫𝔤𝔡𝔬𝔪𝔰 𝔞𝔫𝔡 𝔈𝔰𝔱𝔞𝔱𝔢𝔰   107

was to grant naturalization (which they called *jus civitatis*) and to grant it in the highest degree : that is, not only *jus commercii, jus connubii, jus hæreditatis*, but also *jus suffragii* and *jus honorum :* and this not to singular persons alone, but likewise to whole families; yea, to cities, and sometimes to nations. Add to this, their custom of plantation of colonies; whereby the Roman plant was removed into the soil of other nations. And putting both constitutions together, you will say, that it was not the Romans that spread upon the world, but it was the world that spread upon the Romans. And that was the sure way of greatness. I have marvelled sometimes at Spain, how they clasp and contain so large dominions with so few natural Spaniards : but sure the whole compass of Spain is a very great body of a tree, far above Rome and Sparta at the first. And, besides, though they have not had that usage to naturalize liberally, yet they have that which is next to it : that is, to employ, almost indifferently, all nations in their militia of ordinary soldiers, yea, and sometimes in their highest commands. Nay, it seemeth at this instant, they are sensible of this want of natives ; as by the Pragmatical Sanction, now published, appeareth.

It is certain that sedentary and within-door arts, and delicate manufactures (that require rather the finger than the arm), have in their nature a contrariety to a military disposition. And generally all warlike people are a little idle, and love danger better than travail. Neither must they be too much broken of it, if they shall be preserved in vigour. Therefore it was great advantage in the ancient States of Sparta, Athens, Rome, and others, that they had the use of slaves ; which commonly did rid those manufactures. But that is abolished, in greatest part, by the Christian law. That which cometh nearest to it is to leave those arts chiefly to strangers (which, for that purpose, are the more easily to be received), and to contain the principal bulk of the vulgar natives within those three kinds, tillers of the ground; free servants; and handicraftsmen of strong and manly arts, as smiths, masons, carpenters, &c.; not reckoning professed soldiers.

But, above all, for empire and greatness, it importeth most that a nation do profess arms as their principal honour, study, and occupation. For the things which we have formerly spoken of are but habilitations towards arms: and what is habilitation without intention and act? Romulus, after his death (as they report or feign), sent a present to the Romans, that above all they should intend arms; and then they should prove the greatest empire of the world. The fabric of the State of Sparta was wholly (though not wisely) framed and composed to that scope and end. The Persians and Macedonians had it for a flash. The Gauls, Germans, Goths, Saxons, Normans, and others, had it for a time. The Turks have it at this day, though in great declination. Of Christian Europe, they that have it are, in effect, only the Spaniards. But it is so plain that *every man profiteth in that he most intendeth*, that it needeth not to be stood upon. It is enough to point at it; that no nation which doth not directly profess arms, may look to have greatness fall into their mouths. And, on the other side, it is a most certain oracle of time, that those states that continue long in that profession (as the Romans and Turks principally have done), do wonders. And those that have professed arms but for an age, have, notwithstanding, commonly attained that greatness in that age which maintained them long after, when their profession and exercise of arms hath grown to decay.

Essay 29] of Kingdoms and Estates

Incident to this point is for a State to have those laws or customs which may reach forth unto them just occasions (as may be pretended) of war. For there is that justice imprinted in the nature of men, that they enter not upon wars (whereof so many calamities do ensue), but upon some, at the least specious grounds and quarrels. The Turk hath at hand, for cause of war, the propagation of his law or sect; a quarrel that he may always command. The Romans, though they esteemed the extending the limits of their empire to be great honour to their generals when it was done, yet they never rested upon that alone to begin a war. First, therefore, let nations that pretend to greatness have this; that they be sensible of wrongs, either upon borderers, merchants, or politic ministers; and that they sit not too long upon a provocation. Secondly, let them be prest and ready to give aids and succours to their confederates; as it ever was with the Romans; insomuch as, if the confederates had leagues defensive with divers others States, and, upon invasion offered, did implore their aids severally, yet the Romans would ever be the foremost, and leave it to none other to have the honour. As for the wars which were anciently made on the behalf of a kind of party, or tacit conformity of state, I do not see how they may be well justified; as when the Romans made a war for the liberty of Græcia; or when the Lacedæmonians and Athenians made war to set up or pull down democracies and oligarchies; or when wars were made by foreigners, under the pretence of justice or protection, to deliver the subjects of others from tyranny and oppression, and the like. Let it suffice, that no estate expect to be great, that is not awake upon any just occasion or arming.

No body can be healthful without exercise, neither natural body nor politic: and certainly, to a kingdom or estate, a just and honourable war is the true exercise. A civil war, indeed, is like the heat of a fever : but a foreign war is like the heat of exercise, and serveth to keep the body in health ; for in a slothful peace, both courages will effeminate, and manners corrupt. But howsoever it be for happiness, without all question for greatness, it maketh to be still for the most part in arms : and the strength of a veteran army (though it be a chargeable business), always on foot, is that which commonly giveth the law, or, at least, the reputation, amongst all neighbour States ; as may be well seen in Spain ; which hath had, in one part or other, a veteran army almost continually, now by the space of six-score years.

To be master of the sea is an abridgment of a monarchy. Cicero, writing to Atticus of Pompey's preparation against Cæsar, saith, *Consilium Pompeii plane Themistocleum est ; putat enim, qui mari potitur, eum rerum potiri ;* and without doubt, Pompey had tired out Cæsar, if upon vain confidence he had not left that way. We see the great effects of battles by sea. The battle of Actium decided the empire of the world. The battle of Lepanto arrested the greatness of the Turk. There be many examples where sea-fights have been final to the war : but this is when princes, or States, have set up their rest upon the battles. But thus much is certain, that he that commands the sea is at great liberty, and may take as much and as little of the war as he will. Whereas those that be strongest by land are many times, nevertheless, in great straits. Surely, at this day, with us of Europe, the vantage of strength at sea (which is one of the principal dowries of this kingdom of Great Britain) is great ; both because most of the kingdoms of Europe are not merely inland, but girt with the sea most part of their compass ; and because the wealth of both

Indies seems, in great part, but an accessary to the command of the seas.

The wars of latter ages seem to be made in the dark, in respect of the glory and honour which reflected upon men from the wars in ancient time. There be now, for martial encouragement, some degrees and orders of chivalry (which, nevertheless, are conferred promiscuously upon soldiers and no soldiers); and some remembrance perhaps upon the escutcheon; and some hospitals for maimed soldiers; and such like things. But in ancient times, the *Trophies* erected upon the place of the victory; the funeral laudatives and monuments for those that died in the wars; the crowns and garlands personal; the style of *Emperor*, which the great kings of the world after borrowed; the *Triumphs* of the generals upon their return; the great donatives and largesses, upon the disbanding of the armies, were things able to inflame all men's courages. But above all, that of the *Triumph* amongst the Romans was not pageants, or gaudery, but one of the wisest and noblest institutions that ever was. For it contained three things, honour to the general, riches to the treasury out of the spoils, and donatives to the army. But that honour, perhaps, were not fit for monarchies; except it be in the person of the monarch himself, or his sons: as it came to pass in the times of the Roman emperors, who did impropriate the actual triumphs to themselves and their sons, for such wars as they did achieve in person; and left only for wars achieved by subjects some triumphal garments and ensigns to the general.

To conclude. No man can by *care-taking* (as the Scripture saith) *add a cubit to his stature*, in this little model of a man's body; but in the great frame of kingdoms and commonwealths, it is in the power of princes, or estates, to add amplitude and greatness to their kingdoms. For by introducing such ordinances, constitutions, and customs, as we have now touched, they may sow greatness to their posterity and succession. But these things are commonly not observed, but left to take their chance.